William E. Studwell
D. F. Lonergan

The Classic
Rock and Roll Reader
Rock Music
from Its Beginnings
to the Mid-1970s

Pre-publication
REVIEW

"*The Classic Rock and Roll Reader* is a delightful book that brims with the little-known lore and fascinating stories of the birth and classic expression of a new popular art form. The book includes over 100 song annotations. Every annotation includes marvelous tidbits that explore the popular music scene from the birth of rock in the mid-1950s to the demise of classic rock in the 1970s. Rock is placed in historical context by the inclusion of annotations of other popular music. The essay on 'Tom Dooley,' for example, examines the folk music movement that paralleled the heyday of rock. Rock's forebears are also examined, as are (briefly) its descendants. A typical annotation examines an aspect of the rock scene. The essay on the Beatles' *Sergeant Pepper's Lonely Hearts Club Band* contains a fascinating discussion of the economics of popular music and how 'the most important album ever made' changed the course of popular music by its refusal to pay attention to Top 40 mentality. The book also highlights 'One Hit Wonders,' 'The Megastars,' 'The Best Songs That Never Made Number One,' and 'Novelty Songs.' Another interesting feature is the authors' views on the best and worst classic rock songs. This book is a fun read that no classic rock lover will want to miss."

Bruce R. Schueneman, MLS, MS
Co-Interim Director,
Texas A&M University,
Kingsville, TX

The Classic Rock and Roll Reader

Rock Music from Its Beginnings to the Mid-1970s

HAWORTH Popular Culture
Frank W. Hoffmann, PhD and B. Lee Cooper, PhD
Senior Editors

New, Recent, and Forthcoming Titles:

The Classic
Rock and Roll Reader
Rock Music
from Its Beginnings
to the Mid-1970s

William E. Studwell
D. F. Lonergan

The Haworth Press
New York • London • Oxford

The Haworth Press, Inc., 10 Alice Street, Binghamton, NY 13904-1580

Cover design by Jennifer M. Gaska.

Library of Congress Cataloging-in-Publication Data

Studwell, William E. (William Emmett), 1936-
  The classic rock and roll reader : rock music from its beginnings to the mid-1970s / William E. Studwell, D.F. Lonergan.
      p.   cm.
  Includes an index.
  ISBN 0-7890-0151-9 (hc. : alk. paper).—0-7890-0738-X (pbk. : alk. paper).
  1. Rock music—History and criticism. I. Lonergan, D. F. (David F.) II. Title.
ML3534.S82   1999
781.66—dc21   99-15102
                                                                              CIP

CONTENTS

The Best Songs That Never Made Number 1, or, Time Heals All Aches, Mistakes, and Bad Breaks — 99

CLASSIC ROCK MEETS DISCO, AND BOTH DISAPPEAR

ABOUT THE AUTHORS

William E. Studwell, MA, MSLS, is Professor and Principal Cataloger at the University Libraries of Northern Illinois University in DeKalb. Mr. Studwell is the author of *Barbershops, Bullets, and Ballads: An Annotated Anthology of Underappreciated American Musical Jewels, 1865-1918; College Fight Songs: An Annotated Anthology; Publishing Glad Tidings: Essays on Christmas Music;* and *State Songs of the United States: An Annotated Anthology* (Haworth); as well as thirteen other books on music, including reference books on popular songs, national songs, Christmas songs, ballets, and operas. He has also written three books on cataloging and almost 340 articles on library science and music. A nationally known expert on carols, college fight songs, and Library of Congress subject headings, he has made approximately 425 radio, television, and print appearances in national, regional, and local media.

D. F. Lonergan, PhD, is Associate Professor and Reference Librarian in the Libraries of Northern Illinois University in DeKalb, Illinois. He is the author of nine journal articles and approximately seventy-five encyclopedia articles on anthropological subjects as well as popular music and rock and roll.

Preface

Before the mid-1950s, the most famous rock in music was perhaps "Rock of Ages," the outstanding eighteenth-century hymn. The significance of the word "rock" in the hymn was to suggest strength and stability in times of trouble.

In contrast, the term "rock" in "rock and roll" had a much different meaning. When rock music burst on the American scene in the mid-1950s, there was nothing stable about it and many adults viewed the new type of music as troubling. Since rock had a heavier or stronger beat than its predecessors, the word "rock" could have reflected the increased hardness of the music. Yet the music of 1953 to the mid-1970s, the focus of this volume, was relatively soft in comparison with the various forms of hard rock that followed it, making earlier rock more of a sandstone rather than marble or granite. Also, since rock had a more active style than the majority of its predecessors, the work "rock" could refer to the energetic motions of its rhythms. At the same time, however, since rock music particularly appealed to younger people and since so many of its performers were teenagers and young adults, another famous song with "rock" in the title and in addition suggesting motion might be appropriate—"Rock-a-Bye, Baby." But who could sleep with all that noise!

The authors of this volume have attempted to maintain the same playful and irreverent tone employed in the preceding paragraph throughout this set of essays on the classic or early rock period. The senior author was finishing senior high school when the first rock songs appeared, giving him a good perspective on the first decade or so of the period. The junior author was in junior high school in the mid-1960s, giving him a good perspective on the last decade or so of the period. In addition, the senior author, a cultural historian with ties to classical and other "mainstream" music, has approached the topic from one angle, that of a general music commentator. On the other hand, the junior author, an anthropologist with ties to folk music, looks at the topic from a different angle, more that of an intimate narrator of the period's musical phenomena.

The backgrounds and personalities of the authors combine to provide an informative yet quite readable and, it is hoped, entertaining survey of early rock in its cultural and historical context. Touching on the music that preceded early rock, the music that followed early rock, and the numerous nonrock songs that flourished during the classic rock period, a wide spectrum, yet in-depth view, of rock and its neighbors will be offered by means of well over 100 essays on various songs. Hundreds of rock and nonrock compositions will be covered in one way or another. In format and style, this book is similar to the senior author's related volume, *The Popular Song Reader*, though there is relatively little overlap with that publication. On the other hand, there is little similarity between this volume and other histories or surveys of rock music, including one with the title "Rock of Ages."

THE EMERGENCE OF ROCK MUSIC, OR, WAKING UP THE 1950s

ROCK'S NOT-SO-DULL PREDECESSORS

In the Mood

Dance music has been a vital and active part of American popular culture throughout the twentieth century. Starting before the beginning of the century and continuing to about World War I, ragtime was the craze of the day. With the creation of Cecil Mack and Jimmy Johnson's "Charleston" in 1923, that dance became the fad for several years. And with the beginning of the swing era in the late 1920s, much of America either danced or listened to dance music played by big bands.

The swing era was a time for dancing. With increased emphasis on orchestration and larger instrumental ensembles than before, the songs of the swing or Big Band era, whether fast or slow, tended toward rhythms suitable for fun and romance on the dance floor. If you had a good beat, it wasn't necessary to have great lyrics. For instance, two of the finest pieces of the period, Glenn Miller's "Moonlight Serenade" (1939), a very smooth slow composition, and Joe Garland's "In the Mood" (1939), a very active and playful composition, have lyrics that are seldom used. In fact, one of the top songs of the 1940s, Sy Oliver's "Opus One" or "Opus Number One" (1944), not only doesn't have words but really doesn't have a title.

The big bands, led by famous musicians such as Duke Ellington, Count Basie, Benny Goodman, Tommy Dorsey, Harry James, and

Glenn Miller, hit their peak in the late 1930s and early 1940s. After World War II they declined somewhat and after 1955, when "Rock Around the Clock" shocked the nation, were pushed well into the background by the loud and brash sounds of rock and roll. But the transition from swing to rock was not as drastic as it might appear. Swing, like rock, was frequently loud, often quite lively, and in many cases characterized by a strong beat. "In the Mood," composed fourteen years before "Rock Around the Clock" was created in 1953, was in its way as rebellious as the later song, especially in the devil-may-care recording by Glenn Miller. That is why a New Year's Eve retrospective on American dance music, broadcast in 1993 by a radio station in a major American city, blended together the rhythms of "In the Mood" and "Rock Around the Clock" in an effort to suggest the stylistic similarities. The shift from one song to another was smooth, natural, and almost friendly.

Of Thee I Sing

The swing or Big Band era lasted from the late 1920s until the early 1950s, or about one generation. It spanned the Great Depression of the 1930s, the big war of 1939 to 1945, and the post World War II baby boom.

The classic rock era lasted from 1953 to about the mid-1970s, again about one generation. Although it was also associated with the baby boom, the bigger booms came from the volume of the music. Classic rock was, in addition, intensely involved with the social upheavals and cultural revolution of the 1960s, that in a real way were a war between "the establishment" (which essentially was a fiction) and the counterculture and dissident groups. Since these two dominant types of American popular music each lasted roughly one generation, it is possible that the punk rock, heavy metal, and rap that succeeded classic rock may also only last one generation. If so, what may follow these musical styles at about the one generation mark, around the turn of the century, can only be viewed with a guess and with apprehension. Since rap was the fad at the time this volume was written, and rap is characterized by often questionable lyrics and a monotonous military-style beat to mesmerize its adherents, the future of popular music does not seem to be in good hands.

But the music of the Big Band era was crafted by many good hands. Four of the most talented hands of that period belonged to the great Gershwin brothers. Lyricist Ira and composer George (who unfortunately died at the age of thirty-nine in 1937), wrote a number of fine songs, typically for Broadway musicals. Some of those songs were very lively, loud, and even brash. "I Got Rhythm" (1930), "Love Is Sweeping the Country" (1931), "Strike Up the Band" (1930), and "Of Thee I Sing" (1931), all classics, were like prototypes for the rock songs that came on the American scene about two decades later. There were, of course, differences between these Gershwin songs and the earlier rock songs, but it was more a matter of degree than of style. "Of Thee I Sing," for example, was not only highly active it was also quite playful, for the "baby" in the line "Of thee I sing, baby" was the Statue of Liberty. Furthermore, it wasn't just the Gershwins who wrote such lively fine and dandy songs. Lyricist Paul James and composer Kay Swift were equally impertinent in their 1930 rouser "Fine and Dandy," which, like the Gershwin songs, paved the way for the rock songs about a generation later.

In the matter of playfulness, if the Big Band era and the classic rock era were compared overall for their playfulness and sense of humor, the Big Band era, and even the generation before it (around 1900 to the late 1920s), would clearly surpass the classic rock era. The rebellion inherent in rock did not necessarily carry along with it twinkles in the eyes and smiles in the feet. For good or bad, rebels have something to prove, and humor is not usually at the top of their agenda. This doesn't mean that classic rock was without humor. Far from it. But classic rock and its harder successors have never been described as repositories of mirth and merriment.

Night and Day

There has been some tendency to contrast the music of the rock era and of the preceding era as if they were night and day. Older people tend to view rock and roll, particularly the later versions, as a dark night that followed a bright sunshiny day in American popular music. Younger people tend to view rock music as a new dawn after the dark ages of earlier times. (As an aside, prerock music and earlier rock music started to be successfully revived among youth starting in the late 1980s, so not every young person regards these earlier styles of music as something moldy and antiquated.)

In reality, the transition from prerock to rock was more like the gradual shifts from daytime to nighttime and nighttime to daytime. Whether the mid-1950s were a dawn or a dusk depends on one's age and attitude, but just as the sun doesn't appear and disappear in a few moments, the change from the swing era to the rock era wasn't accomplished by a few somewhat revolutionary rock songs. Rock was certainly different, but early rock didn't just pop up out of nowhere.

One of the traits of rock is that it is more direct and deals with sex more openly than earlier songs. In classic rock, sex was less subtle and restrained than in the swing era of the 1930s and 1940s, but the songs of the 1950s, 1960s, and early 1970s were mild and reserved in sexual tone in comparison to the often explicit and vulgar sexuality of later songs.

However, the shift in sexual content and emphasis that was a characteristic of classic rock was relatively gradual, such as the rest of the change from prerock to rock. Many earlier songs, for instance Cole Porter's "Night and Day" (1932), had a high sensation of sexuality in the lyrics and/or the melody. Another prime example is Howard Dietz and Arthur Schwartz's "Dancing in the Dark" (1931). Even without Dietz's lyrics, the implied eroticism of Schwartz's melody matched the more explicit sexuality of any early rock composition.

7

Bewitched, Bothered, and Bewildered

There is no doubt that "Bewitched, Bothered, and Bewildered," from Richard Rodgers and Lorenz Hart's smash 1940 musical *Pal Joey*, was a classic love song. The lyrics by Hart were very well crafted and the melody by Rodgers, with a strong slow beat and deep tones, had a large dose of sexuality. Tame by later standards, "Bewitched" and other Rodgers and Hart creations such as the more blatant "The Lady Is a Tramp" from their 1937 musical *Babes in Arms*, were nevertheless indicators that prerock songs were anything but dull.

Also anything but dull would be an effort to precisely and concisely define what rock and roll actually is. Somewhat bewitched, bothered, and bewildered about attempting to capture in a few words the elusive phenomenon of rock, the authors instead prefer to discuss the tendencies in rock that made it different from earlier music. These include a stronger beat, louder volume, increased sexuality, and more of an orientation toward teenagers and preteens. Even though classic rock was in some ways revolutionary, it also was in other ways more simple, more ingenuous, and less sophisticated. Popular music before the mid-1950s was directed mostly toward those over the age of eighteen, and younger people more or less accommodated themselves to the situation.

In contrast, classic rock fit in well with the tastes and aspirations of the young, although older people were not necessarily alienated by it. This focus on the teen and preteen resulted in a curious blend of increased sexual emphasis, but at the same time was more tenuous, more naive, and more sexually inconclusive.

Oklahoma!

Although Richard Rodgers and Oscar Hammerstein had both written outstanding musicals before 1943, for example, Rodgers had collaborated with Lorenz Hart on *Babes in Arms* (1937) and *Pal Joey* (1940), and Hammerstein had collaborated with Sigmund Romberg and Otto Harbach on *Desert Song* (1926) and with Jerome Kern on *Showboat* (1927), they had never worked together prior to their creation of *Oklahoma!* in 1943. Therefore, whether the new team would work out was unknown until the opening of the show.

As it turned out, not only were the duo successful in their joint efforts, they became the most successful creators of Broadway musicals ever. In addition, *Oklahoma!* was quite possibly the best musical in American theatrical history, with perhaps *My Fair Lady* (1956) surpassing it somewhat. *Oklahoma!* reached the heights for two reasons: an almost flawless score of fine songs, and a plot emphasizing everyday people in everyday situations with touches of social consciousness. For these reasons, *Oklahoma!* started a new era in American musicals.

Yet the style of *Oklahoma!* was not drastically different from that of prior productions. The changes in the 1943 show involved just a shift in emphasis, not a totally new style. The same type of shift took place in the mid-1950s when "Rock Around the Clock" and other songs started what has been called the "rock revolution." There certainly was a change when rock came on the scene, but not as drastic as it might appear. Even a decade before the advent of rock, in the above-mentioned mainstream and socially acceptable *Oklahoma!*, there were songs that contained some of the ingredients of rock. "I Cain't Say No," about a young woman who couldn't refuse the sexual advances of men, was in some ways more sexually explicit than early rock. Furthermore, the show's title song, "Oklahoma!" was as energetic as any early rock song, including "Rock Around the Clock," whose force and strength triggered the new era in popular music.

Show Business

The classic rock era had a number of composers who created multiple hit songs. Brian Wilson of the Beach Boys, John Lennon and Paul McCartney of the Beatles, Eddie and Brian Holland and Lamont Dozier who wrote for the Supremes, Tony Hatch who wrote "Downtown" and "Don't Sleep in the Subway," Neil Diamond, Paul Anka, Paul Simon, Carole King, and several others were successful far more than once.

However, the classic rock era had relatively fewer dominant songwriters than the decades preceding it. The better known composers of the rock period, furthermore, were those that recorded at least some of their own material. Wilson, Lennon, McCartney, Diamond, Anka, Simon, and King, in different degrees, have gained much of their fame by singing as well as by composing. (To a significant degree, this combination of composition and singing has tended to inhibit the song production of these people and many others because the more time one spends recording and touring, the less time there is for creativity. On top of that, writing for oneself limits the songwriter to the artistic characteristics of the singer.) In contrast Hatch, the Hollands, and Dozier, who did not record, are not well-known to the general public.

Another characteristic of the composers of the classic rock era was their relative youth. A number of successful rock composers wrote their first hit while in their teens or early twenties. Among these youthful composers were the above-mentioned Lennon, McCartney, Anka, and King as well as others such as the Everly Brothers and Ritchie Valens.

Perhaps the most prominent trait of rock composers is that so many were one-hit or one-shot authors. One-hit wonders have always existed in popular music as well as in classical, but the percentage of one-hit composers increased after the mid-1950s. In contrast, the previous generation had so many lyricists and musicians whose names have endured because of repeated successes. Jerome Kern, Oscar Hammerstein, Sigmund Romberg, Richard Rodgers, Lorenz Hart, Leroy Anderson, Duke Ellington, Harold Arlen, Johnny Mercer, Hoagy Carmichael, Frank Loesser, George and Ira Gershwin, Cole Porter, Irving Berlin, and others provided a star-studded quarter century or so of top songwriters.

Irving Berlin is a classic example. From before World War I to well past World War II, Berlin continued to crank out pop masterpieces such as "Always" (1925), "Easter Parade" (1933), "God Bless America" (1939), "White Christmas" (1942), and "Show Business" (1946). The last song, also known as "There's No Business Like Show Business," was only one of many excellent numbers from Berlin's top Broadway show *Annie Get Your Gun*, which Berlin created at the ripe old age of fifty-eight. Could you imagine a rock composer being at the top of his or her game at such a time of life?

The Cry of the Wild Goose

Among the obvious characteristics of many rock songs are a hard driving beat, a high level of energy, and high volume. However, intense, active, and loud songs were by no stretch of the imagination the exclusive property of the rock era. Perhaps as a sort of warmup for the upcoming "rock revolution," the late 1940s and early 1950s had more than its share of strident, noisy, or brash songs.

Terry Gilkyson's 1949 hit "The Cry of the Wild Goose," with hard-driving lines such as "I must go where the wild goose goes," is one prime example. Another is the energetic, intense, and high volume ballad of the same year, "Riders in the Sky," also known as "Ghost Riders in the Sky." Stan Jones' haunting musical description of an otherworldly cattle drive roaring across the horizon helped liven up our lives in 1949. Apparently not satisfied with the two other attention-getting pieces of 1949, "Mule Train," a much slower, but just as intense, song was not slow in attaining artistic and financial success. (The authors of "Mule Train" were Johnny Lange, Hy Heath, and Fred Glickman.)

The early 1950s saw at least three more songs that were far from gentle. In 1950, Teresa Brewer unabashedly and with much energy belted out "Music, Music, Music," asking us to "Put another nickel in, In the nickelodeon." (Authors Stephan Weiss and Bernie Baum saw many a nickel from that recording.) That same year, Johnnie Lee Wills and Deacon Anderson produced the lively novelty "Rag Mop," a raucous bit of lovable nonsense that sold a million records. In 1952 the theme from the classic film *High Noon*, also known as "Do Not Forsake Me," matched the intensity of the exciting story. The creators of this fine ballad were lyricist Ned Washington and composer Dmitri Tiomkin who were later to portray a real cattle drive in the splendid and rousing theme for the 1959 to 1966 television series *Rawhide*.

These and other compositions of the time loudly demonstrated that music prior to the beginning of rock and roll was hardly boring. They made adjusting to the shock of rock much easier, smoothing the way for a generation of classic rock soon to begin. After the advent of rock, of course, there were some definite changes. The cry of the wild goose changed to the wild chords of the electric guitar, specters in the sky changed to spectacles on stage and, in the audience, the mule train changed to a steaming locomotive for youth, nickels for the nickelodeon changed to thousands of dollars in fat bank accounts, the rag mop changed to a brusque broom that swept away old cultural conventions, and the shootout at high noon changed to boom boxes twenty-four hours a day.

THE PIONEERING ROCK SONGS, OR, THREE CREATE A CROWD

Rock Around the Clock

"Rock Around the Clock" was not the first rock and roll song, but it was the first great one. There were several songs with "rock" in their titles before "Rock Around" was written in 1953 by Max C. Freedman and Jimmy DeKnight. These predecessors included: "Rocket 88" (1951), written by Jackie Brenston; "Rock Me All Night Long" (1952), by Jimmy Ricks and Bill Sanford; and "Rock a-Beatin' Boogie" (1952) by Bill Haley, whose lyrics began with the line "Rock, rock, rock, everybody, roll, roll, roll, everybody." In addition, all rhythm and blues songs were predecessors, for rock and roll is essentially a derivative or adaption of that earlier type of music, along with elements from mainstream popular music and country-western music.

Initially "Rock Around" went unnoticed. Even after Bill Haley and the Comets recorded the song in June 1954, it gained little attention. Then "Rock Around" was inserted into the sound track of the 1955 movie *The Blackboard Jungle* due to some very fortunate circumstances. One of the song's composers, DeKnight, was a technical advisor for the film. After the film's release, the song became a very big hit, reaching Number 2 in record sales in 1955. It made Bill Haley, who was not particularly attractive in either appearance or style, the first rock star, and opened up the gates for more songs of this style.

In other words, "Rock Around the Clock" was the song that really started the rock revolution, although some other rock songs came before it. It was the first rock song to make a strong impact on American society, and therefore in effect was the inspiration for a generation of classic rock. For good or bad, "Rock Around the Clock" burst the dam of American popular music.

Sh-Boom

Because "Rock Around the Clock" was not successful until 1955, the 1954 song "Sh-Boom" was the first recording of a rock composition to score high in the charts, reaching Number 3 in record sales in 1954. Fortunately for "Sh-Boom," too many cooks did not spoil its broth, for the song had almost as many authors as it had letters in the title. No less than five people created the piece— James Keyes, Claude Feaster, Carl Feaster, Floyd F. McRae, and James Edwards.

Also known as "Life Could Be a Dream," "Sh-Boom" is one of rock's finest pioneers. But at the time it came out, there was no strong indication that a new style of music was about to attack American culture. In fact, the name of the group that made the first widely-heard recording, the Crew-Cuts, suggests mainstream normalcy. In 1954 the senior author was finishing up high school and remembers that "Sh-Boom" was popular, but that it did not create any kind of sensation. When the more lively "Shake, Rattle and Roll" appeared later in 1954, there was a definite feeling that it was something quite different, especially after Elvis Presley recorded it. By the time "Rock Around the Clock" hit the proverbial fan in 1955, the nation was shocked into believing that popular music might be on the threshold of radical change, if not already over it.

Shake, Rattle and Roll

Elvis Presley, the King of rock and roll, came on the scene at the right time. "Shake, Rattle and Roll," written by Charles Calhoun, was first recorded by Joe Turner in 1954. The song, which was quite active and on the boisterous side, might have done quite well even if nobody else besides Turner had recorded it. But with the distinctive talents of Elvis applied to a later 1954 recording, the pioneering song became one of rock's finest.

The term "roll" in the title suggests that it may have influenced the establishment of the phrase "rock and roll." But the phrase had come into common usage by 1951 when Alan Freed, later an extremely popular disc jockey at WINS radio in New York City, called his Cleveland radio music show *Rock and Roll Party*. Freed said he got the idea for the phrase from a rhythm and blues composition. Yet as far back as 1934, there had been a song with the title "Rock and Roll" in the movie *Transatlantic Merry-Go-Round*, starring Jack Benny. (This meaningless linking of Benny and his low-key humor with rock and roll and its less than subtle style seems a bit out of place and somewhat ridiculous.)

Although Freed popularized the phrase before "Shake, Rattle and Roll" and "Rock Around the Clock" were recorded, the great success of both helped turn what could have been a temporary music fad into a full blown music industry. "Shake" and "Rock Around" did not invent the phrase "rock and roll," but did much to imprint the concept into the minds of the American public. In a real way, then, "Rock Around the Clock" was the lasting inspiration for the term "rock," and "Shake, Rattle and Roll" the lasting inspiration for the term "roll."

OLDER-STYLE SONGS AMIDST THE ROCKS

All the Way

There was a "rock revolution" in the mid-1950s, or more exactly, a shift in the style of popular music. But the emergence of rock did not mean that earlier style songs totally disappeared from the popular scene. In fact, even in the period of hard rock and rap after the mid-1970s, sentimental ballads and other older style compositions still continued to be created and flourish. One of the reasons that the term "rock revolution" is somewhat misleading is that it suggests a more or less total upheaval of earlier musical styles. Such is not true. Rock did alter artistic patterns, but did not go all the way and annihilate other pathways to the hearts of the American public.

In reality, early rock was rather benign, although many older people probably didn't think so. The first years of rock were rather frantic ones in the history of American culture, but there was plenty of room for opposing creative viewpoints. For example, Frank Sinatra continued in his old ways with much success. From the mid-1950s to the mid-1960s, Sinatra had several top hits that were not in rock style. Teaming up with lyricist Sammy Cahn and composer Jimmy Van Heusen, Sinatra recorded their "Love and Marriage" (1955), "The Tender Trap" (1955), "Come Fly with Me" (1958), "High Hopes" (1959), "The Second Time Around" (1961), "My Kind of Town" (1964), and "All the Way" (1957). Singing these pieces, and many others, Sinatra remained somewhat popular all the way into the 1990s.

A different career path developed for Sinatra's younger counterpart Tony Bennett, who is most famous for his rendering of Douglass A. Cross and George Cory's masterful 1962 ballad "I Left My Heart in San Francisco." Bennett, like Sinatra, favored the older-style songs. For several years, however, Bennett's entertainment career suffered from the onslaught of hard rock, but in the late 1980s and early 1990s, his career was revived by a new set of adoring fans, teenagers and young adults, most of whom were not even born in 1962. Another revival at about the same time, incidentally, was the use of Cahn and Van Heusen's "Love and Marriage" in the controversial television series, *Married with Children.*

Rock shook up the world of popular music, but despite the mild artistic earthquake, nonrock music survived and prospered far beyond the end of the classic rock era.

Chances Are

There's an old expression, "The more things change, the more they stay the same." Another way of saying this is that classic works and classic modes never really go out of style. Dante and Shakespeare are still widely read in spite of the passage of several centuries. Leonardo da Vinci and Michelangelo are still very much appreciated in spite of the appearance and disappearance of many later styles in art.

Furthermore, fine love ballads are always appreciated no matter whether the times are prosperous or economically depressed, whether there is war or peace, or whether popular culture is stable or turbulent. Even after the mild cultural upheaval created by early rock in the mid-1950s, older style ballads continued to be written and flourish. And it wasn't just older singers who presented the new ballads to the public. Johnny Mathis is a prime example of a newer face and voice.

Starting around the advent of rock, young Mathis recorded several first rate hits, including "The Twelfth of Never" (1956), "A Certain Smile" (1958), "Wonderful, Wonderful" (1957), "It's Not for Me to Say" (1956), and "Chances Are" (1957). "Twelfth" was written by lyricist Paul Francis Webster and composer Jerry Livingston who adapted the melody from a Kentucky folk song. "Certain" was also written by Webster in collaboration with musician Sammy Fain. "Wonderful" was written by lyricist Ben Raleigh and musician Sherman Edwards. "It's Not for Me to Say" and "Chances Are" were created by lyricist Al Stillman and composer Robert Allen, who also created three other top sentimental ballads in the mid-1950s. The Christmas classic "Home for the Holidays" (1954), the nostalgic "Moments to Remember" (1955), and the love song "No, Not Much" (1956) were other successful compositions by the duo.

Perhaps the most interesting facet of the music of Stillman and Allen is that they were of two different generations, Stillman being born in 1906 and Allen in 1927. Their compositions, in addition, enhanced life for at least two additional generations. Now we're back to the saying at the beginning of this essay.

I Could Have Danced All Night

When times change, some people adjust and some don't. However, not adjusting to new trends and fads doesn't always mean failure. Two examples from Broadway can help illustrate this. Frank Loesser, a very successful songwriter and creator of musicals in the 1940s, 1950s, and early 1960s, mostly ignored the advent of rock. Since he had an established and appreciative postteen audience, he didn't have to convert to the world of gyrating youth and electronic guitars. On one notable occasion, however, he passed over into the domain of rock and created the delightful "Standing on the Corner" for the 1956 show *The Most Happy Fella*.

Other prerock composers of musicals didn't even seem to blink after rock arrived. Wordsmith Alan Jay Lerner and tunesmith Frederick Loewe, one of the top Broadway teams in the history of American theater, didn't make any apparent adjustments in style after rock appeared. From their first top musical to their last, they remained old-fashioned and classic in approach and historical in theme. *Brigadoon*, a very charming 1947 production that gave us "Almost Like Being in Love," dealt with a Scottish village in the mid-eighteenth century. *Paint Your Wagon* (1951) had its locale in the American West of the nineteenth century. Their best show, and perhaps the best ever, was *My Fair Lady* (1956), that presented life in London around the turn of the twentieth century. The 1956 show had a handful of excellent songs, including "The Rain in Spain," "I've Grown Accustomed to Her Face," "On the Street Where You Live," and most of all "I Could Have Danced All Night." Their last hit musical was *Camelot* (1960), which reversed Lerner's trend toward increasingly more recent history and plunged the audiences back into the Middle Ages.

The breaking up of the team of Lerner and Loewe had nothing to do with changing tastes due to the intrusion of rock into American culture. There were many Americans who probably would have continued to appreciate the creations of Lerner and Loewe if the pair hadn't let their personalities and egos split them up. Long after the demise of classic rock, quality works in all types of musical genres still found a warm reception in some segment of American society.

Moon River

Jazz and its forerunners predated classic rock by close to a hundred years. With several variants, including the blues, ragtime, swing, and progressive, jazz was a major component of American popular culture for decades before rock was conceived. In spite of the immense popularity of rock after the mid-1950s, jazz, which appealed to a much different audience, continued to prosper.

A prominent example of this is the theme for the 1958 to 1961 television detective series, *Peter Gunn*. Its excellent dramatic jazz score was probably the most outstanding feature of the program. A few years later its composer, Henry Mancini, wrote a lighter but still top rate jazz theme for the series of *Pink Panther* movies, which started in 1964. These compositions demonstrated that rock had not overwhelmed the potent strains of jazz and that mainstream America was still seduced by jazz's long-lived appeal.

Mancini was one of the best known and most successful of a body of composers who began to create hits after the start of rock and who shunned the style of rock. In addition to his composing in the jazz idiom, Mancini also created in more reflective and gentler modes. His fine theme for the 1959-1960 television program, *Mr. Lucky*, about a gambling boat, reflects this, as does his "Moon River" (1961), "Days of Wine and Roses" (1962), and "Charade" (1963). "Moon River," from the movie *Breakfast at Tiffany's*, won one Oscar and two Grammys, as did "Days of Wine and Roses" from the film of that name. The lyrics for these three songs were written by Johnny Mercer, who in collaboration with various composers had previously created a variety of hits including "Hooray for Hollywood" (1938), "Blues in the Night" (1941), "That Old Black Magic" (1942), and the much-recorded "Laura" (1945).

For many musicians, life as it was continued on without incident after the mid-1950s. People were still interested in detectives, gamblers, moons, rivers, wine, roses, and playing charades of all types, and in the traditional style pop music that touched upon these motifs.

Rocky Mountain High

Not every popular song with "Rock" in the title is a rock song. For example, "Rockabye Your Baby with a Dixie Melody," created by lyricists Joe Young and Sam M. Lewis and composer Jean Schwartz, goes all the way back to 1918. In more recent years, "Rocky Mountain High," a top 1972 hit sung and written by John Denver, is an old-fashioned ballad and not a rock song. Denver also recorded other similar-style ballads at about the same time. These included "Leaving on a Jet Plane" (1969) and "Annie's Song" (1974), both written by Denver, and "Take Me Home, Country Roads" (1971), by Denver and Bill and Taffy Danoff. Not only were these songs a departure from the classic rock-dominated music of the period, but also a marked contrast from the reggae and hard rock that was starting to make its presence known.

In the light of songs such as Denver's, this volume not only covers songs that fall into the category of classic rock compositions, but in addition explores to some extent all of the popular music of the classic rock era. To truly understand classic rock, one must also understand the cultural environment in which it evolved, developed, and disappeared. Not every important or highly successful song of the classic rock period was a rock song, nor was every song by a rock composer a rock song, nor was every song recorded by a rock group a rock song. The classic rock era was undoubtedly dominated by rock compositions, but the rest of the pop music mob of the time must be touched upon, too.

Top of the World

In practicality, the distinction between rock songs and nonrock songs is often debatable or fuzzy. How does one, for example, distinguish between a hard beat rock song or a rhythm and blues song? Or how does one separate an old-fashioned ballad from a folk rock piece from a soft rock song? For instance, "Love Me Tender," the 1956 blockbuster recorded by Elvis Presley and written by Elvis and Vera Matson, used the almost hundred-year-old melody of a Civil War era song, "Aura Lea." Yet no one, to the authors' knowledge, denies that "Love Me Tender" is a rock song. Most people would probably describe it as soft rock.

The many songs that fall into the cavernous limbo between songs that are clearly rock and those that are clearly not are usually categorized by who wrote them, who recorded them, and when they came to life or were revived. Songs that have any resemblance to rock and that appeared or were revived in the classic rock era tend to be described as classic rock compositions.

The songs recorded by the Carpenters in the 1970s and early 1980s are among the inhabitants of musical limbo. Lead singer Karen and her older brother Richard grew up during the early years of rock and their songs could well be labeled soft rock. At the same time, the top recordings by the Carpenters could just as easily be described as tender ballads. "Close to You" (1970), written by composer Burt Bacharach and lyricist Hal David, "Rainy Days and Mondays" (1971), written by Roger Nicholls and Paul Williams, and "Top of the World" (1973), written by Richard Carpenter and John Bettis, were all on the soft and sentimental side. The unique sound of Karen's smooth and golden voice combined with very well-designed arrangements made these songs resemble the sweet flow of honey, so categorizing the songs themselves is made more difficult. However, even if the placid-toned Carpenters had recorded an undeniably classic rock piece such as "Rock Around The Clock," there still would be no doubt that the song belonged to the umbrella genre called rock.

Whatever Will Be, Will Be

Three of the finest singers of the early rock period and the years before it were Nat King Cole, Harry Belafonte, and Doris Day. More at home with old-fashioned ballads and novelties than with rock, the three recorded a number of fine songs in their individual styles.

Nat Cole did most of his best recordings before 1953, including "The Christmas Song" (1946), by Mel Torme and Robert Wells; "Nature Boy" (1948), written in 1946 by Eden Ahbez; "Mona Lisa" (1948), by Jay Livingston and Ray Evans; "Too Young" (1951), by Sylvia Dee and Sid Lippman; and "Unforgettable" (1951), by Irving Gordon. But he continued to produce excellent recordings after the start of rock, including "Darling, Je Vous Aime Beaucoup" (1955), written in 1935 by Anna Sosenko, and "Ramblin' Rose" (1962), by Joe and Noel Sherman.

Belafonte, on top of other things, popularized calypso music in the 1950s. His two big calypso hits were "Matilda, Matilda" (1953), by Harry Thomas, and the delightful "Day-O," or "The Banana Boat Song" (1957), written by Erik Darling, Bob Carey, and Alan Arkin.

Day sang the Academy Award winning "Whatever Will Be, Will Be" or "Que Sera, Sera" for Alfred Hitchcock's movie thriller *The Man Who Knew Too Much* (1956). That song plus "Everybody Loves a Lover" (1958), by lyricist Richard Adler and composer Robert Allen; "Love Somebody" (1947), by Joan Whitney and Alex Kramer; and "Sentimental Journey" (1944), by Bud Green, Les Brown, and Ben Homer, were the mainstay of Day's ballad repertory.

All three were part of the rock era, yet all three were more or less apart from rock music. Although it is not known what their initial attitudes toward the brash new rock and roll phenomenon may have been, perhaps they might have responded "whatever will be, will be" or in contemporary parlance "you can't fight it, so why try!"

A GENERATION OF CLASSIC ROCK, OR, ROCK ROLLS ON

THE MEGASTARS
AND MEGAGROUPS, OR,
THE BOLDER AND THE BOULDERS

Are You Lonesome Tonight?

Elvis Presley burst onto the American pop music scene in 1956, ushering in the classic rock and roll era, and starting a run of rock achievements that is unlikely ever to be surpassed. Elvis had the most Number 1 records, most charted singles, most double-sided hits, and most starring roles in motion pictures (over thirty). He charted Top 40 hits every year from 1956 to 1977, the year of his death. Of the thirteen highest-selling singles of the classic rock era, he personally accounts for five. (The next-best number is the Beatles' two.)

However, few lives better illustrate the cliche that fame and wealth do not necessarily bring happiness. There is no need to recapitulate Elvis' sad life story here, so much already having been written about it. A few observations are worth making, though. Elvis recorded and released several singles for Sun Records before RCA-Victor bought his contract in 1955. Sun, a Memphis-based label specializing in R&B performers, was far too small to distribute his records or promote Elvis on a large enough scale. His stardom was guaranteed by several national television appearances in early 1956, months before RCA released his debut single on their label. Elvis was the first and biggest rock and roll star, and the first pop music star whose success was a direct result of television exposure. The physical gyrations in his live performances—in retro-spect, fairly tame—were at that time an unprecedented shock. They earned him the nickname "Elvis the Pelvis," but they also earned him great notoriety. Elvis Presley was literally a household name after his first television appearance; those who missed it could watch another just a week later, and talk about him in the meantime.

Elvis' stardom was well-established, after more than two years and nine hit singles, when he was drafted in March 1958. Over the next two years RCA-Victor released five singles from their store-house of Elvis recordings, three of which reached Number 1. At this point Elvis had not had an unsuccessful record. Upon his discharge from the Army in March 1960, he recorded new material and had three Number 1 singles in a row. These were "Stuck on You," "It's Now or Never," and "Are You Lonesome Tonight?," three of his very best songs. The third might serve as a sort of Elvis anthem; he was perhaps the loneliest musical celebrity imaginable, a Howard Hughes of rock and roll.

In 1961 two new Elvis movies and four singles were released. Only one of these, "Surrender," reached Number 1. During 1962 there were three new films and three Top Five singles, while 1963 featured two movies and three singles. The latter included "Devil in Disguise," a respectable Number 3 hit, but also two mediocre songs from that year's films. "Bossa Nova Baby" reached Number 8, while "One Broken Heart for Sale" peaked at Number 11. It had finally happened—a release by Elvis had failed to crack the Top Ten, and rightfully so. Without the advantage of Elvis' name recog-nition, some of his lesser singles from 1963 and successive years probably would not have made the charts at all.

Elvis is sometimes cited as an American performer who was hurt by the British Invasion of 1964, but in reality his singing career was already in trouble by 1963. Too much effort was being expended in filmmaking, and too little in finding and recording good songs. Not that Elvis was doing either of those things. His handlers chose the movies and most if not all of the songs; all too often the latter were substandard, but they were recorded for the movies he made. From 1961 on, the songs Elvis performed in his movies ended up as B- or even A-sides on his singles. Earlier movie songs had been released as singles successfully, such as the Number 1 "Jailhouse Rock" in 1957, but those were *good* songs.

Eventually even Elvis' handlers could read the writing on the wall, and movie-generated singles became less common after 1965. By then RCA-Victor, seemingly desperate for decent material, was releasing songs that Elvis had recorded years earlier. This practice started in 1964, when Elvis released six singles. Only one of these was both new and nonfilm related, "Witchcraft," which barely charted at Number 32. The next single was "Kissin' Cousins," from the film of the same name, stalling at Number 12. Elvis didn't break the Top Ten that year, for his other movie tie-in reached Number 21, and the release of three songs recorded up to six years earlier earned a Number 34 and two Number 16s. The next year was both worse and better—worse because the five singles released were all either film or archival material, better because "Crying in the Chapel," recorded in 1960, went to Number 3 in 1965. It was his only successful single that year.

Between 1956 and the end of 1962, Elvis released 24 singles. Of these, eight placed in the Top Five, while the other 16 went all the way to Number 1. There were no A-sides rated lower than Number 5. From 1963 to the end of 1970, Elvis released 30 singles. Among all of these there were only four Top Five records and a sole Number 1; eleven of them would even fail to reach Number 30. Most performers would have been happy with the record sales experienced by Elvis in those later years, but most performers hadn't enjoyed his early career. It was a tragedy that it continued. One can only assume that while Elvis himself didn't need more money, and clearly didn't need to perform, his avaricious handlers always wanted more money, so the singles, films, and live performances in Las Vegas kept coming just as long as he had a pulse.

The sad thing is, rock and roll listeners were predisposed to like what Elvis recorded. Even his poor stuff sold reasonably well. On those rare occasions when he was given good material, Elvis' songs did very well indeed, for example, 1969's "Suspicious Minds," his last Number 1 song and the same year's Number 3 "In the Ghetto," or the Number 2 hit from three years later, "Burnin' Love." The pathetic wreckage of Elvis' later career was unnecessary, a result of those he trusted using him contemptibly.

Blue Suede Shoes

When Elvis Presley was born in Tupelo, Mississippi, in 1935, the son of a poor farmer, his parents could not easily afford to buy him a decent pair of shoes. By the time he recorded "Blue Suede Shoes" at age twenty-one, he could have bought the whole shoe factory. Starting with a blues number recorded for Bluebird in August 1954, "That's All Right" (written by Arthur Crudup), and followed by "Good Rockin' Tonight" for Sun (written by Roy Brown), Elvis soon zoomed into national prominence and super stardom.

Among his early recordings were "I Want You, I Need You, I Love You" (1956), by Maurice Mysels and Ira Kosloff; "My Baby Left Me" (1956), by Arthur Crudup; "Any Way You Want Me" (1956), by Aaron Schroeder and Cliff Owens; "Blue Suede Shoes" (1956), by Carl Lee Perkins, performed by Presley in the film *G.I. Blues*; plus several songs by Jerry Leiber and Mike Stoller. Although Elvis himself contributed to several of the songs he recorded, Leiber and Stoller were perhaps the main supplier of songs for the early Elvis. They wrote "Hound Dog" (1956), "Treat Me Nice" (1957), "Loving You" (1957), and "Jailhouse Rock" (1957).

Leiber and Stoller also wrote several other songs that were not recorded by Elvis, including: "Kansas City," a top hit in 1959; "Charlie Brown" (1959); "Yakety Yak" (1958); "There Goes My Baby" (1959), with Benjamin Nelson, Lover Patterson, and George Treadwell; and "On Broadway" (1963), with Barry Mann and Cynthia Weil. Returning the focus back to Elvis, another Mann, Kal, also wrote "The Cha Cha Cha" (1962), with Dave Appell, "The Wild One" (1960), with Bernie Lowe and Appell, "The Wah-Watusi" (1962), with Appell, and "Teddy Bear" or "Let Me Be Your Teddy Bear" (1957) with Lowe. "Teddy Bear" was of course one of Elvis' best discs, which was probably not recorded when he was "bear" footed.

Bridge over Troubled Water

He wasn't a long-term Senator from Illinois or a presidential candidate as was his namesake, but songwriter and entertainer Paul Simon certainly was a top candidate for best folk rocker of the late 1960s and early 1970s. In marked contrast with much of the popular music of the period, Simon's compositions were a sort of stroll back to the gentler songs of earlier years.

His 1970 creation, "Bridge over Troubled Water," was perhaps the top song by Simon. It was Number 1 in record sales in 1970, plus it won a Grammy Award. Another Grammy winner was "Mrs. Robinson" (1967) which was a big hit in 1968. Other good songs by Simon that did not win Grammies included "The 59th Street Bridge Song" (1967), better known as "Feelin' Groovy," "The Sounds of Silence" (1966), and "Scarborough Fair/Canticle" or "Parsley, Sage, Rosemary, and Thyme" (1966), coauthored by Arthur Garfunkel, with whom Simon recorded all the above pieces.

Although "Bridge over Troubled Water" was probably Simon's biggest success, the song that most exemplified the emotions of the brilliant and highly successful singing duo of Simon and Garfunkel had to be "Feelin' Groovy." However, that sentiment was short-lived, for in 1969, Simon and Garfunkel broke up not long after they recorded "Bridge over Troubled Water." There must have been something in the water around 1969 and 1970, for two other megagroups, the Beatles and the Supremes, also parted company at that time.

Can't Help Falling in Love

If there was a poll as to which was Elvis Presley's best recording, "Can't Help Falling in Love" would surely get its share of votes. The excellent 1961 ballad, written by George David Weiss, Luigi Creatore, and Hugo Peretti may be the finest rock era song performed by Elvis. (The melody, incidentally, was probably adapted from an eighteenth-century French love song, "Plaisir d'Amour," by Martini il Tedesco.) Elvis introduced "Can't Help Falling in Love" in the film musical *Blue Hawaii*, in which he appeared with Angela Lansbury. A later and more famous role for Lansbury would be that of writer and detective Jessica Fletcher in the 1980s to 1990s television program, *Murder, She Wrote*. (Sleuth Jessica, being a very clever person, probably never tried to investigate whether Elvis actually died in 1977 or was still alive in hiding years later.)

Although "Can't Help Falling in Love" was perhaps the best known song by Weiss, Creatore, or Peretti, they also wrote "The Lion Sleeps Tonight" or "Wimoweh" (1952) with Albert Stanton. That song was popularly revived in both 1962 and 1972, and was a key number in the 1994 Disney animated film hit, *The Lion King*. Weiss' songwriting credentials also include "Cross over the Bridge" (1954) and "Wheel of Fortune" (1952), both with Bennie Benjamin; "What a Wonderful World" (1968) with George Douglas; and "Mr. Wonderful" (1956) and "Too Close for Comfort" (1956) both with Jerry Bock and Larry Holofcener. The last two songs were from the Broadway musical *Mr. Wonderful*, starring a wonderful performer, Sammy Davis Jr.

Of course, this list of "wonderful" things should include Elvis' outstanding rendering of "Can't Help Falling in Love."

Crazy Man, Crazy

Being the first rock and roll act, the first performers to have a Number 1 hit with a rock song, and thus launching the rock era—all this would be a daunting responsibility. Especially if none of it were true.

Many disc jockeys and rock historians trace the beginning of rock and roll to 1955, or even more specifically to early July of that year. That was when Bill Haley and the Comets had their Number 1 hit with "Rock Around the Clock," the first time a rock and roll song took over the Number 1 position. It's a major date in rock history, without question. However, to somehow claim that rock and roll began at that point is ludicrous.

It is simply wrong to exclude all the songs recorded previous to a certain date as somehow not being real rock and roll, even if they sound enough like rock to pass. For example: Fats Domino had several hits on the R&B charts, starting in 1950, in his very distinctive style. Is one to believe that his music only "became" rock and roll when he started hitting the pop charts in 1955?

Various pundits have adopted different, equally arbitrary dates to define the beginnings of rock and roll, and each can be argued without resolution. The stance taken here is that some songs dating well before the fabled start of rock and roll are clearly part of the rock canon, and that each should be judged on its own merits. That is why this book speaks of the rock and roll *era*, the period when rock was clearly recognized as a different and important genre, and dominated the airwaves. Even here it is possible to adopt differing views, but the most logical starting point would seem to be the beginning of Elvis Presley's national career in January 1956. To say that the classic rock era began in 1956 does not exclude earlier recordings from being recognized as rock and roll; they are merely preclassic.

The use of Bill Haley's "(We're Gonna) Rock Around the Clock" as the opening and closing theme music in the 1955 film

The Blackboard Jungle was a turning point in rock and roll. Millions of people heard the music in a matter of weeks; its use by Hollywood legitimized rock and roll, to some extent; the teenagers in the film were mostly hoodlums, extending their risky cachet by association to the new, innovative theme music.

"Rock Around the Clock" hadn't even made the Top 40 when first released in June 1954. It was only when public awareness of the song got it some airplay, and Decca rereleased the single, that it soared to Number 1. (The song became a hit all over again in 1974, due to its adoption as the theme of the popular television program, *Happy Days.*)

Bill Haley was born in Michigan in 1925, but began his musical career as the singer in a country band in New England. By 1948 he had his own group, the Four Aces of Western Swing. In 1949 he renamed his band the Saddlemen. They recorded a cover of "Rocket 88" in 1951, for the Holiday label; nothing came of it. The following year he signed with Essex, and in 1953 the once-again renamed Bill Haley and the Comets had their first hit, the Number 15 "Crazy Man, Crazy." According to some rock historians, this was the first record that can fairly be described as rock and roll to ever appear on the pop charts.

The band took its new name to the Decca label in 1954. Their first release of "Rock Around the Clock" failed to chart, but "Shake, Rattle and Roll" went to Number 7 in the summer of 1954, the Comets' first real hit, first Top Ten, and first gold record. In November they released "Dim, Dim the Lights (I Want Some Atmosphere)," a forgettable tune that nevertheless went to Number 11, a sign that Bill Haley now had some real name recognition.

In March 1955 the two-sided minor hit "Mambo Rock"/"Birth of the Boogie" earned Number 17 and Number 26, not so good compared with Number 7 and Number 11. Two months later, though, "Rock Around the Clock" was rereleased and finally charted, becoming Number 1 in the land on July 9, 1955. It held Number 1 for eight weeks, a considerable achievement. America was not all *that* rock-conscious yet, however; Bill Haley's successor at Number 1 was Mitch Miller's "Yellow Rose of Texas"—for six weeks, too.

Haley's next singles, the material he had recorded most recently, were "Razzle Dazzle" (Number 15) and "Rock-a-Beatin' Boogie" (not charted). This is quite a comedown from two months as Number 1, with a recycled record at that. "Burn That Candle" (November 1955) and "See You Later, Alligator" (January 1956) did a lot better, at Number 9 and Number 6. (It was at about the time of "See You Later, Alligator" that Elvis Presley began his strategically-planned series of television appearances, ushering in the new era.)

In 1956, Bill Haley and his band were featured in two movies, Alan Freed's *Rock Around the Clock* and its sequel, *Don't Knock the Rock*. Haley performed more songs in the first film, which was after all named for his big hit, than any other band ever did in any rock exploitation film (of which this was the first). The Comets played the title tune, as well as "See You Later, Alligator," "Mambo Rock," "Razzle Dazzle," "Rock-a-Beatin' Boogie," "Rudy's Rock," and "R-O-C-K." The latter two were among his listless singles in 1956, peaking at Number 34 and Number 16, respectively.

The B-side of "R-O-C-K" did fairly well, however, for a flip. "The Saints Rock 'N Roll" went to Number 18 on its own, beating the A-side "Rudy's Rock" hands down. It is a very bad sign when neither the performers nor the producers know which one of their works best merits promotion. Worse yet, that Number 16/Number 18 record sold fewer copies than the Number 16 would have alone, which is very bad for business.

For *Don't Knock the Rock*, Haley performed a much more typical two songs, the title theme and "Hot Dog Buddy Buddy." "Hot Dog" was released as a single, but did not chart. The Comets' other single for 1956 was a cover of Little Richard's "Rip It Up;" a lackluster Haley version that went to Number 25. The group kept trying, with ditties such as "(You Hit the Wrong Note) Billy Goat," but they failed to chart even one time in 1957. There were to be no further movie appearances either.

The Comets finally charted again in April 1958. "Skinny Minnie" reached Number 22, a poor last showing for a historic group, but not that far off their career average of Number 16 (charitably leaving out numerous singles that completely failed to chart).

Bill Haley kept rocketing up and skidding down the charts because he never really understood rock and roll. With his own roots in country swing, he brought a contagious enthusiasm and relaxed attitude to his music, but as rock evolved and changed, Bill Haley himself wasn't headed anywhere in particular.

His song titles used current buzzwords like protective mantras; the words *rock* and *roll* appear frequently, but so do *mambo* and *boogie*. He also uses rhyming titles (four times), repetition of words (three times), and alliteration (five times; some titles use more than one effect, however). Only one or two song titles can be said to actually mean anything decipherable, not necessarily a deficit in rock and roll.

If one wishes to accord primacy to Bill Haley and the Comets as the "first" rock and roll group, it isn't accurate to do so on the basis of "Rock Around the Clock," or at least not solely. An R&B group called the Chords had a crossover pop hit in June 1954, "Sh-Boom." Their version went to Number 9, at the same time that "Shake, Rattle and Roll" was going to Number 7. The Crew-Cuts, a Canadian vocal group that specialized in covering R&B hits, took "Sh-Boom" to Number 1 on July 28, 1954, almost a full year before "Rock Around the Clock" ended up there, and—by the way—about when the original release of "Rock Around the Clock" was failing even to chart.

Any way you look at it, "Sh-Boom" qualifies as an early (pre-classic) rock and roll song. The Crew-Cuts weren't very original or very famous, didn't do a movie theme, or perform in an Alan Freed film, but *they* had the first rock and roll Number 1 hit on the pop charts.

Honor Bill Haley and his band instead for the first rock song ever on the pop charts ("Crazy Man, Crazy"), for an early rock and roll Top Ten appearance ("Shake, Rattle and Roll"), for one of the first rock Number 1 records ("Rock Around the Clock"), for the first major rock and roll career, and for his important task of spreading the word through two timely movie appearances. His achievements are big enough that he does not need spurious ones added to the total. Rock and roll history, on the other hand, needs to move away from comfortable and familiar mythology, and into the bright light of day.

Diana

The age of sixteen sure was sweet for Paul Anka. After visiting New York at age fourteen, he was so captivated by the excitement and scope of the "Big Apple" that he returned somewhat before he was sixteen with the intention of marketing some songs he had written. To describe his return as successful would be a gross understatement.

The son of a Canadian restauranteur of Syrian descent, Anka became an international star in 1957 at age sixteen. On top of obtaining a long-term recording contract, he recorded one of his own compositions, "Diana," which became a megahit, topping the charts for thirteen weeks in a row and selling nine million discs that year and the next, three million in the United States. By 1963, "Diana" had sold a total of thirteen million copies, approaching the huge financial success of the all-time champion, Bing Crosby's 1942 recording of Irving Berlin's "White Christmas."

Although none of his later songs did as well as the "Diana" phenomenon, several other songs that Anka wrote and recorded were also very well received. "You Are My Destiny" and "Crazy Love" were very popular in 1958. The best selling song "Lonely Boy" (or "I'm Just a Lonely Boy") (1959) appeared in the musical film *Girls' Town*. "Put Your Head on My Shoulder" (1959) was in the Top Ten in record sales in that year and was successfully revived in 1969. "Let the Bells Keep Ringing" (1958), "It Doesn't Matter Any More" (1959), "It's Time to Cry" (1959), "Teddy" (1960), "Puppy Love" (1960), "She's a Lady" (1971), "(You're) Having My Baby" (1974), "I Believe There's Nothing Stronger Than Our Love" (1975), and "I Don't Like to Sleep Alone" (1975) were all hits, as were the Eastman Kodak commercials that featured Anka's very good piece, "The Times of Your Life" (1975).

After "Diana," perhaps the most famous Anka compositions were associated with other celebrities. He wrote the very often heard instrumental theme for Johnny Carson's *Tonight Show* on television. "Johnny's Theme" (or "Here's Johnny") (1962) supposedly was coauthored by Carson. Anka also wrote the lyrics for the 1969 classic "My Way" to accompany the melody by Jacques Revaux. Frank Sinatra made that song famous and the song helped make Sinatra even more famous. Most of all, the song allowed the mature vocalist and actor Sinatra and the still quite young vocalist and composer Anka to both claim, in their pursuits of fame and fortune, that "I did it my way."

Dream Lover

Two years before Walden Robert ("Bobby") Cassotto from the Bronx, New York, leaped toward international fame and success after his 1958 recording of his own song "Splish Splash" became a smash hit, he had decided to adopt another name. Reportedly, in 1956 twenty-year-old Bobby browsed through the phone book (in New York City, that's a lot of browsing) and came up with the name "Darin." Whether he just liked the sense or sound of it, or whether he consciously or subconsciously was thinking of the similar words "darin[g]" or "dar[l]in[g]," "Darin" was the name he was to be known as after that, a name that would be at a superstar level for years after his death at age thirty-seven in 1973 from chronic heart problems.

"Splish Splash" was not Darin's first recording, but it was the first of many top hits sung by him, of which his 1959 Grammy-winning rendition of "Mack the Knife" (words by Marc Blitzstein, 1954, music by Kurt Weill, 1928) was by far the most famous. In 1956 he had recorded "My First Love," written by Darin with Don Kirshner. After he made a big splash in the musical bathtub with "Splish Splash," he wrote and recorded "Dream Lover" (1959). Perhaps the best song written by Darin, and one of his very best recordings, "Dream Lover" went far in making his dreams come true. If one of his dreams was becoming an outstanding film actor, it was at least partially a reality because he was nominated for an Oscar in 1963 for his supporting role in *Captain Newman, M.D.* If one of his dreams was to romance a beautiful actress, that at least temporarily became a reality because of his several-year marriage to Sandra Dee during the 1960s.

However, if one of his dreams was to be a great popular composer, his dream bubble would have burst. Although he wrote over 150 songs, only "Splish Splash," "Dream Lover," and perhaps his 1961 instrumental "Come September" (lyrics added in 1966 by

Cy Cohen), are really outstanding, with just "Dream Lover" perhaps approaching the status of a rock classic. Among his other compositions were: "Queen of the Hop" (1958) and "Early in the Morning" (1958), both with Woody Harris; "This Little Girl's Gone Rockin'" (1958), with Mann Curtis; "I'll Be There" (1959); "Multiplication" (1961), with Kirshner and George M. Shaw; "Things" (1961); "You're the Reason I'm Living" (1962); "18 Yellow Roses" (1963); "Look at Me" (1964), with Randy Newman; "You Just Don't Know" (1965); "We Didn't Ask to Be Brought Here" (1965); "Long Line Rider" (1968); and "Me and Mr. Hohner" (1969).

Although not a truly outstanding writer of songs, Darin was a good actor and a splendid vocalist. His entertainment career from 1956 to 1973 almost perfectly matched the span of years of the classic rock era, and his contributions to that era were major. He was a rock superstar, and to use the title of one of his most successful albums, "That's All" we need to know.

Good Vibrations

Good timing is one of the key ingredients for success in life. It also was the name of two different songs. In 1960 Clint Ballard Jr. and Fred Tobias wrote "Good Timin'," and in 1979 Brian Wilson and brother Carl Wilson created another "Good Timin'." It is ironic that the Wilsons wrote their "Good Timin'" in the late 1970s, for during the 1960s they, by the whim of fate, had bad timing.

Brian, Carl, and brother Dennis, cousin Mike Love, and friend Al Jardine were the original Beach Boys. After their recording of Chuck Berry's "Surfin' USA" in 1963, the Beach Boys became a national phenomenon. In the years following, they recorded several other hits, including Brian Wilson's classic "I Get Around" (1964), "California Girls" (1965), another classic by Brian, "Help Me, Rhonda" (1965) and "Sloop John B" (1966), both also by Brian, and "Barbara Ann" (1966), written by Fred Fassert. ("Sloop John B" should not be confused with "Hang On Sloopy" (1965), by Bert Russell and Wes Farrell, and "Hang On Sloopy" should not be confused with the famous cartoon dog clinging to his dog house or his World War I aircraft.) "Snoopy vs. the Red Baron" was in turn a major hit for the Royal Guardsmen in 1966.

The Beach Boys probably hit their peak in 1966 when they recorded "Good Vibrations," by Brian and Mike Love. Possibly the best rock song ever created, "Good Vibrations" brought very good vibrations to the group and to adoring audiences. With a casual and breezy manner, complex harmonies, use of high falsetto, and a series of good to outstanding songs, the Beach Boys would have been the top male vocal group of the 1960s except for the invasion of the English foursome, the Beatles. The Beach Boys' fabulous rise to fame in 1963 was followed the very next year by Beatlemania hitting the United States, resulting in the Beatles' fame overwhelming all other rock artists for several years. Unfortunately for the Beach Boys, the timing of their initial stardom was just about the worst that one could imagine.

In the long term, however, the Beach Boys survived and continued to be a notable group into the 1990s, while the Beatles didn't last beyond 1970. Maybe that's why the Wilsons wrote their "Good Timin'" in 1979, proclaiming to the world that while other groups may disappear, *they* were still having fun and "good times." In fact, times were so good in 1979 that their trademark song "Good Vibrations" became the musical theme of a national advertising campaign.

I Want to Hold Your Hand

The year 1964 was extraordinary in the history of rock music. That was the year that Beatlemania swept over the United States. The Beatles had become the rage of Great Britain in the second half of 1963, and in early 1964 became the spearhead of the "British Invasion" of the states in the mid-1960s.

The four lads from Liverpool, John Lennon, Paul McCartney, George Harrison, and Ringo Starr, had started as a group only a few years earlier, in 1960. Originally, the drummer was Peter Best, but in 1962 Best was replaced by Starr. (Another original Beatle, Stu Sutcliffe, left the group in 1962 and died soon after.) The addition of Starr seemed to be the catalyst for catapulting this brash, boyish, and unconventional foursome into the international limelight and making them all fabulous superstars by 1964.

They were met by mobs of screaming fans when they arrived at Kennedy Airport in February 1964, and during that year appeared twice on *The Ed Sullivan Show*, the top American television variety program. One of the songs they sang on the Sullivan show was "I Want to Hold Your Hand." That composition, created by Lennon and McCartney, was the Number 1 record in sales in 1964 and also won the British Ivor Novello Award. Several years later, the prestigious Boston Pops Orchestra, noting the touches of classicism in the song, included "I Want to Hold Your Hand" in one of its concerts.

"I Want to Hold Your Hand" was perhaps the best song by the Beatles, but they had plenty of additional good compositions. In 1964 alone, Lennon and McCartney also produced "Can't Buy Me Love," "A Hard Day's Night," and "She Loves You," all three Novello winners, plus "Do You Want to Know a Secret?" and "Love Me Do." On top of this the Beatles had another big 1964 hit with their recording of "Twist and Shout," by Bert Russell and Philip Medley, which was first recorded in 1962.

In 1964 and for several years after, much of America wanted to hold hands with the four Beatles.

In My Room

Surf music was a short-lived but powerful trend in rock and roll, providing brief careers for numerous bands in the early 1960s. The Beach Boys got their start with surf songs, as well as a few drag strip ditties; of all the surf groups, they alone were able to transcend that genre classification and become a truly successful rock and roll band.

In large part this was made possible by the efforts of Brian Wilson, their composer, arranger, and bass player. The Beach Boys consisted of Brian, his brothers Carl and Dennis, their cousin Mike Love, and their high school friend Al Jardine; none were particularly talented instrumentalists, and only the tunes and their wonderful vocal harmonies stood out.

Brian Wilson brought close vocal harmony to 1960s rock and roll. There had always been doo-wop and soul singing, but Wilson's approach to harmony wasn't like that of the Four Tops, with a front man and a backing vocal group or choir. What the Beach Boys featured was often a multivoiced "lead," reminiscent more of the Four Lads than of the Four Tops. "Good Vibrations" (1966) is an excellent example of this.

While many of the Beach Boys' early songs were typical teenage ballads, some of the better efforts were characterized by a wistful, often unhappy attitude toward life. Brian Wilson reached many listeners with his tales of insecurity and sadness. A good example would be "Don't Worry, Baby," a popular B-side from the summer of 1964. It tells of a drag racer who is in way over his head in a dangerous race. (All the Beach Boys' many car-related songs were flip sides.)

A-sides such as "When I Grow Up (To Be a Man)," a Number 9 hit from the autumn of 1964, "Wouldn't It Be Nice?" (Number 8 in summer 1966), and the 1965 Number 1 hit "Help Me, Rhonda" expressed a gamut of teen emotions and situations. Perhaps the best

Beach Boy song of this sort is the lovely B-side ballad "In My Room," a Number 23 in late 1963. It was the flip of the popular but vacuous "Be True to Your School" (which peaked at Number 6). "In My Room" reflected Brian Wilson's frequent reclusive withdrawals into his bedroom for days at a time. This was at the point of his greatest popularity and musical success, probably not an unrelated observation.

Wilson is America's closest equivalent to Sir Paul McCartney, the member of a beloved group whose musical talents far overshadowed the others', whose musical vision and determination often reached the point where his colleagues were manipulated and played like mindless instruments, without creative input. Brian Wilson was not always able to achieve the scope and grandeur of those visions, perhaps due in part to the mediocrity of the materials with which he was forced to work. Even so, the results were always worth hearing.

It Ain't Me, Babe

Many composers and performers in the world of popular music have experienced greater influence on their colleagues than their record sales, however large, would suggest. This can happen when the person's own songs are performed by others, when his/her concerns are echoed by other artists in their compositions, and when even the composer's personal style is imitated. (For an example of the latter, listen to any song by Buddy Holly, and then to "Sheila" by Tommy Roe. This is sincere flattery indeed.) Bob Dylan is a great example of the musician influential beyond surface appearances. He has gone through a number of discernable periods, but only the first few years are relevant to this topic, for his greatest influence was during his early folkie/protest period. Political and social protest songs have been around for a long time; in mid-twentieth century America they were largely a part of the folk tradition, as exemplified by Woody Guthrie, Pete Seeger, Malvina Reynolds, and many other performers.

It seems peculiar to say of a composer that he or she works in "folk" music; isn't folk music traditional and orally transmitted, not created by composers? But all music has to come from somewhere, and a folk performer such as Joe Hill or Huddie Ledbetter may create by putting new words to an old tune, or may compose an entirely new song, but in authentic folk idiom. Bob Dylan began his career as a folkie, writing new songs in a folklike style. Some of his early subject matter was clearly protest music in nature. Some was fairly straightforward music of love affairs and relationships, though always of the doomed sort. And some of his songs were self-consciously paradoxical, like zen koans, devoid of any surface meaning that uninitiate, square, adult (or whoever) might understand, but evidently just *packed* with deeper meanings for the cognoscenti.

In the early 1960s, Dylan performed his own songs in coffeehouses, in concert halls, and at folk festivals. He recorded albums that received virtually no radio airplay. More important for his career, other folk artists, ones with good voices and more name recognition, began to sing his songs. A few went so far as to record Dylan's music; finally, in 1963, one of his songs was released as a single. The song was "Blowin' in the Wind," performed by the folk trio Peter, Paul, and Mary. Their political and musical credentials were impeccable. In the preceding year they had enjoyed a Number 10 hit with "If I Had a Hammer," and in 1963 their recording of "Puff, the Magic Dragon" had reached Number 2. Most important of all, but little known, they, like Bob Dylan, had New York show business heavyweight Albert Grossman as their manager. Grossman, the absolute antithesis of a folk figure, put together this deal that was so profitable to Dylan, to PP&M, and, of course, to himself. "Blowin' in the Wind" reached Number 2, made all involved a great deal of socially conscious money, and—of chief significance for popular music—was heard by people from all walks of life. For the first time, average Americans listened to Bob Dylan's words and music, before they had ever heard of him by name.

Peter, Paul, and Mary immediately followed up their Dylan debut with another of his songs, "Don't Think Twice, It's Alright." It went to Number 9 on the charts, increasing his name recognition. During 1964, none of Dylan's songs were successfully released as singles; he sold a lot of albums, however, and other performers continued to use his music.

Nineteen sixty-five would prove to be the big year in Bob Dylan's career. His album *Bringing It All Back Home* was released to a great deal of critical unease. In it he employed electric guitars and a rock and roll sensibility for the first time, causing some commentators to fear that Dylan was deserting his musical roots, the folk tradition. Of course, they were correct, but at a deeper level the critics were irrelevant. By adopting a more popular genre, Dylan was newly accessible to millions of listeners, influencing that genre, and making even more money than before. What he did was now called folk-rock.

Among its other main progenitors were the Byrds, whose earliest singles were released in 1965 as well. Their very first release was Dylan's "Mr. Tambourine Man," reaching Number 1 in the summer of 1965. The song is vintage Dylan—it isn't about young love, fast cars, or much of anything coherent, but people liked it. It seemed to assume a lot of insider knowledge and secret significance, and you almost can't go wrong with that combination in music for teenagers.

Next, Dylan himself finally released singles of his compositions. "Like a Rolling Stone" was issued in August 1965, reaching Number 2 on the charts, his best performance ever. The preceding May his first effort, "Subterranean Homesick Blues," just barely charted at Number 39; while his songs, and to a lesser extent their titles, became more accessible after that, Dylan only ever reached the Top Ten on four occasions. While one may say that his was album music, or that he wasn't concerned with the 45 rpm market, it still remains that he tried on several occasions to break into that market and never truly succeeded.

Just a week after "Like a Rolling Stone" was issued, the Turtles released their own first single, Bob Dylan's "It Ain't Me, Babe." The Turtles made it to Number 8 that time; "Happy Together," their fourth single, would be their only Number 1 hit.

The next Dylan self-recording to chart was "Positively 4th Street," reaching Number 7 in the fall of 1965. In early 1966 he released "Rainy Day Women 12 & 35," which unfortunately peaked at Number 2, rather than at Number 12 (or Number 35). Due to the vagaries of time and chance, the much better "Just Like a Woman" stalled at Number 33 when it was released later that year. Even Cher got into the act with a version of "All I Really Want to Do" in late 1965, peaking at Number 15.

In 1967 the Byrds once again turned to Dylan for "My Back Pages," their seventh and last single. It was a pretty decent record, but only reached Number 30 despite the classic Dylan line "I was so much older then; I'm younger than that now." This served as a clear sign that the Dylan era was ending. Manfred Mann, the South African that everybody always calls a Briton, released "The Mighty Quinn" in 1968, just breaking the Top Ten. Both songs had lots of unintelligible lyrics, but the old magic just wasn't there anymore. It wasn't everybody's cup of meat.

Nineteen sixty-nine saw the appearance of yet another face of Bob Dylan. *Nashville Skyline* was a highly successful album, and its single "Lay Lady Lay" reached Number 7 on the pop charts. However, it was a new kind of countrified Dylan, singing in a new (awful) way, almost as bad as McCartney's phlegmy performance on "Get Back" that same summer.

Dylan was not to release many more singles, or ever hit the Top Ten again during the rock era. His influence, like that of any innovative composer (or the innovator in any field) is impossible to accurately measure; it becomes a matter of strong opinion, no more. We do not have a control group, a twentieth century in which he never made a record. However, it is probably fair to say that Dylan was one of the defining figures of 1960s popular music. Had, say, Creedence Clearwater Revival never released a record, 1960s popular music would have been little different. If the Beatles, Dylan, or especially Elvis Presley had not recorded, who can say where we would be now?

Last Train to Clarksville

In 1966 an interesting thing happened. Producers at Columbia Pictures' television division created a program about a rock and roll group, and then they created the group. The name of the TV series was *The Monkees*, and it featured four young men as a mythical struggling rock and roll band. Unlike the band they portrayed, the young men known as the Monkees quickly became famous and sold many records.

The Monkees were—probably—the first example of a musical group put together at the whim of producers. They were emphatically not the last. Their primary task was to portray musicians in a comedy series, a job at which the four young men were quite good. Two of the Monkees came from a background of modest success as actors (Mickey Dolenz and Davy Jones), while the other two actually were struggling musicians (Peter Tork and Michael Nesmith). Interestingly, the lead vocals on every Monkees hit were sung by the actors Jones and Dolenz, not the musicians.

The genesis of the Monkees is well documented. The Beatles, the other group with a misspelled animal name, had created a market for films with a mixture of knockabout comedy and high-quality rock and roll. *A Hard Day's Night* in 1964 and *Help!* the following year greatly exceeded previous teen-exploitative rock and roll movies in quality, imagination, and profits. Elvis Presley had starred in a number of films, some reasonably good, but never playing himself, as the Beatles pretended to do. The combination of motifs unique to their films was: real musicians playing idealized versions of themselves, lightweight plots, lots of laughs, and Top 40 music.

By 1966 it was clear that reasonable facsimiles of Beatles movies could make somebody a lot of money—in other words, a niche stood open, waiting for exploitation. *The Monkees* aired on ABC from 1966 to 1968, in which time the group had several major hits. Each Monkees episode included at least two performances of good rock and roll tunes.

A major controversy, then and now, was whether the Monkees played the musical instruments that they, as actors, appeared to be playing during the programs. It is known that Don Kirshner and other creative types associated with the series had studio musicians play the tracks on the earliest Monkees' singles; it is known that Dolenz and Jones have never shown a great tendency to play any instruments professionally since then. One does not get the feeling when watching the show that real music is being made, but Nesmith and, to a lesser extent, Tork, have shown that they are professional quality musicians themselves. Later in the life cycle of the program and the group, the Monkees played at least some of their own music on tour and on vinyl, and recorded their own songs; sales dropped off and the group disbanded.

When the show was in the planning stages, new songs were commissioned from successful rock and roll composers such as Neil Diamond, Carole King, and Boyce and Hart. From the first, the program was a big hit, and many of the songs that debuted on various episodes went straight to the Top Ten. Almost from the first, there was confusion between the Monkees as actors and the Monkees as performers of music, made worse by the Beatle-emulating pattern of calling the Monkee-actors by their real names, not character names. They really acted in the show, they sang the songs, but they didn't play the instruments; within a few weeks they were somehow the biggest "group" in America. The situation was guaranteed to produce resentment toward the actors, centering around their unworthiness for such sudden fame and success, and their perceived lack of musical ability. Even the band's having access to songs by major composers was a basis for complaint.

It might be worth the effort to set the record straight on a few points. On the issue of producers commissioning original music from composers: this happens all the time, even for bands that have not yet recorded a note or sold a single record. Lots of musicians are incapable of writing good music themselves. The Monkees were not noticeably worse off than the average group produced by Phil Spector in this regard.

There was a major stigma attached to being a Monkee—that it was necessary to audition, Hollywood-style, for the part. In truth, it's hard to know what's real in show business. Sloan and Barri wrote and recorded a 45 rpm single themselves as the Grass Roots (the song was "Where Were You When I Needed You?"), and when it went gold in 1966, they happily hired an obscure L.A. band to play their music on record and on stage, and voila, the Grass Roots was a real band! They went on to a successful, multiyear recording career. Are they more authentic than the Monkees, or just more secretive?

Even the Beatles have something shameful in their past. Producer George Martin and manager Brian Epstein forced the other three to dump drummer Pete Best, replacing him with Ringo Starr. (It would be easy to say that they forced "the Beatles" to dump Pete Best, but until the moment it happened, Pete Best *was* a Beatle.) Even then, Martin lacked faith in Ringo and used a studio drummer on several early Beatles tracks. Are the Beatles a *real* group, given that they engaged in such shenanigans to please powerful producers, and let promises of wealth persuade them to behave so foully?

And what of the Partridge Family, a television "musical group" so false and saccharine as to make the Monkees seem like grizzled Delta bluesmen by comparison? Nobody made a similar fuss over the Partridges, even when "their" records went to the Top Ten.

Finally, on the Monkees as musicians. The intervening years have provided perspective on this issue. Michael Nesmith has written, performed, and produced successful rock and roll music, along with being one of the developers of the modern music video. One of his compositions, "Different Drum," was the first Top Ten hit by Linda Ronstadt, even while *The Monkees* program was still on television. The lead vocals of Dolenz and Jones were better than most Top 40 performers of their era, and remain popular on oldies shows.

It is true that, apart from Nesmith, none of the Monkees appear to be particularly gifted as instrumentalists. So what? This is far from a unique situation in rock, where many bands get by on fame and cannot play adequately in live performances. On many occasions the "back-up" musicians on stage will far outnumber the so-called band. Plenty of musicians are only good in the studio, where they only have to get it right once.

Unfortunately for the Monkees, many people—themselves included—confused their roles with their realities. Under a Faustian contract to Columbia, and the subjects of a massive publicity campaign, the four affable young men became famous overnight, while still pegged at low salaries. Their success at portraying musicians led to a desire to be recognized as an actual musical group, which they were not. Over time the four lads (called by one wit, and thousands of half-wits, the "Pre-Fab Four") became a group if not quite a band, under the shared pressures of the exploitation they experienced.

The laugh is on Columbia, for more than three decades after the series was summarily cancelled, the Monkees remain popular—not as actors or individuals, but as a band. Even in the 1960s, Columbia and its subsidiary Colgems didn't know what they had. In September 1966, as the show debuted, the song "Last Train To Clarksville" rocketed to Number 1 on the charts. It probably would have been a major hit even without the television series or the publicity; to this day it is a wonderful song and a much-loved oldie, even by people who have never *seen* the program.

The Monkees went on to have a total of eleven chart hits in less than two years, with nine in the Top Twenty, six in the Top Five, and three at Number 1. Very few groups have done as well, even with careers of five or more years. However, it is even more impressive when one considers that the Monkees only ever released seven singles. Four of their hits were B-sides, always a sign of serious popularity. If Colgems had cooperated and compromised with the Monkees, nurturing their desire to be a real group, while retaining a degree of creative control, it is probable that the group's place in rock history would have been even larger—as would Colgems' earnings.

Certainly they were never overexposed, curious in a group that came into being on and for television. In 1966 the Monkees released two singles, three in 1967, and two more in 1968. During this period it was not uncommon for major recording artists to release two or three times that many singles per year. To judge from their early performance, the Monkees could have been major, but Columbia allowed their momentum to stall, and their careers to end, from pique.

Let It Be

Was there some kind of subconscious code in the last songs of the Beatles? You judge for yourself from the titles of the following John Lennon and Paul McCartney compositions. In 1968 there were the Ivor Novello Award winners "Hello Goodbye" and "Hey Jude." In 1969 there was the Novello winner "Get Back" plus "Come Together." And in the departure year for the Beatles, 1970, there was "The Long and Winding Road" plus the Novello winner "Let It Be." The last two, tied for Number 5 in record sales in 1970, were to be the Beatles' final hits.

"Hello Goodbye" could well describe the relatively short existence of the group, forming in 1960 and dissolving in 1970. "Come Together" and "Get Back" could have been predictions of the public's outcry for the Beatles to get back together after the breakup. "The Long and Winding Road" could have been a metaphor for the difficulties of a group resisting the divisive forces that often accompany great success. And "Let It Be" could have been a recognition that the group's impending breakup was not going to be resolved, or a sort of resignation to the whims of fate.

The 1970 dissolution of the Beatles, which became legal in 1975, did not mean the end of creative activities by the four ex-Beatles. McCartney, with his wife Linda, wrote several later songs (although Linda's contributions are questioned by some people). Starting in the 1980s, McCartney reemerged as a star on his own, including the composition of creditable classical work. George Harrison, who had written a 1969 Beatles hit, the Novello winner "Something" or "Something in the Way She Moves," collaborated with Ringo Starr on the 1973 hit "Photograph," sung by Starr. And Lennon, who was the most controversial Beatle, was involved with various and sundry things. "Instant Karma" and "Imagine" were among eight major hits for Lennon as a solo act.

In spite of much sentiment to reunite the Beatles throughout the 1970s, however, the reunion never happened. With the death of Lennon in 1980, all hope for a reconciliation disappeared. This brings us back to the possible subliminal messages of the last Beatles' songs.

Love Me Tender

Elvis Presley is known for a number of things, including versatile and fantastically successful singing, the onstage gyrations of Elvis the Pelvis, mobs of adoring fans, and a questionable lifestyle. Lesser known are Elvis' contributions to several of the most famous compositions he recorded.

In 1956 he wrote the fine ballad "Love Me Tender" with Vera Matson, the melody being borrowed from an 1861 song, "Aura Lea." (George R. Poulton wrote the music for the Civil War era favorite.) In the same year, Elvis collaborated with Tommy Durden and Mae Boren Axton to create "Heartbreak Hotel," and with Otis Blackwell to produce "Don't Be Cruel." The next year, 1957, Presley and Blackwell cowrote "All Shook Up." Although Elvis will never be regarded as a great songwriter, his participation in the creation of four of his top songs cannot be overlooked. Perhaps if he hadn't had the very appealing voice and personal style that brought him so much adoration, he might have been a songwriter of note. On the other hand, if he hadn't been so very popular, maybe his four compositions would not have been nearly as successful as they were.

Otis Blackwell also wrote two other well-known rock songs. With Jack Hammer (that can't be a real name!), he wrote "Great Balls of Fire" which Jerry Lee Lewis sang in the 1957 film musical *Jamboree*. With Winfield Scott, Blackwell wrote "Return to Sender," which Elvis performed in the 1962 film musical *Girls! Girls! Girls!* As a result of the last-mentioned song and movie, Elvis probably received the adoration of even more girls, girls, girls who wanted to love him tender and every other way.

Michelle

At the ninth annual Grammy awards ceremony, held in Los Angeles in March 1967, John Lennon and Paul McCartney were given their third Grammies. The category of the award was Song of the Year, for their ballad "Michelle;" that particular Grammy goes to the composer(s) of a song, not the performer(s). The Beatles as a group were to win four Grammies, while Lennon and McCartney shared a fifth; it is curious that each award was in a different category.

Perhaps the most noteworthy aspect of the award for "Michelle" is that the song was an album track. The Beatles released the Capitol Records album *Rubber Soul* on January 8, 1966, in the United States; Beatle material generally came out in Great Britain first, naturally. While "Michelle" and a few other tracks on the album certainly had Top 40 potential, the Beatles did not choose to release them as singles. (This was the first, but not the last time the group would release an album without the simultaneous release of 45 rpm singles, but in the later cases (*Sergeant Pepper's Lonely Hearts Club Band* and the White Album) the material was far less commercial.)

It cannot be said that the Beatles went unrepresented on the radio during this period. Their very next album, *Yesterday . . . And Today*, came out in July 1966, collecting four Top Ten hits from late 1965 and early 1966.

"Michelle" was in fact issued as a single in 1966, by David and Jonathan. Biblical reference aside, they were really British songwriting team Roger Greenaway and Roger Cook, authors of, among others, "Long Cool Woman (In a Black Dress)" and "You've Got Your Troubles." Their version of "Michelle" was released on January 29 of that year, just three weeks after the album came out in America. Pretty fast work; it helped that they recorded for the same labels as the Beatles, and the single was produced by the "fifth

Beatle," George Martin. However, a Beatles song without the Beatles was just a curiosity, and "Michelle" went to Number 18 instead of the Number 1 the Beatles would have earned. That Number 18 certainly wasn't responsible for the Grammy.

The listening public became aware of "Michelle," probably the sweetest song the Beatles ever recorded, by hearing this album track on the radio—those that didn't automatically buy the new Beatles album, that is. While the Beatles ignored the Top 40 radio stations in their decision to release no singles from *Rubber Soul*, the radio could not get away with ignoring them. (It wasn't exactly the first time this had happened, for the Beach Boys and a few other groups had grown so popular that even some of their album tracks ended up on the radio, but it was the first time that the recording artists had not deigned to release *any* track from an album.)

For an album track to become quite so popular was unprecedented. In the then eight-year history of the Grammy awards, Song of the Year honors had invariably gone to highly publicized tunes. They had been awarded to two pop favorites (best-selling 45 singles), two numbers from beloved musicals (one a best-selling single), and four movie themes (all available on popular singles as well). "Michelle" was unique.

The Grammy Awards had a somewhat spotty reputation as far as rock and roll went. In its second year, the Best New Artist award went to Bobby Darin, perhaps on the strength of the Record of the Year, "Mack the Knife." That was good. But, when in 1961 a new category debuted, Best Rock and Roll Recording, it went to "Let's Twist Again." With no disrespect to Chubby Checker, there were dozens of much better (and better remembered) songs on the charts in 1961.

In the next two years, the rock and roll Grammy went to "Alley Cat," by Bent Fabric, and "Deep Purple" by the sibling act April Stevens and Nino Tempo. Those are both fine songs, but it is ludicrous to call them the best of rock and roll. It appears that the selection committee didn't really *like* rock and roll, usually picking a pop rather than a rock song.

The very next year, 1964, the Beatles won their first two Grammies. It was inevitable that they would receive the award for Best New Artist(s), and they were also voted Best Group Vocal Performance, a much less convincing award. Worse, the Best Group Vocal Performance was given for "A Hard Day's Night," far from their best work in 1964. It was the last of the Beatles' five American Number 1 records that year, as well as the title song to their popular first movie, so there is no mystery as to why the Grammy selectors would have been aware of the song.

However, "I Want to Hold Your Hand," "She Loves You," or "Can't Buy Me Love" would have made much more appropriate songs to merit an award. Considering the heady days of early April, 1964, when the Beatles occupied the entire Top Five, when "Can't Buy Me Love" was Number 1 only two weeks after its American release, *that's* the song that should have won a Grammy.

In 1966 "Michelle" won its Song of the Year award, but the award for Best Rock and Roll Recording went to "Winchester Cathedral," a forgettable piece of fluff—and in no sense a rock song—by the New Vaudeville Band. The following year things went somewhat better. "Up-Up and Away" won in the categories of Best Vocal Group, Best Single, and Record of the Year for the Fifth Dimension, and Song of the Year for its composer, the great Jim Webb. Best Male Vocalist went to Glen Campbell, singing "By the Time I Get to Phoenix," also written by Webb. The Best New Artist and Best Female Vocalist awards were given to Bobbie Gentry, for her electrifying "Ode to Billie Joe."

So, 1967 was a great year for rock and roll at the Grammy Awards. The best part, though, was the Best Album category. That award went to *Sergeant Pepper's Lonely Hearts Club Band* by the Beatles. The lads from Liverpool really didn't give the Grammy selection people any choice; if ever an album deserved the title "Best," that was the one. It was the most influential, most innovative, and other mosts as well.

The nine earlier Grammies in the category had gone to Judy Garland, Henry Mancini, Barbra Streisand, Stan Getz, two comedians, and Frank Sinatra (he got three of them). *Sergeant Pepper* was quite a change of pace for the Grammy, and 1967 was the year that the Grammy committee finally acted as if it recognized and maybe understood rock and roll.

In 1969 the Fifth Dimension once again took Best Recording and Best Performance by a vocal group, this time for the flawless

"Aquarius/Let the Sunshine In," their recording of the *Hair* show-stopper. And in 1970 the Beatles won yet another Grammy category, in the final year that they would be eligible. The soundtrack album of the last film, *Let It Be*, won in the film/television division. Only once before had Top 40-type music been so honored, Paul Simon's 1968 soundtrack for *The Graduate*.

Some of it is just timing. By the late 1960s, the Grammy committee was falling all over itself giving awards to pop stars. A few years earlier, back when Elvis Presley was at his career height members of the hoi polloi (such as Elvis) rarely if ever received awards. So, Elvis never got a Best Male Vocalist or Best Rock and Roll Performance Grammy. (Chubby Checker did, but that's another story.)

Photograph

The Beatles announced their breakup in early 1970, before their last film, *Let It Be*, premiered in May. It was evident that the group had disbanded much earlier, however, for only a little new Beatle material was trickling out of Apple headquarters. As early as August 1969 John Lennon was releasing singles under the much-loathed name the Plastic Ono Band, also on the Apple label; "Give Peace a Chance" went to Number 14. "Instant Karma" did better in the spring of 1970, peaking at Number 3; people were beginning to figure out that they'd have to get their Beatles individually from then on (and they were beginning to realize that, knock on wood, Yoko Ono's input in Lennon's music was essentially nonexistent).

Lennon continued to issue records, occasionally to great success, until his death in late 1980. (He stayed with the Apple label until about a month before he was murdered, when he switched to Geffen.)

John's no-longer-quite-so-friendly rival and former partner Paul McCartney released the album *McCartney* in May 1970, within days of the debut of the Beatles' last single (a McCartney-dominated song titled "The Long and Winding Road," with lush strings arranged by Phil Spector). In the logical next step from his increasingly self-absorbed work as a Beatle, Paul recorded *McCartney* as a solo project. He wrote, played, sang, recorded, and engineered every note on the entire album, which gratifyingly went to Number 1.

Ringo Starr rushed a quickie album into production at about the same time. *Sentimental Journey* went to Number 22, producing no singles at all. Ringo's second album was much better. *Ringo* went to Number 2 in 1973, with several successful singles on it. His "It Don't Come Easy" and "Back Off the Boogaloo" had reached Number 4 and Number 9, while "Photograph" was his first solo Number 1 record. It's a wistful tune that spoke of a lost relationship; for some listeners, it was hard not to connect the song with the story of the Beatles. Alone of all post-Beatle records, *Ringo* contains the work of all four ex-Beatles; the jovial Ringo remained on good terms with all three of his mates—separately, of necessity.

Some of Ringo's later singles were covers of good old rock and roll. "Only You" dated from 1955, when the Platters had a major hit with the song; it was covered twice in the 1950s, then by Ringo in 1974. The previous year he had also covered the Johnny Burnette song "You're Sixteen" from 1960; both were successful for him, "You're Sixteen" giving Ringo his second and last solo Number 1. Covers were a familiar venue for him, since most of his singing as a Beatle had been B-sides and album fodder such as "Act Naturally" and "Honey Don't," old rock or country tunes.

The last ex-Beatle to release solo records was George Harrison, whose massive boxed triple album *All Things Must Pass* came out in December 1970, quickly becoming the best-selling album in the world. Singles such as "My Sweet Lord" and "Isn't It a Pity" (both Number 1) and "What Is Life?" were released from the album as well.

All four ex-Beatles were active recording artists after the breakup. Lennon's career was ended by death, Starr's perhaps by the fact that he was not driven to write new material, although what little he created was generally good. Harrison and McCartney have stayed active well into their fifties. The latter is of course the most successful performer of all time, when his Beatles, Wings, solo, and composing credits are all considered.

P.S. I Love You

In early 1964, the Beatles arrived in America as the first wave of the legendary British Invasion. Their astounding record sales worldwide made them the most successful musical group of the century, for by their breakup in 1970 the Fab Four had released thirty singles (it would be wrong to include here "My Bonnie" or "Ain't She Sweet") and numerous gold albums. As only Elvis Presley had frequently done before them, the Beatles were often able to place even the B-sides of their singles on the charts, sometimes in the Top Ten. Indeed, in the first months of 1964 it sometimes seemed as though the Beatles *were* the Top Ten, for they had so many singles in the stores, selling well, at the same time.

A listener to rock and roll Top 40 radio stations in 1964 would often hear many different Beatles records on any given day. Relatively few recording artists have two or more records on the same charts; only Elvis and the Beatles did it routinely. Sometimes the Beatles had singles out in such profusion that it must have hurt, not helped, the sales of each individual record. Only if one bought all their records, or at least paid close attention to the Billboard Top 40 charts, was the reason for this odd phenomenon made clear. The 45 rpm rights for the American release of several early Beatles hits were scattered among a variety of record companies, and these firms all tried to cash in on what they feared might turn out to be a brief craze, Beatlemania.

Capitol released all Beatles singles in America from mid-1964 until the Beatles themselves, in the death throes of their collaboration, founded the ill-conceived Apple Records in late 1968. The first half of 1964, however, saw Beatles singles in the American record stores from Vee Jay, Tollie, and Swan as well as the Capitol label. The various nonCapitol singles were by any reasonable criteria as good as the Capitol songs, and included "Please Please Me," "She Loves You," "Twist and Shout," "Do You Want to Know a

Secret?," and "Love Me Do," all of which are still quite popular examples of the early Beatle period. Due to the confusion of this period, one of the best of the early Beatles songs, "From Me to You," never made it to the Top 40 in the United States.

When, back in 1964, it looked as if Beatles records were being released at insanely short intervals, this was true. Four different companies were attempting to make as large and fast a profit as possible from the Beatles, and they got in one another's way during the feeding frenzy. In retrospect, it seems clear that a large part of the apparent inevitableness of Beatlemania in the United States was fueled by this mindless corporate competition, flooding the airwaves as never before with the music of one group. In the end, this behavior cost the Beatles and various record companies significant amounts of money, but helped provide quite a ride for the rest of us.

During a three-and-a-half-month period in 1964, the Beatles had ten major hits on seven singles on four different record labels. Nothing like that had ever happened before or has happened since. (In the equivalent period of Elvis Presley's career, RCA released a mere three of his singles.)

The popular perception of the Beatles' performance on the American Top 40 charts has several components. That they released a counterproductive number of singles in 1964, has been adequately discussed above. Another, that even the Beatles' B-sides made the charts, is attributable to at least two more factors. Record buyers and radio stations couldn't get enough Beatles, even with three singles released in one memorable five-week period, so B-sides were given serious consideration. (It had happened to Elvis eight years earlier.) And, when they were played, the quality of these B-sides was appreciated. In fact, few big-name recording groups have enjoyed as much success as the Beatles' B-sides did by themselves.

If 1964 was a record-setting year for the Beatles, including the release of twelve of their career thirty singles, it was a curiously unsuccessful year at the same time, by Beatles standards. A total of twelve singles and twenty-four songs were released, of which seven songs failed to chart at all. There were six songs at Number 1, and four more in the Top Five. A total of fourteen of their seventeen 1964 hits placed in the Top Twenty. Nobody ever complained about performances like that. And yet, if the warring record companies had been somewhat less crazed, and had given each single a better chance at individual success, the Beatles would probably have set significantly greater records that year.

In later years the group released fewer singles, all under the Capitol label, and achieved more with less. During 1965, for example, the Beatles released five singles and had five Number 1 hits. One B-side went to Number 5, but the others languished in obscurity, as a proper B-side should. One cannot help but wonder whether, given half a chance, the Beatles might not have equaled Elvis' greatest feat. His fourth RCA release, the best-selling single of all time, was the only two-sided Number 1. First "Don't Be Cruel" went to the top of the charts, and then the B-side, "Hound Dog," followed. Clearly the Beatles were the only group in the rock and roll era that had a chance at tying, or besting, Elvis, but the chaos created by four contending record labels ruined their chance at the ultimate rock record.

Perhaps the Tollie single that carried "Love Me Do," the Beatles' last non-Capitol, pre-Apple single, would have been able to achieve this greatness. "Love Me Do" was the Beatles' only nonCapitol song of 1964 to reach Number 1, and its B-side was a Beatles classic, "P.S. I Love You." Fully worthy of A-side status, "P.S. I Love You" almost certainly would have topped the chart if released a month or so later, after the worst excesses of Beatlemania had passed. As a B-side, during the frenzied first half of 1964, it reached the Top Ten even while competing with its own A-side, not to mention the eight other Beatle hits released in the preceding three months. Tollie, Swan, and Vee Jay should be forgiven for putting "A" material on both sides of their Beatles records; they didn't have any lesser material by the group at hand.

It may be that the Beatles' many and varied recordings are best perceived collectively, as the outstanding creative achievement of popular music. Surely no other group, and no other individual apart from Elvis Presley, ever had a similar impact as performers; the Beatles' achievements as composers and innovative recording artists put them on a par with, or above, Brian Wilson and his very few peers. That being said, it still would be satisfying to know how well an underrated song like "P.S. I Love You" would have performed, given the level playing field it did not in reality receive.

Respect

Appearances to the contrary, Aretha Franklin did not suddenly burst upon the pop music scene one day in a blaze of glory. Her impressive string of hits for Atlantic Records, starting in 1967, quickly made Aretha a leading contender for Queen of Soul; almost nobody realized that she had been recording unsuccessfully for years. The truth is, Aretha Franklin's career, despite her considerable talent, went nowhere until she was taken under the wing of producer Jerry Wexler.

Signed by Columbia at age eighteen, Aretha was misused by their production department. Her only charted single from the Columbia period was a cover of "Rock-a-Bye Your Baby with a Dixie Melody" in 1961; it had been a major hit for Jerry Lewis—the comedian, not the piano player—five years earlier, but a less appropriate song for Aretha Franklin to record would take some discovering. Her version scarcely charted, with two weeks at Number 37. Even so, it was more successful than her debut single. "Won't Be Long" was well-named; it wouldn't be long before it was completely forgotten. Peaking at Number 76 on the Hot 100, it literally was never heard by most rock and roll fans of the day.

Six years later, with Aretha recording for Atlantic under the watchful eye of Jerry Wexler, her career took off. Wexler (the man who created the phrase "rhythm and blues" (or R&B) to replace the more offensive terms "race," "colored," or even "sepia" music then used by *Billboard*) handpicked and arranged the tunes, hired the musicians, and produced all of Aretha's singles. A lot of performers came to resent that strong presence on the producer's part; in Aretha's case, her talent was lying fallow, and Wexler truly made her career and reputation. A wonderful list of singles resulted from their collaboration, including "Respect," "A Natural Woman," and "Chain of Fools." Aretha had nine straight Top Ten hits (on eight singles) in one and a half years.

In late 1968 she began to do less well. Her next two singles landed at Number 14 ("See Saw") and Number 19, not tragic but definitely a bit of a comedown. The number 19, her cover of "The Weight," was a song that had failed to chart for two different acts just months before. For some reason, Wexler and Aretha seemed to believe that she could now make a decent career out of covers. This is almost always a mistaken conclusion; it was in her case, at least for a while. "The Weight," "Call Me," and even "Eleanor Rigby" were just a few of the mediocre recordings released by Aretha Franklin from 1969 into 1971.

In the latter year, covers finally began to pay off for her. "Spanish Harlem" and "Bridge over Troubled Water" brought her back to the Top Ten after a three-year, ten-single exile. A couple of new songs kept her there for a while yet, but after 1968, hits were the exception rather than the rule.

Aretha's sole Number 1 record was "Respect," her second single with Jerry Wexler; it too was a cover, but most people didn't realize that. "Respect" had been released two years earlier, in 1965, in a version by its author, a twenty-four-year-old singer who recorded for Volt. The single got very little attention in its original release, peaking at Number 38. Its composer retained faith in the song. In 1967, when he was associated with Memphis' Stax Records, itself under contract to Atlantic Records, somehow he got Wexler to bring the song to Aretha. They didn't even bother to alter the lyrics to reflect the gender change, which is why Aretha says that when her man comes home from his job, they spend *her* money. Anyway, it worked the second time around, and Otis Redding finally made some money from his song "Respect."

Redding was a dynamic performer and a workaholic. His one big hit "(Sittin' on) the Dock of the Bay," was released posthumously, as he died in an airplane crash shortly after recording the song. The success of that single was to some extent propelled by the knowledge that the singer had died, but had he lived, "(Sittin' on) the Dock of the Bay" would almost certainly have made Redding a star at last.

His first single for Volt was back in 1963. "These Arms of Mine" did not chart; only seven of his many singles would, before his death, including two duets with Carla Thomas. His best solo performers were a couple of Number 21s. Three more posthumous—but mediocre—records were released in 1968.

Otis Redding involved himself in nearly every aspect of the recording industry. In addition to performing, he wrote music for himself and others. This led to his founding a publishing firm. He began to produce other artists' singles, which led in turn to a management firm. Eventually he started his own record label as well, Jotis. When he died, after all these activities, Redding was only twenty-six.

(I Can't Get No) Satisfaction

Some of the biggest myths of rock and roll have grown up around the Rolling Stones. For instance, many people believe that the Stones benefitted significantly from the British Invasion of 1964. The Invasion started in January 1964 with the Beatles' "I Want to Hold Your Hand"; many British groups subsequently made it in America only because of a pronounced Anglophilia resulting from Beatlemania. Billy J. Kramer and the Dakotas are a prime example of this trend; they released three singles in a five-month period during mid-1964, placing two songs in the Top Ten, and then were never heard from again in the United States.

The Rolling Stones *tried* to cash in on the British Invasion, but it didn't really work for them. They released two singles in the summer of 1964, neither of which reached the Top Twenty. (Many British Invader debut singles went straight to the Top Ten.) In November 1964 the Stones' third American record finally succeeded. That single was "Time Is on My Side"; in retrospect, after well over thirty years of the Rolling Stones, this was perhaps the best title for a single ever. It reached Number 6, and suggested that there was indeed a market in American pop music for the Rolling Stones' bad boy act.

Thus, the Stones didn't make it effortlessly as invaders, but had to fight for public acclaim; success was hard-won. Their fourth release in America even stalled at Number 19, before they achieved a triumphant run of nine straight Top Ten hits in a two-year period. The second of these was their all-time most famous record, "(I Can't Get No) Satisfaction," later picked in a *Rolling Stone* magazine poll as the greatest single of the rock and roll era. The song is often cited as an example of teenage angst—which it is—but it also, and primarily, is outstanding rock and roll. "Satisfaction" was the first of five Number 1 records the Stones would have throughout the later Sixties.

Another major Rolling Stones myth is that they were in competition with the Beatles. It is true that, aside from the Beatles, the Stones were the biggest British rock and roll band of the decade. However, this is a lot like saying that, apart from Goliath, David was the biggest guy in the battle. No band, British or otherwise, presented a serious challenge to the Beatles while they were together, or in the decades since. The Stones also lacked many of the true marks of superstardom; for example, only two of their B-sides ever saw much airplay, and neither broke the Top Twenty. Their production of Number 1 singles was impressive for a rock band, but not really impressive for superstars.

It often seemed that the Stones were imitating the Beatles, not competing with them. When the Beatles created a colorful (and very complicated) album cover for *Sergeant Pepper's Lonely Hearts Club Band*, or when they "went psychedelic," the Rolling Stones were among the many groups that emulated them. The Stones shouldn't be blamed for this; *everybody* copied the Beatles. That's what set the Beatles apart; other bands, such as the Stones, might be their equals or even superiors as musicians, but none were their peers at musical or cultural innovation.

Another way in which the Rolling Stones seemed to emulate the Beatles was by creating their own record label. Apple, starting in 1968, was a good idea gone bad. The Beatles wanted more creative control and a higher percentage of the profits; what they got instead was an economic fiasco. The Rolling Stones, starting their own eponymous label three years later, appeared to somehow avoid the pitfalls that brought Apple down. In actuality, their label was only a minor part of Atlantic Records, who played on the Stones' conceit by giving them what looked like a label of their own, and so lured them away from London Records, their long-time home.

The Stones kept up a busy schedule of writing and recording songs during the mid-1960s, rarely going more than three months between single releases. However, the Number 1 single "Ruby Tuesday" was not followed up until seven months had passed, and then only by the lackluster "Dandelion" (Number 14 on the charts) in September 1967, and "She's a Rainbow" (Number 25) in early 1968. From that point on, the Rolling Stones released fewer singles. While Top Ten or even Number 1 success did not completely elude them, a large proportion of their records were relative failures, especially for what was by then being billed as "the world's greatest rock and roll band."

What was great about the Rolling Stones? Mick Jagger was the famous one, prancing about on stage, as one commentator wrote, "like a rooster on amphetamines"; he could be a very good and effective singer, but usually only in studio recordings. His writing was one of the Stones' greatest assets, although often overlooked. Keith Richard's guitar playing was perhaps the only absolutely great thing about the band; he was, in his prime, one of the handful of superior rock and roll lead guitarists, with Eric Clapton, Steve Cropper, and just a few others. The guitar riffs to "Satisfaction" and their other giant hits were among the best ever produced.

What kept the Stones interesting was the quality of their best music. Those who believe otherwise, that it was Jagger's fame, rumors of the band's drug problems, Jagger's on-stage strutting and preening, and so on, might ask themselves why so many of the Stones' singles from the Seventies and subsequent decades failed. The fame, the stage act, and so on were all present, but the singles lacked something and did not succeed. When the music worked, the records sold. The Rolling Stones are exasperating and praiseworthy in roughly equivalent degrees; the former because they continued to release cheesy singles when other musicians their age were retired to a life of quiet debauchery, and the latter because, once in a while, the Stones proved that they still had what it takes to create a superior rock and roll song.

Scarborough Fair/Canticle

Sir Thomas More, a famous figure in early sixteenth-century England, has been known as "the man for all seasons." Simon and Garfunkel, the highly acclaimed singing duo of the late 1960s, could be dubbed "the men for four seasons." Although they were briefly together before 1966, their effective existence as a top group lasted from 1966 to 1969, just four years. After their breakup, both Paul Simon and Arthur Garfunkel were to have moderately successful careers by themselves, especially Simon. In the 1970s, Simon wrote and recorded two songs of some note, "Fifty Ways to Leave Your Lover" (1976) and "Slip Slidin' Away" (1977), and in the 1980s and 1990s continued to please audiences.

Ironically, probably the best recording by Simon and Garfunkel was released after they parted ways. "Bridge over Troubled Water," which was first in record sales in 1970 and earned a Grammy, was a curious reminder that Simon and Garfunkel could not bridge their own troubled water. In the several years before they split, however, they were a most pleasant duo popularizing the folk rock songs written by Simon (and in one case also by Garfunkel).

Although another piece, "Feelin' Groovy" (1967), officially "The 59th Street Bridge Song," was also a very fine composition, Simon and Garfunkel were probably at their peak in the outstanding 1967 film *The Graduate*. In the movie's score were three top hits by Simon and Garfunkel, Grammy winning "Mrs. Robinson" (1967), "The Sounds of Silence" (1966), and "Scarborough Fair/Canticle" (1966), also known as "Parsley, Sage, Rosemary, and Thyme." "Scarborough Fair" was the only famous Paul Simon song co-authored by Garfunkel, which might explain why Simon's favorite themes, the number "fifty" and the word "bridge" did not appear in the title. It also made Simon and Garfunkel, "the men for four seasons," also, in a way, "the men of four seasonings."

Sergeant Pepper's
Lonely Hearts Club Band

In the 1960s it was not uncommon for a rock and roll album by a successful group or solo act to be made up of two or three hits from recent singles, along with eight or ten nonhits. These other songs might be the B-sides of the original hit singles, the A-sides of failed singles, covers of other people's hits, show tunes, or in fact just about anything musical. A very successful group might have as many as six hits on a typical album's twelve songs; any more hits than that would be bad economics, because more money could be made later by releasing an all-successes "greatest hits" album.

Album cuts didn't get played on Top 40 radio stations. Albums could help make an artist rich, and give true fans a lot more of their favorite music than singles alone could ever do. However, chart position, real fame, and frequent airplay on the major radio stations were all reserved for a few successful singles at any given time.

Sometimes a group might release an album of holiday songs or thematically-related cover tunes, such as Elvis' Christmas album or the Supremes' *We Remember Sam Cooke*. These were never new, never intended to compete in the singles scene. The idea of an entire album of new songs, by a major group, with no single releases was rock and roll heresy. But in 1967, ushering in the Summer of Love, the Beatles released what has been called the most important album ever made, *Sergeant Pepper's Lonely Hearts Club Band*. It is unlikely that anyone would have even used the phrase "most important album" in speaking of rock and roll before 1967, although after the release of Sgt. Pepper the accolade was virtually automatic.

First, one saw it—the album cover was a visual treat, with its stunning originality of design and wonderful colors. The Beatles in bizarre band uniforms. The impenetrable album title. The anticipation—it had been three months since the Beatles released "Penny Lane," their latest single (Number 1, of course). As it turned out,

"Penny Lane" with its powerful nostalgic appeal, and the Number 8 B-side "Strawberry Fields Forever," with *its* electronic experimentation and seemingly random lyrics, were very good preparation for Sgt. Pepper.

The music was wonderful—maybe a bit harder to warm up to than most Beatle records to that point. It repaid repeated listening (a certainty anyway), like such earlier album tracks as "Norwegian Wood." People eventually would call Sgt. Pepper a unified work, or the very first "concept" rock and roll album. It was neither, which in no way denigrates its achievements. (The first real concept album, also released in 1967, was *Days of Future Passed* by the Moody Blues; its obsession with time was expressed both by the songs' themes and their linear progression from dawn to midnight. Now that's a concept album.)

Sgt. Pepper songs had several common threads, but no unifying theme. Nostalgia for and interest in the past is present in several numbers, beginning with the first lyric: "It was twenty years ago today, Sergeant Pepper taught the band to play," and continuing with Ringo's big-band-like vocal to "With a Little Help from My Friends" and the old-timey air of "Being for the Benefit of Mr. Kite!" But it is difficult to find a nostalgic aspect to "I'm Fixing a Hole" or "Lovely Rita, Meter Maid," while "When I'm Sixty-Four" looks ahead, not back—but does so, admittedly, in an old-fashioned mode.

The main thing that sparked discussion about the album back in the Summer of Love was its "lack" of even one single. Rock and roll criticism was in its infancy then, and many commentators missed something that now seems obvious: Sgt. Pepper was tied together by that very lack of interest in Top 40 success and chart-topping singles.

The Beatles, after three and a half years as the most successful group in rock history, the undefeated champions, were bored by the Top 40 mentality. They chose to redefine the basis of the competition. They produced an album to be listened to in its entirety, not merely mined for three minutes of radio glory at a time. For the first time, the *album* was the unit of consumption and of comparison; even the cover photo began to tell us that on first viewing. Later album covers would desperately bid for our attention, but Sgt. Pepper commanded it. (The Beatles would continue playing with public sensibilities when they released the White Album, which had the effrontery to bear a completely blank cover.)

The album did go on to produce a single—sort of. Elton John covered "Lucy in the Sky with Diamonds" in 1974, going to Number 1. In 1969 Joe Cocker gave a marvelous, historic performance of "With a Little Help from My Friends" at Woodstock. Back in 1967, when Sgt. Pepper was new and fresh, Johnny Rivers recorded the prettiest of all his songs, "Summer Rain." It is for many people the real anthem of that summer; its lovely refrain repeats "And the juke box kept on playing/Sergeant Pepper's Lonely Hearts Club Band," a nice reference to the Summer of Love and the hugely influential album. However, no 45-rpm juke box *could* play songs from Sgt. Pepper, precisely because there were no singles. Not that the album went unheard. For the first time, many radio stations began to regularly play album cuts. They had to, or miss out on an entire Beatles album.

The release, two months after Sgt. Pepper, of "All You Need Is Love"/"Baby You're a Rich Man" was no consolation for the lack of singles from the album. "All You Need Is Love" is the worst single in Beatles history, rising to Number 1 only because that's what happened to Beatles singles. (Even "Come Together," with its self-indulgent claptrap for lyrics, is a gem by comparison.) One can scarcely imagine how the same band could produce those two records successively.

Apparently the Beatles enjoyed remaking the form of popular music with their $3.99 masterpiece, for they twice more released albums without singles. *Magical Mystery Tour* was a mildly successful album, though a catastrophic failure by Beatles standards. One side collected older singles such as "Penny Lane," while the other featured new, nonsingle music from the *Magical Mystery Tour* film, a flop by anybody's standards. The ultimate Beatle album, however, may be the White Album. At least that's what it's called, but really it is a featureless white-covered double album, entitled for shipping and ordering purposes *The Beatles*. It is packed with "noncommercial" songs that nonetheless became huge hits—on the radio, but not on the charts.

Stop! In the Name of Love

The Supremes were supreme in the mid and late 1960s. The singing threesome from Detroit, Diana Ross, Mary Wilson, and Frances Ballard, were the dominant female group of the decade. With ten records that at least fleetingly hit the top of the pop charts between 1964 and 1967, they brought themselves and their hometown label, Motown, great success.

In the 1964 to 1967 period, the Supremes recorded a number of songs created by Eddie Holland, Brian Holland, and Lamont Dozier. These included "Baby Love" (1964), "Come See About Me" (1964), "Where Did Our Love Go?" (1964), "Stop! In the Name of Love" (1965), perhaps their best, "Back in My Arms Again" (1965), "I Hear a Symphony" (1965), "You Can't Hurry Love" (1966), "You Keep Me Hangin' On" (1966), "The Happening" (1967), and "Love Is Here and Now You're Gone" (1967). (In 1966, another song by the Hollands and Dozier, "Reach Out, I'll Be There," was recorded by the Four Tops.)

By 1968, there were signs of trouble in the group. Its name had changed to Diana Ross and the Supremes, and Cindy Birdsong had replaced Frances Ballard. In that year they recorded "Love Child," written by Frank E. Wilson, Deke Richards, Pam Sawyer, and R. Dean Taylor. Ross made her last recording with the Supremes in 1969 and her last public appearance with them in 1970.

After Ross' departure, the group declined, but Ross went on to become a superstar. Two other songs by Frank Wilson, "You've Made Me So Very Happy" (1969), written with Berry Gordy Jr., Brenda Holloway, and Patrice Holloway, and "Keep on Truckin'" (1973), written with Anita Porce and Leonard Caston, might have represented Ross' mood at the time. The 1969 song, recorded by Blood, Sweat, and Tears, could have expressed Ross' sentiments at her entrance into stardom, and the 1973 song could have expressed her determination to maintain her ongoing star status.

Surfin' USA

In the early 1960s there were a number of beach and surfing songs. Inspired by the 1961 beach film *Where the Boys Are,* with its song of that title by lyricist Howard Greenfield and composer Neil Sedaka, surfing songs were up even in places without an ocean. Among the surfing songs were "Surfin' Safari" (1962) by Mike Love and Brian Wilson; "Surf City" (1963), by Brian Wilson and Jan Berry; and the best of all "Surfin' USA" (1963) by Chuck Berry. Actually "Surfin' USA" was a reworking of Berry's 1958 composition "Sweet Little Sixteen," with new lyrics by Brian Wilson.

Note that the name Brian Wilson came up often in the previous paragraph, just as great waves come up frequently at good surfing locations. That's because Wilson was the head honcho and chief songwriter for the Beach Boys, one of the megagroups of the 1960s and a quite respectable group well into the 1990s. Although "Surfin' USA" was the piece that shot them into the rare atmosphere reserved for superstars, and other early recordings were connected with surfing, none of the five original Beach Boys, Brian, Carl, and Dennis Wilson, cousin Mike Love, and friend Al Jardine, were reportedly surfers.

Yet they rode the big wave of success with an innovative vocal style and a low-key demeanor reminiscent of those who perpetually inhabit West Coast beaches. Several excellent songs by Brian also helped them ride the crest, including "I Get Around" (1964), "California Girls" (1965), and the superlative "Good Vibrations" (1966), with Mike Love.

Let us not forget Charles Edward "Chuck" Berry whose "Sweet Little Sixteen" piece provided the Beach Boys with their initial surfboard to fame. Berry, one of the top composers and performers of early rock, also concocted several other songs, including "Maybellene" (1955) with Russ Fratto and Alan Freed; "Johnny B. Goode" (1958), which was featured in the 1985 film *Back to the Future*; "Memphis" (1959); "Rock and Roll Music" (1957); and "Roll Over Beethoven" (1956).

Walk Like a Man

Some rock and roll historians believe that the British Invasion of 1964 wantonly destroyed the careers of many innocent American bystanders. In a Darwinian sense, maybe that's true; numerous American acts, already struggling to survive, were finished off by the new competitors a little sooner than they might otherwise have been. However, it really matters which American acts one considers. The Supremes, for example, pretty much got their start during the Invasion, and posted five straight Number 1 records in 1964 to 1965. They couldn't have been much less like the Beatles if they'd tried. Elvis Presley, his career already slumping, fell even further at the hands of the British invaders; he did not have a Top Ten record in 1964, the first year since his 1956 debut that this was so.

For Frankie Valli and the Four Seasons, 1964 was pretty much business as usual. They had Top Ten hits every year from 1962 to 1966, and went on to record into the 1970s, earning a Number 1 as late as January 1976 (with the wonderful "December 1963 (Oh, What a Night)." Valli, as a solo act, recorded from 1966 to 1978, when he had a Number 1 hit with "Grease." The Four Seasons were one of the most durable American bands of the rock and roll era, with their distinctive sound built around Frankie Valli's great vocal range. (Perhaps just to see how high he could go, they recorded a cover of "Don't Think Twice" and released it in 1965 as by "The Wonder Who." It climbed to Number 12; his singing almost went supersonic.

The Four Seasons started out as the Four Lovers in 1956, and required six years and numerous name (and personnel) changes before hitting the big time. When they finally made it, though, it was the sort of Cinderella story that sometimes happens in show business. Their first three singles, "Sherry," "Big Girls Don't Cry," and "Walk Like a Man," all went to Number 1 during late 1962 and early 1963. Not all of their singles clicked with the public, but most did; the group continued to hit the Top Ten with songs such as "Dawn," "Ronnie," "Rag Doll" (a Number 1 in the Beatlemaniac summer of 1964), and "Save It for Me."

After 1964, when the British Invasion could be declared officially over, things paradoxically got a little harder for the Four Seasons. They had only one real hit in 1965; "Let's Hang On" peaked at Number 3, a respectable showing. In 1966 the group had two hits, "Working My Way Back to You" and "I've Got You Under My Skin," both favorite oldies to this day.

At about the same time, Frankie Valli started recording as a solo act. In mid-1967 he had his first hit, "Can't Take My Eyes off You," peaking at Number 2. Although he released several more singles, success eluded Valli until 1975, when his "My Eyes Adored You" went all the way to Number 1. A few singles later, in 1978, "Grease" made it to Number 1 as well. It's not bad to have chart-toppers with your first and last singles, sixteen years apart.

Unlike many bands in the 1960s that saw their fame begin to wane, the Four Seasons did not try to go psychedelic or to dress like hippies, to become socially relevant, or anti-everything. They just kept turning out comparatively simple love songs in good rock and roll arrangements, and every so often one of their tunes would become a major hit. The Four Seasons stayed true to themselves, and perhaps largely for that reason their music remains pure and timeless.

What Becomes of the Brokenhearted?

Here's a hard question: which is the better group, the Temptations or the Four Tops? There are so many different criteria by which one could judge, that it is almost impossible to come up with an objective answer.

The Four Tops and the Temptations have oddly parallel histories. Both first hit the pop charts in 1964, both on Detroit labels controlled by Berry Gordy (Motown and Gordy, respectively). Both were traditional black vocal groups, with a lead singer in front of a strong harmonic chorus. Both groups were popular with white as well as black audiences (a strategic effort on the part of Berry Gordy, because the white record-buying audience was so much larger than the black), just like the stars of Gordy's empire, the Supremes. Both had excellent production values on their recordings, and avoided the rough edges so common on contemporary R&B records.

In fact, for many listeners the two groups tend to blur together, making it difficult to identify from memory which group recorded a particular song. (For those of us interested in rock and roll trivia, it's sometimes safer to talk about the songs and be a little vague about the recording artists.) Most songs recorded by a wide variety of Motown performers were written by the same small stable of composers, so there is not likely to be enough difference in tune or song content to differentiate on that basis.

The whole process isn't made any easier by the huge number of hits produced by the two groups during the classic rock and roll era, or by former members who struck out on their own. All together, there were sixty-two Top 40 hits on the charts from these men between 1964 and 1975. The Four Tops had twenty-one, the Temptations thirty-five, and former Temptations lead singers David Ruffin and Eddie Kendricks had two and four, respectively. (On the whole, leaving the Temptations was not the wisest career move either Eddie or David ever made.)

If you judge by longevity, the Four Tops come out way ahead. During their entire recording history they had no personnel changes. Levi Stubbs, Duke Fakir, Obie Benson, and Lawrence Payton recorded and performed together from the inception of the group to the recent (at this writing) death of Fakir. The Temptations originally were David Ruffin, Eddie Kendricks, Paul Williams, Otis Williams, and Mel Franklin. By 1971 only the three backing vocalists were still in the group, and new lead singers had to be recruited.

If you judge by the hits, the Temptations have it, hands down. They outproduced the Four Tops at every level: more Top 40 hits (35 to 21), more Top Ten (14 to 7), more Top Five (seven to five), and more Number 1 hits (four to two). A large part of the explanation of this differential, however, is simply that performers can't have a hit if they don't release a record.

Berry Gordy, for whatever reason, seems to have always preferred the Temptations, and gave them special treatment as compared with the Four Tops. For example, the Temptations released more singles and albums than the Four Tops were allowed to cut. In the year 1969, when both groups were in their productive prime, the Temptations had three Top Twenty hits. The Four Tops had no hits at all.

It looks as if the Temptations have to be the winners in this little contest. They spent more time on the charts, and that is how success is defined in the music business. And yet, when you look back at the songs themselves, the really memorable hits that helped define the mid-1960s musically, the Four Tops are clearly the winners. Compare the first hits of the two groups: the Temptations' "The Way You Do the Things You Do" versus the Four Tops' "Baby I Need Your Loving"; their second Top Ten hits: "Beauty Is Only Skin Deep" versus "It's the Same Old Song"; the powerful "Bernadette" of 1967 with the lackluster "You're My Everything." It's true that the Temptations had major hits such as "My Girl," but the Four Tops' "I Can't Help Myself," released a few months later, was even stronger. Truthfully, it must come down to personal judgement, but consider how many Four Tops oldies you hear on the radio, or find yourself humming, and then how many by the Temptations.

So, who sang "What Becomes of the Brokenhearted?" back in 1966? It is sometimes attributed to both groups, but was performed by neither. A consummate Motown production, it sounds a lot like the Temptations because it was recorded by Jimmy Ruffin, the brother of the Temptations' original lead singer.

What's Going On

It is an axiom of pop music that performers cannot stay too long in a stylistic rut if they wish to stay at the top. However, there is more than one way to reinvent oneself as a musical performer.

There is the frequent alteration of appearance method, beloved of haircut bands the world over. There is musical growth, the maturation of a composer that one sees in a Brian Wilson or a Stevie Wonder. There is, all too rarely, the development of new forms of musical expression, as seen in the later work of Lennon and McCartney. And finally, there is the gradual growth of social conscience and concern. This is the case with Marvin Gaye, the Motown star who died so tragically and violently at the hands of his abusive father.

When Marvin Gaye began recording in the early 1960s, he was a handsome young black man with a fine voice. He made numerous successful records for Tamla, one of Berry Gordy's labels in Detroit—Motown, Gordy, and Soul were others. Gaye's singles were noteworthy for his smooth styling, but did not particularly stand out in any other way. Had Marvin Gaye and Smokey Robinson traded songs, it probably would not have been noticed.

Among the better of Gaye's singles from his early period is "How Sweet It Is to Be Loved by You;" released in December 1964, it climbed to Number 6 on the pop charts. His next single, "I'll Be Doggone," peaked at Number 8, to be followed two records later by another Number 8, "Ain't That Peculiar?."

Marvin Gaye's second period may be characterized as the time of duets. As early as 1964 he had recorded a double-sided single with fellow Motown artist Mary Wells (whose career spanned four years and ten Top 40 singles), but it was in 1967 that Gaye began to make romantic duets a regular part of his repertoire. Between 1967 and 1969 he recorded eight singles with female Motown stars; in 1973 to 1974 he cut two more with the ultimate Motown songstress, Diana Ross. That totals eleven singles with four different partners.

Gaye's first 1967 duet, with Kim Weston, was punningly titled "It Takes Two." This record made it to Number 14, and has remained popular as an oldie ever since. His next seven duets were made with Tammi Terrell, and included "Your Precious Love" (Number 5), "Ain't Nothing Like the Real Thing" (Number 8), and "You're All I Need to Get By" (Number 7). These records reflect the "new" Motown, with greatly improved production values and a smoother sound, one made for the soulful singing and masterful timing of Marvin Gaye.

Rounding out this second period are a couple of superior singles that Gaye recorded as a solo. "I Heard It Through the Grapevine" eclipsed the rival version by Gladys Knight and the Pips, reaching Number 1 nationally. Knight's version, recorded later but released months earlier by the autocratic Berry Gordy, peaked at Number 2. (This may be the only case in rock and roll history where the "original" version was in truth the cover, and then the apparent cover was the chart-topper.) Both versions are excellent, but Marvin Gaye's is one of the best recordings ever made.

The other major song from this period is "Too Busy Thinking About My Baby," released in May 1969. It peaked at Number 4, and would by itself have been the high point of many a successful rock or soul career. Coming directly after "I Heard It Through the Grapevine," it seems a bit of a letdown, but then almost any song would.

After another Top Ten record in 1969, Gaye released only one charted single in 1970. "The End of Our Road" spent only two weeks on the charts, and never rose out of the basement, by far his worst performance. Perhaps stunned by this abysmal showing, Marvin Gaye released no records during the next several months.

When he came back to pop music in 1971, it was with the first of five straight Top Ten hits, powerful songs evincing a greater social conscience than any of his early works ever had. There is plenty of basis for assuming that Gaye himself was always socially aware, but he does not appear to have previously realized music's potential as a medium of serious expression.

In March 1971 Marvin Gaye released "What's Going On," a song that rises above all his earlier work musically, conceptually, and socially. It is a reflection of his worries about the future of life in America, and is praiseworthy in that right, but it is also a masterful and memorable piece of American vernacular music.

Over the next couple of years Gaye released "Mercy Mercy Me," "Inner City Blues," "Trouble Man," and "Let's Get It On." All four were Top Ten hits, the last a Number 1. Along with "What's Going On," they showed a maturity of composition and execution, and a seriousness of subject matter, beyond almost all his peers. Following these songs Gaye was less successful in his career, and his music reverted to more or less the romantic but vapid form of the middle 1960s. Between November 1973 and his death in 1984, Gaye charted with only four singles, two of which went gold. They were perfectly reasonable recordings, but a big step down from his fluorescent period in the early 1970s. A drug habit and other personal problems gave Marvin Gaye trouble, but he was apparently putting these things behind him in his last few months of life. Gaye was still popular to the end; unlike most artists in rock and soul, he probably would have continued to be creative well into middle age, had his life not been taken from him.

Who's Sorry Now?

Connie Francis signed with MGM Records in 1955, as a sixteen-year-old high schooler. After ten unsuccessful singles and three years of trying, she finally had a Number 4 hit with "Who's Sorry Now?"—and still was barely nineteen. Before her recording career was over, she had released thirty successful singles, with thirty-five hits in the Top 40. Francis recorded sixteen Top Ten hits; three of them reached Number 1.

Her style and material were almost more like those of a big band singer, and Connie Francis is generally forgotten now, but she was the most successful female vocalist of the classic rock and roll era. For over six years, she averaged a new charted hit every ten weeks; it is easy to become confused and overwhelmed by the number of records and the best-selling titles in her past.

All of Francis' major hits came in the four years following "Who's Sorry Now?". One almost could not turn on the radio without hearing her powerful voice. "Stupid Cupid," "Lipstick on Your Collar," and "Everybody's Somebody's Fool," as well as several of her other hits, were very popular in their day.

By the age of twenty-two Connie Francis had added another string to her bow. From 1961 to 1965 she appeared in four movies, lightweight romantic comedies in which, rather than having to carry the plot, as Elvis sometimes strained to do, she was just one of an ensemble of players. *Where the Boys Are, Follow the Boys, Looking for Love,* and *When the Boys Meet the Girls*—the titles fairly well sum up the films.

Francis didn't have any major hits after the summer of 1962. Between then and mid-1964, she released eight singles that averaged an only acceptable Number 24. Connie Francis made no more records after 1964, but performed frequently in hotels, resorts, and similar venues. Her career was halted in 1974, when she was raped in one of the hotels where she was the headliner. After a long legal battle she was awarded three million dollars in damages. Francis made a comeback performance in 1978, and continued to perform thereafter.

World Without Love

One of the rock and roll questions that may never by completely resolved is: who wrote the Beatles' songs? According to the copyright data, almost all of them were cowritten by John Lennon and Paul McCartney. The two decided early on that all their musical compositions would be copyrighted jointly, and so all but a few of the Beatles' songs were listed this way. It has become apparent over time that this simple pattern of attribution means nothing, and a lot of ink has subsequently been spilled trying to assign authorship accurately.

Of course, in some cases there is no mystery. George Harrison wrote a few of the songs on various Beatles albums, including some of the later hits, such as "Here Comes the Sun" and "Something." In the rush to issue more albums and singles back in 1964, when they ran out of original material, the Beatles recorded a number of covers of older songs. Only a few of these were released as singles, but many are still to be found as album filler. (Ringo's country-and-western background asserted itself occasionally on songs such as "Act Naturally," the B-side of the monster hit "Yesterday.") All of these songs are well-attributed.

It is only the Lennon-McCartney songs that are hazy. According to many authorities, their authorship varied from "all John" to "all Paul;" sometimes one wrote the music and both the lyrics, or one added a final polish to the other's work. It appears that the best indicator of authorship is really pretty simple, though; the one who sings lead is probably the chief composer. "Yesterday," for instance, is attributed entirely to McCartney.

Throughout the Beatles' career as recording artists, they were associated with several other groups or performers in very positive ways. Lennon and McCartney provided old friend Cilla Black with one of her first British hits, "Love of the Loved," a song they decided not to record. Her career in the United States never took off. The one hit she had in America was "You're My World," a recording with no Beatle connections; it stalled at Number 26. Later in the decade, Paul McCartney wrote other songs for her, hits in England that, given her previous performance, were not even released in America; these include "It's for You" and "Step Inside Love," Beatle—or at least McCartney—songs that few American Beatles fans have ever heard.

Years later, the Beatles started the Apple label, and set out to become record moguls. They apparently discovered that business wasn't much fun, for they issued only a few records by themselves or others, and lost millions in the process. Among the few groups they found and produced was Badfinger. The band released four good singles on the Apple label in 1970 to 1972; the first, "Come and Get It," was written by McCartney for the film *The Magic Christian* (starring Ringo, with cameos by John and Yoko). Mary Hopkin was another performer who recorded for Apple, with her singles produced by McCartney. "Those Were the Days" was a Number 2 hit in the United States, a lovely, nostalgic song.

The Beatles helped indirectly to launch another band back during the 1964 British Invasion. Their manager, the fledgling impresario Brian Epstein, took on a few more bands before his suicide in 1967. One, the American group Cyrkle, had two promising hits in 1966 and, unfortunately, then faded from view. ("Red Rubber Ball" made it to Number 2, while the follow-up "Turn-Down Day" peaked at Number 16.)

Back in 1964, Epstein managed a second Liverpool group, acquaintances of the The Fab Four. Gerry and the Pacemakers had seven hits between 1964 and 1966, including three in the American Top Ten. "Don't Let the Sun Catch You Crying" and "Ferry Cross the Mersey" were among the best songs of the British Invasion. Even with a good song, known association with the Beatles (and even thicker Liverpudlian accents than George Harrison's), Gerry and the Pacemakers just couldn't catch on as transatlantic stars.

One final British group that the Beatles—or at least *a* Beatle—helped out was the duet of Peter and Gordon. Between 1964 and 1967 the two released ten singles, three of which made the American Top Ten. "Peter" was Peter Asher, since the late 1960s a major record producer, and brother of famous model Jane Asher. In the mid-Sixties Paul McCartney was known as one of the richest and most eligible bachelors in the world, and for a time it looked as if Jane Asher was going to change all that. Paul thoughtfully provided Peter and Gordon with a lovely ballad, "World Without Love," (copyrighted by Lennon and McCartney) to serve as their debut single. It performed very well, reaching Number 1 (their only American chart-topper), and starting their career off with a bang. (Three releases later they reached the Top Ten again, with the Del Shannon-penned "I Go to Pieces," in early 1965.)

"World Without Love" is vintage McCartney, with its clever rhymes and sweet harmonies; at least in this one case it seems clear which Beatle wrote the (non)Beatle song.

Yesterday

"Yesterday" by the Beatles was the Number 1 record in sales in 1965, following up on a similar triumph by the group in 1964 with "I Want to Hold Your Hand." "Yesterday" is also one of the most recorded songs of all time. Yet there are some who consider this song by John Lennon and Paul McCartney to not be as good as a later song with "Yesterday" in the title. "Yesterday When I Was Young," written by Charles Aznavour and Herbert Kretzmer, a hit in 1969, is a fine sentimental ballad. Unfortunately, though, it wasn't enhanced by the mystique of the Beatles.

Beatlemania, which had started in the United States in 1964, continued brashly in 1965, 1966, and 1967. On top of the Ivor Novello Award winning song "Yesterday," the Beatles also sang several other Lennon and McCartney hits in this period. "Eight Days a Week" and "Ticket to Ride" joined "Yesterday" in 1965, "Paperback Writer" plus Novello winners "We Can Work It Out" and "Yellow Submarine" came out in 1966, and "All You Need Is Love," "Sergeant Pepper's Lonely Hearts Club Band," and "Lucy in the Sky with Diamonds" were hits in 1967.

The last song could be interpreted as a sign of impending decline for the Beatles. There was much speculation that "Lucy in the Sky with Diamonds" was an allusion to LSD, the mind-altering drug that was a fad in the turbulent 1960s. Whether or not this speculation was valid, the Beatles had done their best work by 1967 and by 1970 had broken up, never to work together as a foursome again. After 1970, the Beatles could be described as a fantastically successful group of yesterday.

You Send Me

Far too many of the giants of rock and roll have died too young. Sam Cooke, believed by many to have been the first real soul stylist, is another grim example. Born in 1935, he was still six weeks short of his thirtieth birthday when murdered in an altercation.

The son of a Baptist minister, Cooke sang in the church choir from the age of six. While still a child he was a member of a minor gospel group; he went on to join the famed Soul Stirrers as their lead singer in 1950, at the age of fifteen. Cooke remained in this pioneering gospel group for six years, and it was excellent preparation for his later secular work. The chief antecedent of soul and much other black vocal pop music is gospel singing, rather than early black commercial music such as R&B.

Cooke recorded as a solo act with the Specialty label in 1956; to protect his identity as a gospel singer, the first singles were released as by "Dale Cook." (Speciality was the Soul Stirrers' label as well.) He needn't have bothered, for virtually nobody ever heard them. The following year he went to the Keen label, and things started looking up. Cooke's first release there was the marvelous love song "You Send Me," which gave him a powerful Number 1 hit the very first time he reached the Top 40. Specialty still had the rights to an unreleased Sam Cooke single, and rushed it out to capitalize on his big hit. "I'll Come Running Back to You" did acceptably at Number 18, but may have dispelled some of Cooke's momentum from "You Send Me."

Few of his remaining singles for Keen performed particularly well; eight more charted hits averaged Number 25 and less than six weeks on the charts. After a string of so-so releases, even superior songs such as "Only Sixteen" and "Wonderful World," the last two singles Cooke released on Keen, did far more poorly than they should have. Both were very decent tunes, later to be covered successfully; for Sam Cooke they earned a dismal Number 28 and a somewhat better Number 12. Some perfectly adequate acts never charted higher than Number 12, but for a major talent like Sam Cooke, such poor performances verged on failure.

That Number 12 provided him with some career momentum at last, and Cooke was able to move into the majors. He signed with RCA in 1960, and the change was immediately apparent. With more money for production and promotion of his records, his very next single went to Number 2, the moody "Chain Gang."

Cooke's batting average did not really go up all that much at RCA; his nineteen charted songs on sixteen singles still varied in their degrees of success, but the numbers were improved overall. His work at RCA averaged about Number 17, with three Top Ten records and six more from Number 11 to Number 13, for a total of nine strong hits in about four years. Two of his other singles each peaked at Number 17, even though they have proven more popular over the years than several more successful songs. "Cupid" and "Having a Party" should have been bigger hits, somehow.

Cooke's best work at RCA included the Number 9 "Twistin' the Night Away" in 1962, arguably the only good song to come out of the Twist craze, and the following year's humorous "Another Saturday Night," another Top Ten for Sam Cooke.

Cooke's last two singles were issued posthumously in 1965, including his third-most successful song, "Shake." The Supremes subsequently recorded an entire album of his material, *We Remember Sam Cooke*. Many of his songs live on as radio oldies, while many others were covered at one time or another. Sam Cooke was inducted into the Rock and Roll Hall of Fame with the very first group, in 1986.

THE BEST SONGS THAT NEVER MADE NUMBER 1, OR, TIME HEALS ALL ACHES, MISTAKES, AND BAD BREAKS

Ain't That a Shame?

When Pat Boone sang "Ain't That a Shame?" in 1955, he wasn't referring to the popularity of the song by Antoine "Fats" Domino and David Bartholomew. Probably the best song by Domino or Bartholomew, "Ain't That" was one of the top hits of the year. Among the other compositions by the two were "Blue Monday" (1957), "I'm in Love Again" (1956), and "I'm Walkin'" (1957). Bartholomew also wrote "I Hear You Knocking" (1955) with Pearl King.

Domino also made recordings, perhaps the most notable of which was "Blueberry Hill" in 1956. Like many successful rock-era songs, "Blueberry Hill" was not a rock song but a composition from an earlier time that fit in well with the rest of the discs made in 1956. Al Lewis, Larry Stock, and Vincent Rose wrote the piece in 1940.

Staying on the topic of recordings, Domino and Bartholomew directly helped the singing career of young Ricky Nelson. Although Nelson was already familiar to the American public as one of the child stars of the long-running early television series *The Adventures of Ozzie and Harriet*, which portrayed the fictional lives of a real family, Ozzie, Harriet, David, and Ricky Nelson, he gained additional fame as a rock singer. Unfortunately, his life was cut short by a 1985 airplane accident, but he had several successful recordings in the late 1950s, and a respectable career after that. The first disc by Nelson, who was at the time just seventeen, was his gold record of "A Teenager's Romance" (1957) written by David Gillam. On the flip side was Nelson singing Domino and Bartholomew's "I'm Walkin'."

Downtown

If you want an entertaining day or night out, downtown is the place to be in most cities. There are exceptions in some localities, such as Manhattan where midtown is the center for bright lights and amusements of all kinds.

Downtown was an especially interesting place in 1965 after British singer Petula Clark recorded Tony Hatch's "Downtown." The song was Number 3 in record sales, and won the American Grammy Award and the British Ivor Novello Award. As if these three honors were not enough, Clark also recorded "I Know a Place" in the same year, "My Love" in 1966, and "Don't Sleep in the Subway" in 1967. "I Know" (by Hatch) also won a Grammy, "My Love" (again by Hatch) was also Number 3 in record sales, and "Don't Sleep" (by Hatch and Jackie Trent), won the Novello Award.

Clark and Hatch were a part of the British Invasion of the United States in the mid-1960s. The Beatles were, of course, the main body of the invasion force, but Clark and Hatch would also make their mark. Clark became a big celebrity because of her recordings, but Hatch is far from a household name in spite of the previously listed songs and several other notable ones including "Harvest of Love" (1963), written with Benny Bill; "Where Are You Now My Love?" (1965), written with Trent; and "Call Me" (1967). All three of these won the Ivor Novello Award. Hatch was honored by five Novellos and two Grammys in a four year period and yet is basically unknown in the United States. Whether fair or not, composers often receive far less attention than performers.

After the British Invasion subsided and the Beatles broke up, another song called "My Love" won a Novello Award. The 1973 composition was by ex-Beatle Paul McCartney and his wife Linda. In this case, since the song was recorded by Paul McCartney and Wings, the composer and the artist were equally famous.

From Me to You

A frequent topic in these essays is the need for recording artists to change their act, or at least to vary it. Often a newly emerged artist will have one or two highly successful singles, only to quickly lose public favor when the next several songs are too similar to the first. In the early days of rock and roll, the major record labels often acted as matchmakers for performers and songwriters, soliciting new songs for their artists. It had been so from the earliest Tin Pan Alley days until the mid-1950s with little change. Singer-songwriter-producers such as Buddy Holly somewhat reformed the way major labels did business.

Smaller labels did not have the clout to attract songs from big-name pop composers. Many of these labels compensated for their small scale with an openness to new composers and new acts; many famous rock and roll performers started their careers with obscure record labels, doing their apprenticeships in a sense.

Smaller labels encouraged artists to record their own material; recording the work of unknown composers, or covering established hits, were their only options. Unfortunately, many performers either could only write one kind of song, were painfully slow in composing new material, or both. The upshot was that they rarely had any good material left, after recording their first couple of singles.

Between an unvarying performance style and excessively similar songs, some artists had a hard go of it as professional musicians. Del Shannon is almost the ultimate in this category of hard-luck artists. Shannon (born Charles Westover in 1939) was discovered as a performer after a stint in the Army; his first single was released in March 1961, when he was twenty-one years old. It was his own composition, "Runaway," (on the misleadingly-named Big Top label) that became one of the most striking debut songs in rock history. It turned into a Number 1 hit.

Three months later, "Hats Off to Larry" went to Number 5, and Del Shannon seemed well launched as a rising rock and roll star.

Both songs were characterized by Shannon's vigorous attack, his use of falsetto, and the eerie, whiney tones of the primitive Musitron keyboard synthesizer used by Max Crook. Unfortunately, the same could be said of virtually everything that Shannon ever recorded. In the fall of 1961 he released "So Long Baby," a song that bore all his trademarks. Lacking originality, it stalled at Number 28, a poor showing in the context of the two Top Five records that preceded it. The next was even worse, a cover of "Hey, Little Girl." Del Shannon's version stayed on the bottom of the chart at Number 38 for just two weeks.

Worse yet, "Hey, Little Girl" was Shannon's most successful single for an entire year, until early 1963. "Cry Myself to Sleep" (it is hard not to read deeper significance into some of these titles) never got close to the Top 40; *Billboard* maintains a Hot 100 chart, of which the Top 40 is the successful portion, and "Cry Myself to Sleep" spent one week at Number 99, just about the worst possible performance a single could experience.

The next Shannon single was a comeback by comparison. "The Swiss Maid" spent five weeks on the Hot 100, peaking at Number 64 in the fall of 1962. (It should be mentioned that the profits involved in the music industry are so enormous that even a mediocre single makes some real money. Also, especially in the 1950s and 1960s, a single on the charts was adequate justification for a tour; touring profits went mostly to the performer, not to the label, so tours were very desirable.)

Following "The Swiss Maid," Shannon released "Little Town Flirt" in early 1963. It was a vindication of his tenacity, going to Number 12. He followed it with "Two Kinds of Teardrops," which spent nine weeks in the Hot 100 without besting Number 50. At about this time, Shannon toured Great Britain in support of "Little Town Flirt," and found himself playing at the same venue as a very popular British group, the Beatles. They had begun releasing successful records in Britain during 1962, and at the time that Del Shannon met the Fab Four, they were pushing *their* current hit, "From Me to You."

Shannon liked the song, and heard it months before Beatlemania would hit the United States. Upon returning home he recorded his own version, and released it on June 29, 1963. Del Shannon is thus triply historic; he was the first American to cover a Beatles song, his version was the only Beatles song first available in the United States as a cover, and his version was the first Lennon and McCartney song ever recorded in the United States.

None of these firsts helped, and "From Me to You" spent a month on the Hot 100, never rising above Number 77. The trouble was, in July 1963 almost nobody in America yet cared about the Beatles; eight months or so later, when things might have gone differently, Shannon was no longer with Big Top, and the label did not choose to rerelease the record. Shannon's fourth "first" is that he was the first American to fail miserably with a Beatles cover. In November 1963 Shannon issued "Sue's Gotta Be Mine" on his own label, Berlee. It did about as well as "From Me to You." Shortly thereafter he signed with the Amy label, and a different company seemed to help. His first single on Amy was a cover of "Handy Man." It went no higher than Number 22, but perhaps Number 22 looked pretty good by then. The next release was another cover, "Do You Want to Dance?," a real frustration. After seven weeks on the Hot 100, it just missed the Top 40 with a Number 43. (If a record gains enough support from disc jockeys to enter the Top 40, potential fans become more aware of it.)

Del Shannon kept plugging away, and on his next effort struck gold. "Keep Searchin'," a symbolic enough title, earned him a Number 9 in the early days of 1965. His next single, "Stranger in Town," went to Number 30. In May 1965 Shannon tried again. "Break Up" was almost a replay of his worst performance. It "peaked" at Number 95 in its three-week life span.

In 1966 Shannon moved to Los Angeles and, like many over-the-hill recording artists, became a writer-producer instead. He released more singles, but they were not successful by any standards. Shortly after providing Peter and Gordon with "I Go to Pieces," a very nice and quite successful song, Shannon himself covered an inauspicious choice, "The Big Hurt." Miss Toni Fisher had a Number 3 hit with this in 1960, but Shannon's version spent two weeks at Number 94 and succumbed.

During the 1980s there was a rebirth of interest in Del Shannon when he released a few new singles. "Sea of Love," a cover of the oldie by Phil Phillips, went to Number 33. He was also approached to record a new version of "Runaway" as the main theme for Michael Mann's period television series, *Crime Story*. (Almost twenty years earlier, Shannon had foolishly refused to record "Action," the theme of Dick Clark's daily music show *Where the Action Is*. Freddy "Boom-boom" Cannon did so instead, earning a Number 13 on the charts in the summer of 1965, a time when Shannon could really have used a hit.)

Following Roy Orbison's death in late 1988, the surviving members of the supergroup The Traveling Wilburys were hard put to decide what to do: disband, go on as a quartet, or replace Orbison. One of the Wilburys was long-time Shannon fan Tom Petty. According to him, the Wilburys had tentatively decided to invite Del Shannon to join in Orbison's place, when Shannon committed suicide in his southern California home. He was just fifty.

The Traveling Wilburys (George Harrison, Bob Dylan, Tom Petty, and Jeff Lynne) were correct. Del Shannon was the only older rock and roll performer in the world capable of standing in for Roy Orbison. It is sad that nothing came of the notion.

Returning to the song "From Me to You," it is noteworthy, after failing to chart for Del Shannon, that the song also failed to hit the Top 40 for the century's top group, the Beatles. In Great Britain it was a big hit, but never in America. It was during the confusing days of spring 1964, when the rights to many songs the Beatles had long-since released in England were scattered among several companies in the New World. On that famous week when the Beatles held all five positions in the Top Five, the singles were on four different labels: Capitol, Swan, Tollie, and Vee Jay.

Capitol was their long-term label in America, but the backlog of hits on other labels was made up of some of the Beatles' best early songs. Swan had "She Loves You," while Tollie owned "Twist and Shout," "Love Me Do," and "P.S. I Love You." With these songs, Swan scored a Number 1 and Tollie had a Number 1, a Number 2, and even a B-side Number 10. Vee Jay was less fortunate. "Please Please Me" reached Number 3 and "Do You Want to Know a Secret?" went to Number 2 during that hectic spring, almost the only Beatles A-sides *not* to capture Number 1.

Obviously not all of the Beatles' songs could reach Number 1, even for a single week, since there were so many of them. It is less obvious why their Vee Jay releases did so comparatively poorly. The company, a small, R&B-oriented label from Chicago, had insufficient funds for record promotion; clearly the biggest rivals a Beatles single had at that point in time was the other Beatles singles, and advertising helped a lot in the struggle.

Vee Jay also owned the rights to "From Me to You," the only Beatles A-side released in America during the first half of 1964 that failed to even reach the Top 40, much less the Top Ten. Vee Jay had released "Please Please Me" on February 22, 1964, their first entry in Beatlemania. "From Me to You" came out just two weeks later, on March 7. By this time "Please Please Me" was in the Number 4 position, with the Beatles at Number 1 and Number 2 as well. "From Me to You" debuted at Number 86, well below normal for a Beatles single right about then, and spent six weeks on the Hot 100. It reached Number 41, missing the Top 40 by a hair.

One might conclude that there were too many Beatles singles on the market, and that "From Me to You" failed to chart primarily for that reason. One would be wrong. Even more Beatles songs would be released in the weeks to come, and all charted successfully. (Even their embarassing juvenalia, "Why" and "My Bonnie," did pretty well when released by MGM and Atco.) The worst A-side performance among the Beatles' other releases at that time was the Number 3 "Please Please Me" (yes, on Vee Jay). The Beatles had a lot of B-side hits; the worst charted performance of a B-side then was "Thank You Girl" at Number 35 (yes, on Vee Jay).

Vee Jay went on to release "Do You Want to Know a Secret?" in April, at about the worst moment in Beatlemania; it reached Number 2 a few weeks later. On April 4, 1964, the Beatles held all five top spots on the chart; it is less widely known that they also held Number 31, Number 41, Number 46, Number 58, Number 65, and Number 79. The Number 41 was "From Me to You," in its closest approach to glory. Of all the Beatles hits, this song alone still has not charted in America. And it is not a bad song at all; one could safely argue that much poorer Beatles songs were on the chart that spring.

I Feel Good

James Brown obviously felt good in 1966 when he recorded his own composition, "I Feel Good." It was a big hit then and continues to delight today. The song's real title, "I Got You," is not as attention getting as its acquired title and Brown's exuberant rendering of the piece, and therefore the song has become somewhat lost in the passage of time. Also somewhat diminished by time is another of Brown's creations, "Papa's Got a Brand New Bag" (1965), despite the fact that it won a Grammy.

It was a good year for songs. Other excellent recordings in 1966 were Barry Sadler's Number 1 hit, "The Ballad of the Green Berets," which he also wrote; "Georgy Girl," recorded by the Seekers and written by lyricist Jim Dale and composer Tom Springfield; "Winchester Cathedral," an Ivor Novello Award winner sung by the New Vaudeville Band and written by Geoff Stephens; and "Monday, Monday," written by John E. A. Phillips and sung by The Mamas and the Papas. The last song was adopted as one of the themes of The Mamas and the Papas, along with "California Dreamin'" (1966), created by Phillips and his wife, Michelle.

Among the other hits of 1966, but with less long-term impact, were "Cherish," recorded by the Association and written by Terry Kirkman, and "Summer in the City," sung by Lovin' Spoonful and created by John B. Sebastian, Mark Sebastian, and Steve Boone. All this shows that although a man with the very common name "Brown" recorded one of the best songs of the year, devising the names of singing groups continued to be as creative as the writing of new songs.

I'm on the Outside (Looking In)

Back in 1955, Teddy Randazzo and Tony Gourdine were members of rival vocal groups in Brooklyn. Teddy was in the Three Chuckles, and Tony was one of the four Duponts. The Three Chuckles had a Number 20 hit with "Runaround" late in 1954, but after that neither group seemed to be going anywhere. Ten years later, Tony and Teddy would unite to produce two of the best rock ballads ever, but they and their story are largely unknown.

The Three Chuckles never charted again, but they kept trying, and remained part of the New York City music scene. When important New York disc jockey Alan Freed made the first rock and roll movies in 1956 and 1957, he used a lot of local acts; the Three Chuckles were one of them. The films were *Rock Around the Clock; Don't Knock the Rock; Rock, Rock, Rock;* and *Mister Rock and Roll.* The Three Chuckles performed in *Rock, Rock, Rock,* and Teddy Randazzo had a leading role as an actor as well.

Perhaps on the strength of this outing, the Three Chuckles were also cast in *The Girl Can't Help It,* a 1956 Jayne Mansfield vehicle, which was the first rock and roll movie ever to be made in color. The next year Teddy Randazzo was a featured actor in *Mister Rock and Roll.*

Teddy's fourth and last film was *Hey, Let's Twist* in 1961, the biographical movie about—and starring—Joey Dee and the Starliters. (Rock and roll movies had a way of treating contemporaneous events as history.) Teddy Randazzo had third billing in the film, and also performed a musical number.

If one doesn't know one's rock and roll, Teddy Randazzo would appear to have dropped off the face of the earth after 1961. In fact, he went on to occupy a more important position than any he had held previously.

What had Tony been doing all this time? The Duponts tried to succeed in the competitive New York music world, but could never get ahead. They recorded vocal numbers for two different small labels in New York, but neither had the resources to vigorously promote the resultant singles.

Tony quit the Duponts, who replaced him but still couldn't put together a successful act. Tony recorded as a solo, and then joined an existing vocal group, the Chesters. Their efforts to obtain a recording contract worked out, but their new producer thought that the name "The Chesters" on a 45 rpm label would not attract buyers. A name change was definitely called for. In 1958 they began calling themselves the Imperials; before long they became famous as Little Anthony and the Imperials, on End Records. Their first single was the very pretty "Tears on My Pillow," a Number 4 hit.

After such a promising start, Little Anthony still had a hard time finding decent material to record. The singer who rarely, if ever, writes music is literally at the mercy of the record producer. In Little Anthony's case, he cut a large number of singles for End; some were local hits in New York, where the group had a following, but only one ever made it to the national charts after their debut. In January 1960 they released "Shimmy, Shimmy, Ko-Ko-Bop." It was a fun song, nicely arranged and produced, but could not move past Number 24.

Things continued like this until 1964. Then Little Anthony and the Imperials moved to DCP (Don Costa Productions), a United Artists label, and had a brief but powerful comeback. The reason? Old neighbor Teddy Randazzo was by 1964 an established composer, as well as an A&R (artists and repertoire) man for DCP. He teamed up with Little Anthony as both composer and producer.

They started with a pleasant ballad called "I'm on the Outside (Looking In)." Like all of their collaborations, it tells the story of someone at a painful distance from love and happiness; the title may have had other significance for Little Anthony, after a decade spent hammering on the gates of pop music stardom. The song went to Number 15, his second best performance to date.

In November 1964 he released "Goin' Out of My Head," a Number 6 major success. Teddy Randazzo, who wrote or cowrote four straight hits for Little Anthony, knew that he was working with one of rock and roll's most powerful and emotional singers, whose real abilities had scarcely been called into play before.

Three months later came "Hurt So Bad," arguably an even better song than "Goin' Out of My Head" despite a slightly lower (Number 10) finish. The two are what Little Anthony and the Imperials will be remembered for, as long as rock and roll is played.

In the summer of 1965, Little Anthony released his fourth Randazzo tune, "Take Me Back." It is a very pretty song, done to perfection, but seems a bit pallid after the surging emotionalism of the two preceding efforts. "Take Me Back" earned a reasonable Number 16. From this point on, for some foolish reason, Randazzo and Gourdine were separated professionally. Little Anthony and the Imperials were reassigned within United Artists to the Veep label, and then to United Artists itself, presumably to cash in on the success they had enjoyed with Randazzo. That success, although they recorded for many years thereafter, was never approached again.

Teddy Randazzo continued as a journeyman composer and producer, never creating with other artists the perfection that he achieved with Little Anthony. Each brought something to the collaboration that the other was never to find elsewhere.

I'm Walkin'

Antoine "Fats" Domino was not known to most pop music fans before "Ain't That a Shame" became a Top Ten hit for him in 1955. Domino had already been an established star on the R&B charts, however, going back as far as 1950. It was only the emergence of rock and roll, and the relaxation of color barriers on the radio, that made Fats Domino a household name among pop listeners.

His career on the pop charts lasted another eight years, until 1963, but Domino's real hits were between 1955 and 1960. His singing and stylized piano playing did not evolve along with public tastes in the 1960s.

Some of Domino's best-remembered songs are "My Blue Heaven," "Blueberry Hill," and "Blue Monday," all from 1956 to 1957. Then he changed direction, at least with regard to titles, and had big hits with songs such as "I'm Walkin'," "I Want to Walk You Home," and "Walking to New Orleans," up through 1960. Domino had major hits that didn't mention the color blue or the act of walking, but not very many.

Just considering his Top 40 records, and not the numerous R&B releases that preceded them, Domino had thirty-six hits on twenty-eight singles, with ten major Top Ten hits. His role as a rock pioneer is widely recognized. Fats Domino was inducted into the Rock and Roll Hall of Fame in 1986, its first year of operation.

Lookin' Out My Back Door

One of the most famous and successful bands never to have a Number 1 record was Creedence Clearwater Revival, a group of San Francisco Bay-area musicians who managed to sound like swamp denizens. They hit Number 2 five separate times, but always against some serious competition.

CCR, as they came to be abbreviated, had formed in 1959 as the Blue Velvets; the members were four high school students in El Cerrito, California, including John Fogerty and his brother, Tom. By 1964, they were the Golliwogs, signed with a tiny, jazz specialty label in San Francisco, Fantasy Records. Unsuccessful under that name, in 1967 they changed to the much funkier sounding Creedence Clearwater Revival, and their fortunes improved almost immediately. They stayed with the Fantasy label, but changed their name and their material.

Their first release under the new name was a cover of Dale Hawkins' "Susie Q.," a minor hit back in 1957. Creedence's version is one of the best rock and roll records of the 1960s; due largely to their obscurity, the single peaked at Number 11 instead of the Top Five position it deserved. Not that CCR was complaining; for the first time, after nine years of playing music together, they had a hit.

"Proud Mary" came next. It spent three weeks at Number 2, their most successful single. During the year 1969, including "Proud Mary," they had six hits on four singles, and quickly became one of the country's best-known bands. "Bad Moon Rising" and "Green River" also made it to Number 2; the latter's B-side, "Commotion," made it to Number 30 independently.

At about that time, *Billboard* changed its reporting rules to a confusing mess where both sides of a two-sided hit received the same position. This obviously reflects purchase patterns only, not radio play, but that is what rock and roll historians now have to work with.

Thus, CCR's two-sided hit "Down on the Corner"/"Fortunate Son" is a Number 3, while "Travelin' Band"/"Who'll Stop the Rain?" made it, yet again, to Number 2. It was CCR's fault, really; they lost a great deal of money by placing A-quality material on the B-sides of their singles, instead of releasing those songs as A-sides and using innocuous Everly Brothers or Elvis covers as their B-sides.

Their next single was "Up Around the Bend," a Number 4 on the charts. Following that, and rounding out their second full year of recording, was the whimsical "Lookin' Out My Back Door." This was to be their fifth and last Number 2 single. In 1971 the group released two singles, "Have You Ever Seen the Rain?" and "Sweet Hitch-Hiker." These went to Number 8 and Number 6, respectively, intimating that, while America still liked CCR, they weren't royalty anymore.

Also that year Tom Fogerty, the group's rhythm guitarist and John's brother, left to pursue a solo career. (He sank without a trace.) Part of the problem was ego. John Fogerty wrote and arranged the songs, sang lead, played the melody on his guitar, and produced their records. Other members of the band lacked input, which is not to say that their creative abilities were on a par with his.

In 1972 CCR, now a trio, released only one single, the Number 25 "Someday Never Comes," and then disbanded. John Fogerty himself then successfully pursued a solo career, first as the Blue Ridge Rangers (a one-man band, once again with a name and style that distanced him from his California roots), and then under his own name. The "Rangers" had two hit singles in 1973, a cover of Hank Williams' wonderful "Jambalaya (On the Bayou)," a Number 16, and then "Hearts of Stone," a cover of the 1954 hit by the Charms. Like "Susie Q.," these songs were heard primarily by audiences too young to realize that they were covers.

In 1975, John Fogerty began a solo career under his own name. His career has lasted almost twenty-five years at this writing, with some considerable success.

Back in 1971, a CCR song made it to Number 4 without the band's involvement. Ike and Tina Turner had their only real hit in fourteen years of trying, with a cover version of "Proud Mary."

Tina, of course, has enjoyed major stardom since divorcing Ike, but it was "Proud Mary" that first made her well-known in America.

It was not entirely accurate to say that CCR never had a Number 1 record. True, their singles never passed Number 2, but in the highly rewarding arena of album sales they had two different Number 1 records. In 1969 CCR released three albums, placing each in the Top Ten. *Green River* was Number 1 for four weeks, and continued to sell well for months after that. In 1970 the band released two albums, a Number 5 and their all-time best-seller, *Cosmo's Factory*. This was Number 1 for over two months, a major achievement. Two other albums sold well in the early 1970s.

John Fogerty, who has recorded for Warner Brothers since 1975, has also had a Number 1 album under his own name. In 1985 he was once again on the Top 40 with singles, and his album *Center-field* briefly held the Number 1 slot.

Oh, Pretty Woman

Some songs are only successful with one generation. Others, such as "Oh, Pretty Woman," are pretty well-received by later generations. Written in 1964 by Roy Orbison and William Dees, and recorded by Orbison, "Oh, Pretty Woman" would have a second career as the theme of the popular 1990 film, *Pretty Woman*, two years after Orbison's death.

Orbison also had several other top recordings, written with Joe Melson, including: "Blue Angel" (1977), "Only the Lonely" (1960), "Running Scared" (1961), and "Crying" (1961). These half Orbison and half Melson songs, all of which touch upon negative emotions ("blue," "lonely," "scared," and "crying"), were in the long run to be eclipsed by the positive feelings of "Oh, Pretty Woman" that was so pleasantly revived in the 1990 movie.

Curiously, "Running Scared" was not the only 1961 hit with the word "run" in the title. Also appearing in 1961 were "Run to Him," sung by Bobby Vee and written by Gerry Goffin and Jack Keller, "Runaround Sue," sung by Dion and written by Dion (Dion Di Mucci) and Ernie Maresca, and "Runaway," sung by Del Shannon, and written by Max T. Crook and Charles Westover. None of these four "run" songs were a truly runaway hit, yet there sure was a run of them in 1961.

Papa's Got a Brand New Bag

James Brown came to recording relatively late, in a profession where youth and precocity often outweigh actual talent in determining one's success. Brown turned twenty-eight a few weeks after the Federal label released his debut single, "Please, Please, Please." The song, like many of his subsequent releases, was an R&B hit that went gold, but did not reach the more remunerative pop charts. James Brown was not to strike that particular vein of gold for another three years, and even then not with any consistency.

Often called (by his press agent) the hardest-working man in show business, James Brown lived up to his reputation. Records and live performances by Brown were extremely common, even if successful records were not. After getting a few Top 40 hits, Brown still experienced dry spells. He switched labels, going to King Records where things went a lot better. (He would change companies again, eventually charting Top 40 hits on six labels between 1956 and 1974.)

King was a good choice, evidently. Out of forty-three career pop chart hits in the classic rock era, Brown only reached the Top Ten on six occasions (of course, on the R&B charts he was more dominant). All six hit singles were released on the King label from 1965 to 1968, Brown's golden age. These hits ranged from the epochal "Say It Loud—I'm Black and I'm Proud" and "Papa's Got a Brand New Bag" to "I Got You" (the one everybody thinks is called "I Feel Good").

The majority of James Brown's work, not just of his bigger hits, came from King. By 1971, he was lured away to a bigger label, but his output slowed and the quality dropped. Brown is truly an artist whose persistence and high energy performances, rather than any great string of major hits, made him a national star. He was ubiquitous, he had a striking act, and once in a great while he produced a memorable hit.

In 1985, James Brown emerged from relative obscurity to perform the great song "Living in America" in the film *Rocky IV*. (The song was also a hit on the charts.) In 1986, Brown was among the first group of artists inducted into the Rock and Roll Hall of Fame, a great honor. Two years later, the year he turned sixty, Brown became famous once again, in a less pleasant manner. He was sentenced to six years in a South Carolina prison for assault, eventually serving about two and a half years before being paroled in 1991.

Raindrops Keep Fallin' on My Head

In the late 1950s, 1960s, and early 1970s, or roughly equivalent with the classic rock era, good songs kept falling on the heads of wordsmith Hal David and tunesmith Burt Bacharach. Perhaps that phenomenon was the inspiration for the title of their classic 1970 song "Raindrops Keep Fallin' on My Head." Popularized by the excellent movie, *Butch Cassidy and the Sundance Kid*, starring Paul Newman and Robert Redford, "Raindrops," the Academy Award winning song that year, was the highlight of their long-time collaboration.

Other compositions by David and Bacharach would fill a large section of a "what's what" of softer songs of the period. They include "Alfie" (1966), a top hit; "Anyone Who Had a Heart" (1963); "April Fools" (1969); "Are You There?" or "Are You There with Another Girl?" (1966); "Blue on Blue" (1963); "Close to You" (1970), a top hit by the Carpenters; "Do You Know the Way to San Jose?" (1968), another top hit; "A House Is Not a Home" (1964); "I Say a Little Prayer" (1967); "I'll Never Fall in Love Again" (1968), yet another top hit; "The Look of Love" (1965); "Magic Moments" (1958), one more top hit; "Make It Easy on Yourself" (1962); "The Man Who Shot Liberty Valence" (1962); "Message to Michael" (1966); "Odds and Ends" or "Odds and Ends of a Beautiful Love Affair" (1969); "One Less Bell to Answer" (1970), a top hit by the Fifth Dimension; "Only Love Can Break a Heart" (1962); "Paper Maché" (1970); "Promises, Promises" (1968); "Reach Out for Me" (1964); "Story of My Life" (1957); "This Guy's in Love with You" (1968), still one more top hit; "Trains and Boats and Planes" (1965); "Walk on By" (1961); "What the World Needs Now Is Love" (1965), one of their best; "What's New Pussycat?" (1965); "Windows of the World" (1967); "Wishin' and Hopin'" (1964); and "You'll Never Get to Heaven" (1964).

When the style of popular music started to get harder and less subtle in the early 1970s, the fortunes of this outstanding songwriting team declined. Lots of things have changed in the generation since David and Bacharach were at their peak, including the size of the now very large San Jose. Yet at least a half dozen of David and Bacharach's creations have remained classics or standards well into the 1990s.

Rhinestone Cowboy

A rhinestone-covered cowboy is a garish and quite ridiculous sight to behold. With cheap urban ornaments clashing with the more natural clothing of a working man, a glittering rhinestone cowpoke walking down a city street and trying to look sophisticated is bound to evoke stares and laughter.

Yet Glen Campbell's excellent recording of Larry Weiss' 1975 smash hit "Rhinestone Cowboy" did not produce negative responses from the American public. It was one of the top songs of the year, and made Campbell's already significant star status even shinier (like a diamond, not a rhinestone). But there was something symbolic in the song for both Campbell and rock music. For Campbell, it showed that he had drifted somewhat from his folkish earlier image to a more slick, citified image. For rock and roll, it was yet another indicator that rock music was shifting away from the simpler and more spontaneous style of classic rock to the harsher and less natural style of hard rock.

While "Rhinestone Cowboy" is sort of a connector between classic and hard rock, its creator, Weiss, had few connections with other top hits. Even concocting a chain from songwriter to songwriter does little to enhance his reputation as a one hit composer. Weiss collaborated with Scott English on the 1968 song "Bend Me, Shape Me." English collaborated with Richard Kerr on the 1975 hit "Mandy," sung by Barry Manilow. Kerr collaborated with Will Jennings on "I'll Never Love This Way Again" (1979) and "Looks Like We Made It" (1977). With Jennings the chain ends, and so does this essay.

(I'm a) Road Runner

Like Rodney Dangerfield, some performers just get no respect, or nothing like the respect they deserve. Junior Walker and the All-Stars are unfortunately an apt example.

Autry DeWalt, Junior, wisely renamed himself Junior Walker every time he picked up his saxophone. As Junior Walker, he was widely recognized as the best sax player in American pop music, without somehow ever achieving the string of big hits that ought to have accompanied his greatness.

The All-Stars signed with Harvey Fuqua's Tri-Phi label in the early Sixties, but were transferred to Berry Gordy's Soul label when Fuqua and Gordy, brothers-in-law, merged their companies. Junior Walker started out his recording career with a bang, literally, releasing "Shotgun" in early 1965. Like the Number 4 "Shotgun," all his recordings were characterized by good, sometimes excellent, R&B music, modest production values, and mumbled lyrics.

The next two singles did poorly, at Number 36 and Number 29, and even the quite good "(I'm a) Road Runner" reached no higher than Number 20 on the charts. The band's output was then reduced, a serious error; they had only moderate success for the next three years. For a band that could hit the Top Five on their first single, this was a real debacle.

During the summer of 1969 the All-Stars had their second and final big hit, "What Does It Take (To Win Your Love?)." This beautiful, underappreciated tune went no higher than Number 4, perhaps because so few pop music listeners had become established fans of Junior Walker. Among professionals the band was known as a paragon of fluid, give and take R&B musicianship; the Grateful Dead specifically identified the wonderful All-Stars instrumental track "Cleo's Mood" as an inspiration for the Dead's famous long, improvised live jam sessions. Jerry Garcia and other pros loved "Cleo's Mood" (it is indeed a wonderful song); most rock listeners literally have never heard of it.

Some of the blame surely lies with the band. Their music, and especially the singing, can be a bit rough around the edges. R&B is occasionally somewhat raw to the mainstream audience, though it doesn't seem fair to blame the All-Stars for that. They wanted to play their music and let their natural audience—whoever that might be—find them.

A great deal of blame can be attributed to the men who produced Junior Walker's singles and albums. The All-Stars were less appropriate material than most Motown groups for the Berry Gordy treatment. Gordy wanted slick songsters with biracial appeal; they wanted to play the best R&B in the country. In a way, it's too bad that Junior Walker and the All-Stars ended up working for Motown; at a predominantly white label such as Capitol, or an integrated one such as the incomparable Atlantic, the All-Stars might have been given the go-ahead to see what they could produce. At Motown, where they ended up by default, they became the poor relations.

Motown had a small stable of proven songwriters, and of course several of their recording artists were themselves gifted writers. Junior Walker's biggest hit, his signature tune, was "Shotgun," a solo composition by his alter ego, Autry DeWalt. Many of the other songs he was allowed to record, in the autocratic confines of Motown, were recycled Motown standards. "How Sweet It Is (To Be Loved by You)" was a Number 6 hit for Marvin Gaye in 1965, composed by the leading Motown writing team, Holland, Dozier, and Holland. When Walker released a cover version on the Soul label in 1966, it could reach no higher than Number 18. Why? It wasn't his kind of song, plus there had been an excellent original version, and it was too recent, just one year earlier. Covers should improve on the original, or at least reprise an old favorite; Junior Walker could do neither.

The Supremes had a Number 1 hit with "Come See About Me" in 1964, another tune by brothers Eddie and Brian Holland and their partner Lamont Dozier. Junior Walker's version four years later stalled at Number 24. Like "How Sweet It Is," only more so, "Come See About Me" was wildly inappropriate for the All-Stars. Another, even worse song they were forced to record was "Money (That's What I Want)," a boring little tune that kept popping up all over in Motown—perhaps because it was cowritten by Motown founder, the Detroit titan Berry Gordy. Barrett Strong, a Motown composer himself and would-be singing star, had his sole charted hit with "Money" in 1960, a Number 23 song. The Kingsmen covered it in 1964, reaching a slightly better Number 16. Junior Walker's (second) cover of it did not even chart, a real embarassment for all involved.

Harvey Fuqua (nephew of marvelous Ink Spot vocalist Charlie Fuqua) continued to produce Junior Walker on Soul, often with his friend Johnny Bristol; both were would-be singers who ended up as producers. (Fuqua, with his band the Moonglows, charted three times for Chess Records in the 1950s, never rising above Number 20.) However, at least seven men produced the All-Stars' records, part of Junior Walker's problem. At Motown, producers were paid by the number—and success—of the songs cut under their direction. This is normal practice in the music business. Also normal is the fact that all of Motown's producers were at least peripherally involved in songwriting; Holland, Dozier, Fuqua, Bristol, Berry, and Cosby were all major composers on Motown's various labels.

Because Junior Walker was at best a second-class citizen at Motown, he was never able to settle down with only one or two preferred producer/composers. Instead, on the rare occasions when he was finally allowed to cut records, he would be shuttled back and forth between various producers. Unfortunately, those producers were also writers who wanted their own compositions to be produced.

These men rarely brought their best work to Junior Walker; he recorded lesser new songs, and recycled older songs, by some of Motown's best writers. (His own compositions did not always do much better, when he could squeeze them in.) A producer committed to the band's welfare might have solicited appropriate songs from the many capable freelance composers in the business, or from the other great writers in the Motown stable (Smokey Robinson, for example, provided good songs to a wide variety of Detroit groups). A motivated producer might have worked carefully with Junior Walker to create an arrangement that played to the band's strengths, and produced many more Top Ten hits. The All-Stars never had such a producer, however.

They kept trying, releasing singles as late as 1970, but success stayed out of reach. For music cognoscenti, to consider the career of Junior Walker is a lot like watching a world-class painter who was rarely allowed to paint, and even then only with inferior materials and on sunless days. That he managed to create a small number of masterworks is a true testimonial to his abilities; that the number was so small is a major indictment of the soulless, adding-machine ethos of too many recording studios.

Song Sung Blue

You probably have heard the old saying about "pearls before swine." You surely have not previously heard the expression "monkeys before diamonds," because it was first used on this page. Most likely, it will never, ever be used again!

The Monkees, a group of four young men who had never performed together, were brought together in 1966 to star in the television series *The Monkees.* Chosen because they physically resembled the Beatles, the Monkees were intended to be an American counterbalance against the fabulous success of the invading British group. The Monkees managed to absorb some of the magic of the Beatles, although by no means approaching the heights of the Liverpool four. They had several top hits in 1966 and 1967, including "Last Train to Clarksville" (1966), created by Tommy Boyce and Bobby Hart; "Daydream Believer" (1967), written by John C. Stewart; and "I'm a Believer" (1967), written by Neil Diamond. The last-mentioned "believer" song was Number 1 in record sales in 1967.

After a few years the Monkees faded away, but Neil Diamond was a believer in his own considerable talents and by creating several other good songs in the next decade or so became a more permanent star in the pop music constellation. Diamond also wrote "A Little Bit Me, a Little Bit You" (1967), "Sweet Caroline" or "Good Times Never Seemed So Good" (1970), "Cracklin' Rosie" (1970), "And the Grass Won't Pay No Mind" (1970), "Holly Holy" (1970), "I Am, I Said" (1971), "Say Maybe" (1979), "Forever in Blue Jeans" (1979), with Richard Winchell Bennett, and best of all, "Song Sung Blue" (1972). Diamond himself recorded many of his songs, including the top hit "Song Sung Blue," making him a many faceted blue diamond of considerable value.

Standing on the Corner

Everybody is entitled to their personal opinions. There are plenty of them in this book. But when the 1956 hit, "Standing on the Corner" is described as a "hillbilly song," the opinion of that critic has to be seriously questioned. Lots of urban young men of all types stand on the corner "watching all the girls go by." Older men also do this. Plus there is nothing smacking of the hills in the song itself, in its composer, Frank Loesser, or in the Broadway musical for which the piece was written, *The Most Happy Fella*.

Frank Loesser was a completely citified artist. With three other successful shows, *Where's Charley* (1948), *Guys and Dolls* (1950), one of the best musicals ever, and *How to Succeed in Business Without Really Trying* (1961), in addition to *The Most Happy Fella*, composer and lyricist Loesser was a bright light on Broadway at a time there were other competing bright lights such as Rodgers and Hammerstein and Lerner and Loewe.

Possibly what the "hillbilly" critic meant to say was that the song depicted behavior not suitable for gentlemen. At the time, even some of the young men who had stood on the corner and behaved in less than ideal fashion were a bit taken back by the directness and brashness of the lyrics. Songs before "Standing on the Corner" tended to be more subtle. Yet if a similar concept song had been written thirty years later, in 1986, who knows what the lyrics might have been. Quite possibly they would have been much too explicit to print in a book like this.

Tie a Yellow Ribbon Round
the Ole Oak Tree

Accidents can be bad, accidents can be good. When Irwin Levine and L. Russell Brown wrote "Tie a Yellow Ribbon Round the Ole Oak Tree" describing the return of a man from prison, their lively song just happened to come out for public consumption at about the same time that tens of thousands of American military personnel were coming out of Vietnam. Although the composition was excellent, the coincidental timing surely helped the song rise to the top.

Aided by a well-crafted recording by Tony Orlando and Dawn, "Yellow Ribbon" reached Number 2 in record sales in 1973. The same group, with a somewhat different name, Dawn, also recorded another top hit by Levine and Brown, "Knock Three Times" (1971). Levine and Brown collaborated on yet another good song, "My Sweet Gypsy Rose" or "Say Has Anybody Seen My Gypsy Rose?" (1973), and Levine created "Candida" (1970) with Toni Wine.

Tied with "Yellow Ribbon" for Number 2 in 1973 was "My Love," recorded by Paul McCartney and Wings, and composed by McCartney and his wife, Linda. The McCartneys had several other hits, including "Live and Let Die" (1973), "Band on the Run" (1974), and "Listen to What the Man Said" (1975), all three recorded by Paul McCartney and Wings, plus "Jet" (1974), "Let 'Em In" (1976), and "Silly Love Songs" (1976), the last piece gaining Number 2.

Other 1973 hits included "Superstition" and "You Are the Sunshine of My Life," both Grammy winners recorded and written in 1972 by Stevie Wonder, and "The Most Beautiful Girl in the World" or "If You Happen to See the Most Beautiful Girl in the World," recorded by Charlie Rich and written by Rory Bourke, Billy Sherrill, and Noro Wilson. Altogether, it was a sweet, beautiful, rich yellow ribbon year filled with wonder and elevated by the wings of musical talent.

Up-Up and Away

When the Fifth Dimension sang "Up-Up and Away" or "My Beautiful Balloon" in 1967, the blend of the uplifting and upbeat composition and the feel good tones of the vocal group carried it into the hearts of America and all the way to a Grammy Award. Two years later, the Fifth Dimension's splendid rendering of the ethereal "Aquarius" floated home yet another Grammy.

The composer of "Up-Up and Away" was Jim Webb, who seemed to be only successful with songs that had directions or places in the title. Webb also wrote the hits "By the Time I Get to Phoenix" (1967), "MacArthur Park" (1968), "Wichita Lineman" (1968), and "Galveston" (1969). "Up-Up and Away" was created in reaction to Webb's feeling down after losing his sweetheart to another. One wonders whether there were any special events that precipitated Webb's inspiration for his songs about the park and the cities in Arizona, Kansas, and Texas.

The Fifth Dimension wasn't the only group with an interesting name that had hits in 1967. The Young Rascals recorded "Groovin'," by Edward Brigati and Felix Cavaliere. The Boxtops sang "The Letter," by Wayne Thompson. The Doors recorded "Light My Fire," by John Densmore, Robert Krieger, Raymond Manzarek, and James Morrison. And Gladys Knight and the Pips sang "I Heard It Through the Grapevine," by Norman Whitfield and Barrett Strong.

If one sort of combines most of these 1967 titles into one lunatic sentence, you might get "You were groovin' until, as I heard it through the grapevine, you got a dear Jim letter saying that she would no longer light your fire, so you went up up and away to escape from it all." With that, it's time to escape to another essay.

Will You Love Me Tomorrow?

The answer to the question was yes. When husband and wife team Gerry Goffin and Carole King inquired to the pop music world "Will You Love Me Tomorrow?," by means of a recording by the Shirelles, the answer in 1961 and for years after was definitely in the affirmative. It was no wonder that music fans responded so positively. Goffin and King, together and separately, were among the best songwriters of the 1960s and 1970s.

As a pair, they wrote "Take Good Care of My Baby" (1961), "The Loco-Motion" (1962), a top hit of 1963, "Go Away Little Girl" (1963), "Up on the Roof" (1963), "One Fine Day" (1963), and "A Natural Woman" or "You Make Me Feel Like a Natural Woman" (1967), with Jerry Wexler. Their songs attracted several well-known performers and groups. Bobby Vee recorded "Take Good Care," Little Eva sang "Loco-Motion," Steve Lawrence did "Go Away," the Drifters recorded "Up on the Roof," the Chiffons sang "One Fine Day" and Aretha Franklin did "A Natural Woman." By 1968 Goffin and King had split up maritally and artistically. Before that time, Goffin, a lyricist, had collaborated on two hits without King. Although "Who Put the Bomp?" (1961), written with Barry Mann, was a lively and interesting song, it was far from the most literate. "Run to Him" (1961), with Jack Keller, was a more normal song. After 1968 Goffin collaborated on "I've Got to Use My Imagination" (1973) with Barry Goldberg, but did little else.

In contrast, King, the Queen of soft rock composition, shook off a few hitless years and revived with several top songs in the early 1970s, some of which she sang herself. In 1971 King wrote the words and music for Grammy winners "You've Got a Friend" and "It's Too Late," plus "So Far Away" and "I Feel the Earth Move." In 1974, she collaborated with David Palmer on one of that year's top hits, "Jazz Man" or "Jazzman," and in 1975 another collaboration with Palmer produced one of King's finest, "Nightingale." To put all this succinctly, Goffin "bomped" in 1961, Goffin and King "stomped" away from each other in 1968, and King "romped" in the 1970s.

ONE-HIT WONDERS, OR, FLASHES IN THE CHARTS

At the Hop

Teenagers and rock music have been very closely associated over the years. Most teenagers have been big fans of rock music, some rock stars have begun their careers while still in their teens, and teenagers have often been the subject of rock songs. "At the Hop" (1958), by Artie Singer, David White, and John Medora, was clearly a song about teenagers. That top hit, in addition, was recorded by a youthful sounding group, Danny and the Juniors.

Possibly using up too much energy at the hop, neither Singer, White, nor Medora created any more top songs. However, 1958 saw much other activity relating to teens. Phil Everly was still a teenager and Don barely out of his teens when the Everly Brothers recorded two hits "All I Have to Do Is Dream" and "Bird Dog," both written by Boudleaux Bryant. Seventeen-year-old Ritchie Valens, who was to die in an airplane accident early in 1959, had two top hits, "Donna" and the Spanish-language smash "La Bamba," both written by him. Eighteen-year-old Ricky Nelson recorded "Poor Little Fool," written by Shari Sheeley. Frankie Avalon was also about eighteen when he recorded "Dede Dinah" and "Ginger Bread" in 1958. ("Dede Dinah" was written by Bob Marcussi and Peter De Angelis and "Ginger Bread" by Clint Ballard Jr. and Hank Hunter.) Fabian was around fifteen when he recorded "I'm a Man" and "Turn Me Loose," both songs by "Doc" Pomus and Mort

Shuman. And Paul Anka was propelled to fame with his giant hit "Diana" (by Anka) and was an accomplished international star at seventeen in 1958.

Two other rock hits of 1958 that in some way are associated with teenagers were "Sixteen Candles," recorded by the Crests and written by Luther Dixon and Allyson R. Khent, and "Yakety Yak," recorded by the Coasters and written by Jerry Leiber and Mike Stoller. Especially when a telephone is involved, teenagers do tend to yakety yak.

The Battle of New Orleans

There were three battles involved when "The Battle of New Orleans" came out in 1959. The first was the actual battle in 1815, during the War of 1812, in which the Americans beat the British. Almost a century and a half later, an 1815 fiddle tune celebrating that victory was adapted by Jimmy Driftwood, with words added by Driftwood. Recorded by Johnny Horton, the song battled to Number 2 in record sales in 1959 and earned a Grammy. The third battle was a losing one, for Driftwood never created another song that even came close to his smash of 1959.

Another borrowed hit of 1959 was the Kingston Trio's rendering of "A Worried Man," derived by Dave Guard and Tom Glazer from an American folk piece. Yet another 1959 song, "Personality," sung by Lloyd Price and written by Price and Harold Logan, borrowed its title from the better known 1946 song of the same name by lyricist Johnny Burke and musician Jimmy Van Heusen. Price and Logan's other 1959 hit, "Stagger Lee," sung by Price and written by Price and Logan, lent support to "Personality."

The vocal group the Fleetwoods had similar supportive hits in 1959, "Come Softly to Me," written by Gary Troxel, Gretchen Christopher, and Barbara Ellis, and "Mister Blue," written by DeWayne Blackwell. So did vocalist Paul Anka, with "Lonely Boy" and "Put Your Head on My Shoulder," both written by Anka. In addition, Frankie Avalon borrowed from the success of his 1958 hits "Dede Dinah" and "Ginger Bread" by recording "Venus," written by Ed Marshall.

Despite two unborrowed top hits written and recorded by Bobby Darin, "Splish Splash" (1958) and "Dream Lover" (1959), even the original and creative Darin got involved in borrowing in 1959. He was at the center of the most inspired and most complex borrowing of that year. Darin's fantastic recording of "Mack the Knife," that won a Grammy, was associated with three borrowings. "Mack the Knife," with words written by Marc Blitzstein, was from the 1954 musical *The Three-Penny Opera* (borrowing one). The melody for "Mack" was by Kurt Weill, who originally wrote it for the 1928 German opera *Die Dreigroschenoper* (borrowing two). The original idea for the adventures of Mack the Knife, further-more, goes back to the famous 1728 production *The Beggar's Op-era* by John Gay and John Christopher Pepusch (borrowing three). Keeping up with all these borrowings is sort of a fourth battle.

Classical Gas

An old television comedy skit portrayed two mediocre songwriters working against an impending deadline. Finally, one of them, frustrated by his lack of inspiration, proposed, "Why don't we just steal something from Chopin or Tchaikovsky again?" There is a lot of reality in this anecdote, for all throughout the nineteenth and twentieth centuries, American songwriters have been directly and indirectly "borrowing" from the masters. One well-known example of this is the 1918 piece "I'm Always Chasing Rainbows." Harry Carroll, a songwriter of some accomplishment, adapted a passage from the music of Frederic Chopin and with new words by Joseph McCarthy helped create a still performed mini-masterpiece.

The rock era was no exception to such borrowing or influences. Chuck Berry paid homage to Beethoven in his 1956 "Roll Over Beethoven." In 1976 Walter Murphy wrote "A Fifth of Beethoven" based on the great composer's Fifth Symphony. Probably the strangest manifestation was the conversion of Bach's religious classic "Jesu, Joy of Man's Desiring" into a rock piece by a group called Apollo 100 during the 1970s.

Classical influences also were evident in one of the best songs of 1968. Appropriately named "Classical Gas," the innovative and lively instrumental by Mason Williams was a combination of jazz and classical modes. Williams, one of the graduates of the controversial *Smothers Brothers Comedy Hour* of 1967 to 1969, apparently ran out of gas after composing "Classical Gas," for he wrote no other notable compositions.

Earth Angel

Although "Rock Around the Clock" knocked the cultural socks off Americans in 1955, there were plenty of other notable songs in that epic year. One of the top hits was "Earth Angel," written by Curtis Williams. After his success, Williams seems to have buried himself deep in the Earth or become an angel, for he created no other songs of importance.

Other angels of 1955 were the three McGuire Sisters who recorded Harvey Fuqua and Alan Freed's "Sincerely," and Johnny Mercer's "Something's Gotta Give." The other person who recorded "Something's Gotta Give," Sammy Davis, Jr., probably would not qualify as an angel, but Georgia Gibbs, who sang Winfield Scott's "Tweedle Dee," might well make the grade.

Other hits of 1955 were "Cry Me a River" written by Arthur Hamilton, "I Hear You Knocking" written by Dave Bartholomew and Pearl King, plus three pieces that must be described as novelties. "The Ballad of Davy Crockett," sung by Bill Hayes and created by lyricist Tom Blackburn and musician George Bruns, was the theme of the highly successful television series. (Another "ballad" for a successful television series, incidentally, was "Ballad of Jed Clampett," written in 1962 by Paul Henning for *The Beverly Hillbillies*.) The title of the second song, "The Crazy Otto Rag," broadcasts its eccentric nature. ("Crazy Otto" was recorded by Johnny Maddox and written by lyricist Edward R. White and composer Mack Wolfson.) Last, but far from quietest, was "Tutti Frutti" sung by Little Richard (Richard Penniman) and created by him along with Dorothy La Bostrie and Joe Lubin. Although this final sentence may seem to be a misprint, Pat Boone, famous for singing ballads, actually made a recording of "Tutti Frutti" too.

Ease on Down the Road

The ingredients for a top movie were apparently there when the 1978 film *The Wiz* was made. The Broadway production of *The Wiz*, a 1975 black version of *The Wizard of Oz*, had been a smash hit. The songs, with both words and music by Charlie Smalls, were good, particularly the main number, "Ease on Down the Road," which was Smalls' easygoing response to the peppy "We're Off to See the Wizard" in the original 1939 movie.

The star of the movie, moreover, was none other than superstar Diana Ross. After several years as part of, and then lead singer of, the highly successful Supremes, Ross went on her own. Her last record with the Supremes was "Someday We'll Be Together" or "Some Day We'll Be Together" (1970) (written by Harvey Fuqua, Jackey Beavers, and Johnny Bristol), which was recorded in 1969. (That certainly was a strange title for a song that marked the end of the group.) Starting in 1970, Ross had a solo career that was also very successful. Among her hits were "Touch Me in the Morning" (1973), created by Michael Masser and Ron Miller; and "Love Hangover" (1976), written by Marilyn McLeod and Pamela Joan Sawyer.

Unfortunately, the love given to *The Wiz* on Broadway did not hang over into the nation's movie theaters. Some people thought that Diana Ross was too old to portray teenaged Dorothy, and that was perhaps one of the reasons the 1978 film did not do well. Neither the huge pot of gold that was "Over the Rainbow" in the original film, nor the magic of Judy Garland's 1939 adventures with the wizard, were present in *The Wiz*. Just as Charlie Smalls could not duplicate the success of "Ease on Down the Road," it may have been too much to expect another film to even approach the artistic level of the extraordinary 1939 blockbuster.

Gentle on My Mind

Before there was a smooth-talking, saxophone-playing President from a small town in Arkansas, there was a smooth-singing, guitar-playing entertainer from a small town in Arkansas named Glen Campbell. (That is, the singer was named Glen Campbell, not the town.)

Getting his start on the infamous *Smothers Brothers Comedy Hour* that ran from 1967 to 1969, Campbell was one of the most successful singers of the late 1960s and 1970s. The song that brought Campbell into the ranks of stardom was "Gentle on My Mind." Written in 1967 by fellow *Smothers Brothers* regular John Hartford, "Gentle on My Mind" won a Grammy and became, more or less, the theme song of the country boy from rural Arkansas. It also was Hartford's continuing musical signature, for he wrote nothing else of significance.

Campbell tended to sing ballads that were folklike or softer than many contemporary pieces. Among his more famous recordings were "Wichita Lineman" (1968) and "Galveston" (1969), both created by Jim Webb. His biggest hit of the 1970s, Larry Weiss's "Rhinestone Cowboy" (1975), showed that Campbell had drifted away from his earlier style a bit, but "Rhinestone Cowboy" was still far from the hard rock that was starting to push out classic rock by the mid-1970s.

The Great Pretender

After "Rock Around the Clock," the blockbuster by Max C. Freedman and Jimmy DeKnight, appeared in the 1955 film *The Blackboard Jungle*, the song became such a tremendous hit that it was almost inevitable that there would be some kind of follow-up. The next year, 1956, Bill Haley, who had created quite a stir with his recording of the attention-getting song, starred in the musical film *Rock Around the Clock* (could anybody wishing to make money have chosen any other title?).

In that film were two other good rock songs "The Great Pretender" (1955) and "Only You" or "Only You and You Alone" (1955). Buck Ram wrote both songs, with Ande Rand (Ram again, using a pseudonym) collaborating on "Only You." Despite his tough-sounding name, all of Ram's hits showed a vulnerable or tender side. This was certainly true for "The Great Pretender," which showed psychological openness, "Only You," which focused on a tender relationship, and "Twilight Time" (1944), which was a gentle tribute to evening. "Twilight Time," written with Morty Nevins, Al Nevins, and Artie Dunn, tiptoed into the early rock period in a 1958 revival by the Platters (a great name for recording artists). The Platters had another successful revival in their 1956 rendition of "My Prayer," created in 1939 by lyricist Jimmy Kennedy and musician George Boulanger.

Buck Ram straddled two eras, having a big hit in the 1940s, "Twilight Time," and another top song in the 1950s, "The Great Pretender." Although he also wrote "Only You," a somewhat less notable song, Ram was essentially a one-hit composer in the rock era. Perhaps that was for the best, for if he had been one of the most prolific and successful composers of the early rock era, rock and roll might have been dubbed "rock, roll, and ram."

Happy Together

In the wake of the "British Invasion" that began when the Beatles came to the United States in 1964, some rock groups deliberately and consciously tried to emulate and even imitate the "Fab Four." The Turtles, an American group that took advantage of the Beatles phenomenon, sometimes pretended to be British and did manage to sound somewhat like the lads from Liverpool. A casual listener, for example, might think that the Turtles' smash recording of "Happy Together" was made by the Beatles. One of the top hits of 1967 that was Number 4 in record sales, the upbeat "Happy Together" was created in 1966 by Garry Bonner and Alan Gordon, who wrote nothing else of consequence. Their excellent song, however, has endured for over a generation, and has been heard in various media including Hollywood films. Although the Bonner and Gordon composition was honored by having a 1990 movie, *Happy Together*, named after it, the honor was somewhat tainted since the song was a lot better than the film.

Tied for Number 4 in 1967 was a considerably different piece recorded by a considerably different vocal group. "Light My Fire," also a very notable rock piece, was written by the four members of the Doors; Jim Morrison, John Densmore, Robert Krieger, and Raymond Manzarek. The controversial style of the Doors and the intense vibrations of their most famous song contrasted greatly with the relatively clean-cut image of the Turtles and the pleasant, outgoing tones of their most successful recording.

I'm Sorry

There have been many sorry songs in the history of American popular music. That is, there have been a huge number of songs that were terrible, or flops, or both. There have also been a number of songs with "sorry" in the title. The classic song of that type is "Who's Sorry Now?," created in 1923 by lyricists Bert Kalmar and Harry Ruby and musician Ted Snyder.

In 1957, this 1920s wailer became a part of the rock era by being revived in a recording by the then unknown Connie Francis. Three years later, in 1960, came the best-known "sorry" song written in rock style. "I'm Sorry," created by Ronnie Self and Dub Albritton, was a top hit that year. (Much to their sorrow, it was to be their only famous song.) Other "sorry" songs of the era were "Sorry" or "Sorry I Ran the Whole Way Home" (1959), sung by the Impalas, written by Harry Giosasi and Artie Zwirn; "Sorry Seems to Be the Hardest Word" (1975), written by Elton John and Bernie Taupin; and another "I'm Sorry" (1975) by John Denver.

The 1960 "I'm Sorry" was sung by Brenda Lee, who also recorded some other hits. In the same year she proclaimed she was sorry she recorded her plea "I Want to Be Wanted." Originally an Italian song, "Per Tutta la Vita" by lyricist A. Testa and composer Pino Spotti, it was converted into a hit in the United States after Kim Gannon wrote a set of English words. Lee also belted out "Rockin' Around the Christmas Tree" (1958), written by Johnny Marks who also created "Rudolph the Red-Nosed Reindeer" in 1949. "Rockin' Around the Christmas Tree" was one of the few good rock Christmas songs. The best, of course, was "Jingle Bell Rock" written by Joseph Carleton Beal and James R. Boothe in 1957, a hundred years after the original "Jingle Bells."

Jesus Christ, Superstar

Andrew Lloyd Webber, the famous composer of successful musicals in London and New York, can scarcely be described as a one-hit phenomenon. The best known creator of musicals in the 1970s and 1980s, Lloyd Webber wrote the music for several hits, including *Jesus Christ, Superstar* (1971), *Evita* (1978), *Cats* (1982), and *Phantom of the Opera* (1987). Two time-tested songs from these musicals were "Don't Cry for Me, Argentina" from *Evita* and "Jesus Christ, Superstar" from the musical of that name. (Tim Rice wrote the lyrics for both of these exceptional songs.)

Despite the overall notoriety of Lloyd Webber, "Jesus Christ, Superstar" was the only top song written by him that can be described as a real rock piece. In the context of classic rock, his brilliant proclamation of the early 1970s religious revival among youth, unfortunately, was a one-hit wonder. On the positive side, in the same year that *Jesus Christ, Superstar*, the English rock opera and later motion picture first appeared, another similar style production premiered in New York. No doubt inspired by the smash recording of "Jesus Christ, Superstar" that came out months before the opening of the stage version, Stephen Schwartz's off-Broadway production of *Godspell* rocked onto the scene. With its top number "Day by Day," *Godspell* ran for several years.

But instead of spawning other folk rock operas based on religious motifs, *Jesus Christ, Superstar* and *Godspell* apparently were fads just as beach songs and twist songs had been before them. Nineteen seventy-one was a unique spellbinding year with two excellent rock tributes to the greatest superstar of all time.

Na Na Hey Hey Kiss Him Goodbye

One of the more interesting musical occurrences of 1980s and 1990s America is the taunting "goodbye" chant loudly directed at opposing teams and members of opposing teams during sporting events. If the other team loses, if the other team's pitcher has to leave the game, if a player from the other team is ejected, and for other reasons, a chorus of "goodbye" spontaneously fills the stadium or arena. The same song is used to celebrate a home run or other athletic coup by "the good guys," and in addition can often appear in various nonsporting events or situations.

On all the above occasions, some variant of the 1969 rock hit "Na Na Hey Hey Kiss Him Goodbye" is the song of the moment. Written by Gary DeCarlo, Paul Leka, and Dale Fashver, "Goodbye," as recorded by Steam, was Number 5 in record sales in 1969 and was Number 1 for a while. Although the song has endured as a popular icon for over a generation in one form or another, both the vocal group and the creators of the composition never had another top hit. In other words, they completely lost steam after 1969, leaving themselves open to a common variation of the very taunt they created, "Na na na na, Na na na na, Hey hey hey, Goodbye!"

An earlier hit with "na na" in its lyrics was "Get a Job" (1957), written and recorded by the Silhouettes (Earl T. Beal, Raymond W. Edwards, William F. Horton, and Richard A. Lewis). With its famous "sha na na na" line, "Get a Job" was one of the more successful rock pieces of its time. However, the Silhouettes did not have any more big hits, and they all probably had to get a job in the real world.

Save the Last Dance for Me

It's always hard to judge who is great and who is not. At the other end of the spectrum, it's also sometimes difficult to separate "one-hit wonders" from the rest of the pack. Take the case of Jerome "Doc" Pomus and Mort Shuman. They definitely had a top hit in "Save the Last Dance for Me" (1960), sung by the Drifters. They also had a big hit in 1961 with "Surrender," sung by Elvis Presley. But "Surrender" was not original. It was based on an Italian song, "Torno a Sorrento," by G.B. de Curtis and Ernesto de Curtis. Furthermore, they wrote several lesser compositions, "I'm a Man" (1958) and "Turn Me Loose" (1958), both recorded by the teen-aged Fabian, plus "Teenager in Love" (1959) and "Suspicion" (1964). The sum of all this, if you discount the "borrowed" Italian song, is that Pomus and Shuman, in essence, were responsible for only one really notable song, "Save the Last Dance for Me."

However, the year was not a one-hit phenomenon. Other top songs of 1960 included: "Alley Oop," sung by the Hollywood Argyles and written by Dallas Frazier; "Itsy Bitsy Teenie Weenie Yellow Polkadot Bikini," recorded by Brian Hyland and written by Paul J. Vance and Lee Pockriss; "Cathy's Clown," sung by the Everly Brothers and written by Don and Phil Everly; "Stay," recorded by Maurice Williams and the Zodiacs and written by Williams; "Teen Angel," recorded by Mark Dinning and created by Jean Surrey and Red Surrey; "Why," recorded by Frankie Avalon and written by Peter De Angelis and Bob Marcussi; and "Tom Dooley," recorded by the Kingston Trio and adapted by Dave Guard from a Blue Ridge Mountain folk song, "Tom Dula."

Like any year of the classic rock era, there were songs and people still familiar to us today, and songs and people now lost in the fog of obscurity and declining memories.

Singin' the Blues

Gone with the Wind was a one-of-a-kind classic. As a 1936 novel, the only one written by Margaret Mitchell, it won a Pulitzer Prize. As a spectacular 1939 Civil War film, it is probably the best motion picture ever made.

In 1957, there was another one-of-a-kind classic involving a person named Mitchell. The 1957 event certainly did not even begin to approach the importance of either the 1936 or 1939 events, but in its day and in the context of rock music, it was significant. It also was for both the composer and the singer their only rock hit. Guy Mitchell never again duplicated the success of his Number 1 recording, "Singin' the Blues," and composer Melvin Endsley never again wrote a song of consequence. These two "one-hit" cases are doubly interesting since their joint effort managed to surpass three famous songs. Number 2 was "All Shook Up" sung by Elvis, Number 3 was "Teddy Bear" sung by Presley, and Number 4 was "Jailhouse Rock" sung by the King of rock and roll.

This double "one-hit" phenomenon couldn't have been caused by the theme used. Over the years the concept of the "blues" has been employed very successfully by a number of top composers including W.C. Handy ("Saint Louis Blues," 1914); Bud DeSylva, Lew Brown, and Ray Henderson ("The Birth of the Blues," 1926); Lorenz Hart and Richard Rodgers ("Blue Moon," 1934); Johnny Mercer and Harold Arlen ("Blues in the Night," 1941); and Leroy Anderson ("Blue Tango," 1952). Neither was it caused by the song's title, for an earlier "Singin' the Blues" (1931) was written by lyricist Dorothy Fields and composer Jimmy McHugh, and that event didn't seem to stifle the careers of those two notable songwriters.

Sit Down, I Think I Love You

This essay is about one of the less pleasant aspects of popular music, the tendency for "one-hit wonders" and their works to be forgotten. Classic era rock and roll is kept alive largely by two institutions, oldies radio programs and the recording industry. The latter reissues some of the great older 33 rpm albums as compact discs, and occasionally compiles new anthologies of old hits.

On the radio and at the recording studio, one-hit wonders are typically underrepresented. There's nothing odd about this; a singer who released a dozen successful singles is a lot more likely to be remembered than the artist who only had one or two hits. For whatever reason, perhaps their unusual qualities, some one-hitters do manage to remain in the rock and roll collective consciousness.

Two examples from a few weeks on either side of New Year's 1968 will illustrate this. The Lemon Pipers reached Number 1 with their rather odd "Green Tambourine" the first week of February 1968; they never charted again, although they did release more singles during that year. A few weeks earlier, in the last days of November 1967, Strawberry Alarm Clock topped the charts with *their* rather odd "Incense and Peppermints." They did release another single, in January 1968, but it stalled at Number 27 and the group gave up. Both of these songs are heard fairly often on oldies radio stations, even though they are from one-hit wonder bands, but the songs were Number 1, the titles were memorable, and the group names were pretty weird too.

One of the ugly truths about popular music is that an established act can achieve a hit more easily than an unknown act, even with identical material. The public is predisposed to like what a known performer or group will show them; witness how, in the declining months or years of a major act, poor quality material will still sell fairly well. "Hello Goodbye" by the Beatles comes to mind; had this been the debut single by the "Terre Haute Two," it never would have made it on the radio, much less reached Number 1. As "Incense and Peppermints" shows, striking first records may indeed become big hits, but that is not the norm. Groups that fail to build a track record also fail to become memorable.

The saddest part of all this is that a typical band will pick its very best number for the A-side of the first single. (And, far too often, its second-best for the B-side, a foolish waste of good material.) That is one reason there are so many one-hit groups; that one single is often very good, and in a new, distinctive style. When the group cannot produce an equally interesting (but different) next single, or when they are torn apart by internal problems (see Tom Hank's excellent film on the dangers of success, *That Thing You Do*), they are lost in rock and roll limbo.

Having to explain, to some extent, why there are so many fine one hits out there, this essay will celebrate some of the best, yet least known, among them. Not all were hits per se; position rarely reflects the real worth of a first recording. Also, tastes change as time passes, and the canon of great rock and roll is adjusted accordingly. (Just think how few early Rolling Stones songs you hear on the radio, from back when Mick's voice was higher and whinier than in his classic period.)

The Amboy Dukes had a memorable hit that is still played occasionally. "Journey to the Center of the Mind" reached Number 16 in 1968, during the psychedelic rock period. Possibly it remains popular because the group's leader was Ted Nugent, who went on to greater notoriety in the decades to follow, but it's a great song on its own merits.

Hee-Haw co-host and country all-star Roy Clark appeared on the pop charts just once, with the sensitive Jacques Brel ballad "Yesterday When I Was Young." It reached Number 19 in the summer of 1969, somewhat stunning a public that knew Clark in his screen persona as a bumpkin, who just happened to be a champion guitar, banjo, and fiddle player.

Speaking of guitars, Santo and Johnny, the Farina brothers, had one of the most beautiful Number 1 records of the early rock era with the instrumental "Sleep Walk." They tried, but the lightning never struck again. The unique quality of the sound came from a pedal steel guitar played in pop music arrangements.

"Walk Away Renee" by the Left Banke was a Number 5 hit in 1966, a truly beautiful ballad that some contemporary critics called Baroque, perhaps because it featured a harpsichord. The song is still played occasionally, often in the 1968 cover version by the Four Tops. The latter rose to Number 14, is a typically wonderful Four Tops single, and is also that very rare item, the black cover of a white original. The Left Banke released many more singles, but only charted once after "Walk Away Renee." "Pretty Ballerina" made it to Number 15, despite its arguably being a better song than their first hit. Those are the breaks.

"Our Day Will Come" went to Number 1 for Ruby and the Romantics, one of the truly underappreciated groups in pop music. It was among the greatest romantic ballads of the early 1960s. Ruby's next two singles were less successful, and the group's recording career was over in about eight months.

Lonnie Mack was an Indiana country boy but also just about the hottest guitar player in the nation, back in 1963. His instrumental of Chuck Berry's "Memphis" went to Number 5, before being covered by the vocal version Johnny Rivers released.

"Hot Smoke & Sasafrass" is a high energy rocker from one of America's least-known bands, Bubble Puppy. It climbed to Number 14 in the spring of 1969, and is just about completely forgotten now. Bubble Puppy never charted again.

The British group, Status Quo, had a Number 12 hit with the very psychedelic "Pictures of Matchstick Men" in 1968. Like so many other one-hit wonders, they weren't around long enough to miss once they were gone. They did produce several more minor hits in England, however.

Another British import was the lovely ballad "Everyone's Gone to the Moon," by Jonathan King. It was a Number 17 single in 1965. In this case at least, something is known of the artist; King went on to become a successful record producer in London.

The Sopwith "Camel" (that's how they wrote the name) briefly tickled the listening public's interest with "Hello Hello" back in 1967. Their four-week visit to the charts culminated at Number 26, before they too were only a memory.

The final one-hit wonder discussed here is the Mojo Men, once fronted by Sylvester (Sly Stone) Stewart, who had a very brief hit with a very good song in 1967. The song was "Sit Down, I Think I Love You," composed by a not-yet-famous Stephen Stills, and the single "peaked" at Number 36; only real trivia experts recall it now. "Sit Down, I Think I Love You" deserved better. Its author, however obscure at that time, has become a titan of pop music, and the song is a lyrical ballad of rock and roll. The Mojo Men did very well by it. For whatever reason, the single never took off, and cannot truly be called a one-hit wonder. It wasn't a hit, except by the most inclusive of definitions, but it was a great version of a great song. Go figure. Like most of the songs under discussion here, it is almost as lost as if it had never been written or recorded.

Spinning Wheel

Doing any type of physical task can produce blood, sweat, and tears if one works hard enough. Even a relatively docile activity such as using an old-fashioned spinning wheel can result in the emission of those three body fluids. In the case of a 1969 song, however, the exact opposite was true. Blood, Sweat, and Tears produced a recording of "Spinning Wheel."

In contrast with the earthy and nontraditional name of the vocal group, the name of the song's composer, David Clayton-Thomas, sounded elevated and traditional. Clayton-Thomas did not write any more top hits, a phenomenon that is both traditional and contemporary. On the other hand, Blood, Sweat, and Tears probably sweated a lot in 1969, for in addition to "Spinning Wheel" they came out with two other top recordings, "And When I Die," written in 1966 by Laura Nyro, and "You've Made Me So Happy," written by Berry Gordy Jr., Frank E. Wilson, Brenda Holloway, and Patrice Holloway. The varying moods of these last two songs can cause one's head to spin.

But Blood, Sweat, and Tears was not the only group with multiple hits that year. Another ensemble with a drastically different type of name, Tommy James and the Shondells, had two successful recordings. After singing Jeff Barry and Ellie Greenwich's "Hanky Panky" in 1966, James and the Shondells recorded "Crimson and Clover" and "Crystal Blue Persuasion" in 1969. ("Crimson" was written by James and Peter Lucia, Jr., and "Crystal" by James, Mike Vale, and Ed J. Gray.) If you want to make your head spin even more, try to figure out what a "shondell" is.

Finally, the turbulent 1960s was not the only decade that spun. A considerably dissimilar decade, the Depression-plagued 1930s, also had a "Spinning Wheel" song of its own, written in 1931 by Maryan Rawicz.

Tequila

The most famous post-World War II song with an alcoholic beverage in the title is perhaps "Days of Wine and Roses" (1962). The creators of this Oscar and double Grammy winner, lyricist Johnny Mercer and musician Henry Mancini, wrote a number of other top songs. In contrast, Chuck Rio, the composer of "Tequila" (1958), only wrote one song of consequence. Could it be that the potency of the beverage in the title had something to do with the productivity of the composers? Most people can tolerate several glasses of wine in a day, while few can tolerate more than one shot of powerful tequila. Also, the lack of lyrics for the song "Tequila" could be due to the breathless state that a drink of tequila can produce.

"Tequila" was one of the powerful songs of 1958. Recorded by the Champs, it was Number 2 in record sales that year, tied with "Volare." Another instrumental hit of 1958 with a Latin beat was "Patricia," played and composed by Prez Prado. "Patricia" appeared in the film *La Dolce Vita*. Prado also recorded the Latin-flavored "Cherry Pink and Apple Blossom White," the Number 1 disc in 1955. The music for "Cherry Pink" was written in 1951 by Spanish-born Luis Guglielmi, also known as Louiguy, with English lyrics added for the 1955 recording by Mack David. Louiguy also created the melody for another famous song, "La Vie en Rose" (1946), with French lyrics by Edith Piaf and English lyrics (1950) by Mack David.

Volare

Most people familiar with the 1958 smash hit "Volare," or "Nel Blu Dipinto di Blu," would probably point to its excellent melody and dramatic tone as the reasons for its success. There's no denying that Domenico Modugno's melody and Francesco Migliacci and Modugno's original Italian lyrics were major factors in making Dean Martin's rendering of "Volare" a Grammy winner and a tie for Number 2 with another foreign-flavored song, "Tequila." But one other factor that most people are probably unaware of was the lyricist. Yes, we mean the lyricist, not the lyrics, although the words were quite good.

There was something magical and/or mystical about Mitchell Parish, the lyricist for "Volare." Not only did Parish provide successful words for the 1958 hit after the song was originally conceived, but he also did it for several other classics of American popular music. He created lyrics after the fact for Duke Ellington's "Sophisticated Lady" (1933), Peter De Rose's "Deep Purple" (1934), Leroy Anderson's "Sleigh Ride" (1948), and perhaps the best popular song of the twentieth century, Hoagy Carmichael's "Stardust" (1927).

However, Mitch's magic wasn't always there. He wrote "Ciao Ciao Bambina" (1959) with Modugno and Edoardo Verde and the song was nothing special. Another after-the-fact lyricist, Carl Sigman, didn't turn Modugno and Migliacci's "Adio, Adio" or "Goodbye" (1962) into a big American hit, although the Italian version won first prize at the San Remo Music Festival in 1962. One other effort by Migliacci, "Son of a Travellin' Man" (1969), with R. I. Allen and Mauro Lusini, was not particularly notable. Like Chuck Rio, the creator of "Tequila," Modugno and Migliacci were essentially one-hit composers in the United States. A third 1958 hit, "Summertime, Summertime," by Sherm Feller and Tom Jameson, was also its creators' only top song, demonstrating that a composition didn't have to have a foreign flavor that year to fall into the well-populated limbo called "one hit."

NOVELTY SONGS, OR,
UNUSUAL, BUT UNUSUALLY GOOD

Aquarius

The numbers five and one were closely interlinked in 1969. The Fifth Dimension, an excellent vocal group consisting of three men and two women, had two Number 1 hits that year. Their recordings of "Aquarius" and its flip side "Let the Sunshine In" were tied for number one in record sales. "Let the Sunshine In," though the lesser of the two, did not just inevitably and passively ride along to the top with the superb composition "Aquarius." It was a superior song on its own.

Yet there is no doubt which of the two pieces was the dominant one. So perfectly aligned with the mood and style of the free-wheeling and flamboyant 1960s, the Grammy winning "Aquarius" with its famous line "the dawning of the age of Aquarius" was one of the premiere songs of the decade. Although what the age of Aquarius really is has never been clearly defined, its mystic overtones still appeal to us a generation later in the 1990s.

Both "Aquarius" and "Let the Sunshine In" were from the 1967 musical *Hair*, which was one of the scandals of the time because of its onstage nudity. The creators of both songs were lyricists Gerome Ragni and James Rado and composer Galt MacDermot. The musical with its two outstanding songs is the one significant thing for which the three men are known.

The Fifth Dimension, in contrast, were not one-record flukes. They also recorded the Grammy-winning "Up-Up and Away"

(1967), written by Jim Webb. Other successful recordings by the Fifth Dimension were "Wedding Bell Blues" (1966), by Laura Nyro, a hit in 1969, and "One Less Bell to Answer" (1970), by lyricist Hal David and composer Burt Bacharach. The artistic and financial success of the Fifth Dimension may well have caused them to celebrate with high fives, which would be in harmony with the group's original name, "The Hi-Fi's."

The Candy Man

The senior author was first introduced to the 1972 hit "The Candy Man" under not-so-sweet circumstances. A visit by three young nephews and nieces, who couldn't seem to sing anything else but Leslie Bricusse and Anthony Newley's novelty, made the author a little sick. Recovery set in after hearing Sammy Davis Jr.'s much better rendering of the song. Davis also recorded another top song by Bricusse and Newley, the Ivor Novello winner "What Kind of Fool Am I?," from the 1962 British musical *Stop the World—I Want to Get Off*. Another notable recording by Davis was Walter Marks' "I Gotta Be Me" (1968).

Nineteen seventy-two was a very sweet year for tie-in record sales. Tied for Number 1 were "Alone Again" or "Alone Again Naturally," sung and written by Gilbert O'Sullivan, which won an Ivor Novello Award, and "The First Time Ever I Saw Your Face," sung by Roberta Flack and written by Ewan MacColl, which won both a Novello and a Grammy. (Another Number 1 and Grammy for Flack came the next year for her recording of Charles Fox and Norman Gimbel's "Killing Me Softly with His Song.") Tied for Number 2 in 1972 were "American Pie" or "Bye Bye American Pie," sung and created by Don McLean, "I Can See Clearly Now" or "I Can See Clearly Now the Rain Has Gone," recorded and written by Johnny Nash, and "Without You," sung by Nilsson, the original Spanish words and music by Osvaldo Farres, the English words by Ray Gilbert and Charles Wolcott.

"Candy Man" was tied for Number 3 with "A Horse with No Name," sung by America and written by Lee Bunnell, "Lean on Me," sung and written by Bill Withers, and "Me and Mrs. Jones," recorded by Billy Paul and created by Leon Huff, Kenneth Gamble, and Cary Gilbert. If you're not completely tied up in knots by all these ties, we'll offer one more tidbit. Helen Reddy had a Number 5 song in 1972, "I Am Woman" written by Reddy and Ray Burton. It was, of course, tied with another song, as was Reddy's 1973 Number 5, hit, "Delta Dawn," written by Alex Harvey and Larry Collins.

Don't Sleep in the Subway

A homeless person might not have a choice, but why would anyone sleep in the subway of their own free will? Such places are dirty, noisy, and often quite unsafe. Yet the person being sung to in the 1967 composition "Don't Sleep in the Subway" apparently had not only snoozed in the underground, but had also wandered around in heavy rain. Is such an idiot deserving of the love implied in the fine 1967 Ivor Novello Award winner?

Well, British composer Tony Hatch was deserving of the awards he won in the 1960s. In addition to "Don't Sleep in the Subway," written with Jackie Trent and very artistically recorded by Petula Clark, Hatch also wrote the Novello Award winners "Downtown" (1965), "Call Me" (1967), "Harvest of Love" (1963) (with Benny Bill), and "Where Are You Now My Love?" (1965) (with Trent). Other songs hatched by Hatch were "Color My World" (1966) (with Trent), "I Couldn't Live Without Your Love" (1966), and "I Know a Place" (1965).

On top of the Novello Awards, two of Hatch's songs, "Downtown" and "I Know a Place" won Grammy Awards. Also, "Call Me" received another honor of sorts by being used in a later advertising campaign by Bell Telephone systems. With such success in the 1960s, Hatch probably didn't have to sleep in the subway and could well afford a vehicle to keep him protected from the rain.

Hit the Road, Jack

One of the leading candidates for rudest song title is "Hit the Road, Jack." Written by Percy Mayfield and recorded in 1961 by Ray Charles, the title is far from endearing though the song won a Grammy Award for 1961. Another 1961 composition with a "mean" title was "Big Bad John," written and sung by Jimmy Dean, which was also a 1961 Grammy winner as well as Number 2 in record sales.

In contrast, Charles recorded Don Gibson's "I Can't Help Loving You" the following year which was a song with a much better attitude. But the 1962 song was like "Hit the Road, Jack" in one way. It also won a Grammy Award, and on top of that was Number 1 in record sales. Other Grammy winners for Charles were "Let the Good Times Roll" (1961), written by Sam Theard and Fleecie Moore; "Busted" (1963), written by Harlan Howard; and "Crying Time" (1966), written by Buck Owens.

Actually, "I Can't Help Loving You," was only tied for Number 1 in 1962. With Charles' recording at the top were "Big Girls Don't Cry," sung by the Four Seasons, written by Bob Crewe and Bob Gaudio, and "Sherry," also sung by the Four Seasons, and also written by Gaudio (alone). Another 1962 hit was "Don't Know Me" by Cindy Walker and Eddy Arnold, recorded by Charles.

Charles doesn't just sing. He also plays piano, was a television advertisement star for a popular cola, and has written songs. Among his creations are the 1958 instrumental "Sweet Sixteen Bars;" the English lyrics (along with S. K. Russell) for the 1940 Spanish language song "Frenesi," by Alberto Dominguez; "This Little Girl of Mine" (1955), an adaption of the Gospel song "This Little Light of Mine;" "Don't You Know" (1956); and "I Believe in My Soul" (1959). Charles recorded the three last songs, and for "I Believe in My Soul" he not only sang the male part but dubbed in the four female parts using falsetto. All the above-mentioned songs sung and/or written by Charles, that involve rock, rhythm and blues, soul, gospel, and foreign music, demonstrate Charles' wide range of modes.

When you're as versatile and talented as Ray Charles, you probably can get away with saying "Hit the Road, Jack."

Itsy Bitsy Teenie Weenie Yellow Polkadot Bikini

It would not do well in a contest for the best song ever written, or even the best song of 1960, but it probably would be a finalist in a competition for hardest to say song titles. In fact, if you could convert the long title into cloth, it would possibly cover more body than the "Itsy Bitsy Teenie Weenie Yellow Polkadot Bikini" actually did.

The disc by Brian Hyland was a top hit of 1960. The novelty's composers, Paul J. Vance and Lee Pockriss, never again wrote a song touching upon beach life, or a song with as long a title. However, they did, as a team or with others, write several other songs. "Calcutta" (1960) was by composer Heino Gaze and lyricists Vance and Pockriss. "My Heart Is an Open Book" (1959), was by lyricist Hal David and musician Pockriss. "Johnny Angel" (1962) was by Lyn Duddy and Pockriss. "Catch a Falling Star" (1958), "Playground in My Mind" (1973), "Starlight" (1960), "Tracy" (1969), and "When Julie Comes Around" (1970), were by Vance and Pockriss. (Note that a more famous composition called "Starlight" was written in 1931 by lyricist Joe Young and musician Bernice Petkere.)

"Polkadot Bikini" was not a great song, but it was one of the first of the beach songs that were a fad in the early 1960s. The culmination of the beach craze was probably Chuck Berry's "Surfin' USA" (1963) or perhaps Brian Wilson's "California Girls" (1965). Both of these lively winners were sung by the Beach Boys, who possibly got their inspiration from seeing attractive young women wearing itsy bitsy teenie weenie bikinis.

King of the Road

Although being called the "King of the Road" implies that one is a hobo, Roger Miller didn't mind at all. The 1965 song, written and recorded by Miller, won a Grammy and also became Miller's theme. The year before, in 1964, "Dang Me," again composed and sung by Miller, was similarly honored by a Grammy. A third interesting Miller song of the mid-1960s was "England Swings (Like a Pendulum Do)" (1965). For a while, then, Miller was one of the kings of pop music though the real royalty at that time were the Beatles, the Emperors of the 1960s Land of Pop Music.

Other hits of 1965 were: "Count Me In," recorded by Gary Lewis and the Playboys and written by Glen D. Hardin; "This Diamond Ring," also sung by Gary Lewis and the Playboys, and written by Bob Brass, Irwin Levine, and Al Kooper; "Save Your Heart for Me," once again sung by Lewis and the Playboys, and written by Gary Geld and Peter David Udell; "I Got You Babe," sung by Sonny and Cher, written by Sonny Bono (Sonny later went on to be Mayor of Palm Springs and a Congressman from California and Cher, among other things, to be an exercise guru); "I'm Telling You Now," by Freddie and the Dreamers, written by Freddie Garrity and Mitch Murray; "Turn! Turn! Turn!," sung by the Byrds, written by Pete Seeger; and "You've Lost That Lovin' Feeling," recorded by the Righteous Brothers, written by Barry Mann, Cynthia Weil, and Phil Spector.

Nineteen sixty-five witnessed kings, emperors, mayors, gurus, dreamers, playboys getting a lot of play, and righteous siblings. It was also the year for toys and the supreme patriarch of music. One of that year's hits was "A Lover's Concerto," also known as "How Gentle Is the Rain," recorded by the Toys and written by Denny Randell and Sandy Linzer. The music was based on "Minuet in G," by none other than the great Beethoven.

The Last Kiss

Few rock and roll songs deal even in passing with the concept of death; often those that do are excessively sentimental, such as the Righteous Brothers' maudlin "Rock and Roll Heaven." This song, with its saccharine refrain and tasteless allusions to dead rockers, was a Number 3 on the charts in 1974, outperforming all but two of their *good* records from the 1960s.

A small but significant group of rock records deal explicitly with death, that indeed have someone's death as their *raison d'etre*. Some disc jockeys openly refer to the morbid and often bloody nature of these singles by calling them "splatter platters." The earliest of these platters was "Teen Angel," a one-hit-wonder by Mark Dinning. Released in January 1960, it spent two weeks at Number 1. Like many of the death ballads to follow, "Teen Angel" linked teenagers, cars, and death—on the whole, an accurate assessment.

Another early splatter platter came out later in 1960, the overdone "Tell Laura I Love Her" by Ray Peterson. The narrator dies as a result of participating in a car race, but has sufficient life in him to cry out the song's title several times before expiring. It went to Number 7, Peterson's second single and first Top Ten hit; he never bettered that Number 7 performance.

"Patches" may not really qualify as a splatter song—the title character commits suicide, after all—but it *was* morbid enough for anybody. The narrator's girlfriend drowns herself when they are forced to break up due to her lower social class. The narrator clearly plans to kill himself, to join her, making "Patches" the only doubleheader among these records. This sad little song went to Number 6 in 1962 for Dickey Lee, who had two more Top Twenty hits in his brief career.

For some reason, perhaps the then-recent assassination of John F. Kennedy, 1964 was a motherlode of death-theme songs. The Shangri-Las, a girl group with six charted singles from 1964 to 1966, had their greatest success with "Leader of the Pack." In this song the lead singer tells how her parents made her break up with her motor-cycle-riding bad boy. He is killed immediately afterward in a traffic accident, complete with motorcycle engine and crash sound effects on the record. The single went to Number 1, and was wonderfully parodied two months later when "Leader of the Laundromat" by the Detergents (actually Ron Dante, later of the Archies, and two friends) went to Number 19. In the parody, a boy relates how his parents forced him to break up with a girl who worked in a laundry. She is killed by a car while running blindly across the street (carry-ing *his* laundry). It could be claimed that several splatter platters were funny, but only this one was intentionally funny.

Also in 1964, Jan and Dean released their song "Dead Man's Curve," about a drag race that ended in a fatal crash. The Beach Boys' "Don't Worry Baby" from that year is about a young man who fears his coming drag race, perhaps the first rock and roll song to deal with anxiety and the fear of death. "Dead Man's Curve" went to Number 8, while the much superior song "Don't Worry Baby" stalled at Number 24, but then again nobody actually dies in it, so it's not too exciting.

The best death song of 1964, and perhaps of all time, was "The Last Kiss" by J. Frank Wilson and the Cavaliers. This, their only hit, tells of yet another car wreck and the death of the narrator's girlfriend. The tune is excellent, the arrangement and performance praiseworthy, and the bathos kept to a reasonable level. "The Last Kiss" is the most imaginative title yet for a song about young sundered lovers; it's a real shame that this group never hit the charts again, after such a strong debut.

The next (and final) death song of the classic rock and roll era is by all odds the strangest as well. Bobbie Gentry exploded onto the pop scene with the enigmatic "Ode to Billie Joe," a powerful song that spawned a lot of discussion, and eventually a very bad movie. The single was Number 1 for an entire month, a rare achievement for a debut record. The narrator recounts a series of sad, rural Southern vignettes worthy of Faulkner, including her boyfriend's suicide (by drowning).

The clever touch in "Ode to Billie Joe" that oldies fanatics still debate, is the line where someone has seen the nameless narrator and Billie Joe throwing "something" off the Tallahatchie bridge, from which the boy later commits suicide. Murdered adult, aborted child—she never tells, but Billie Joe can no longer live with himself. This unresolved mystery, unique in rock and roll, gives the song lasting power and appeal.

Over the course of the next several years, Gentry released three singles, as well as a few duet recordings with Glen Campbell. None were successful. Like too many other performers of teenage death songs, Gentry was seemingly jinxed, and her career went nowhere fast.

Let's Twist Again

Chubby Checker was the only rock and roll star to have a major career that entirely revolved around dance tunes; it is somewhat surprising after the passage of several decades to see how successful a career it was. Chubby had twenty-two hits on nineteen singles, and released ten albums. Four of the albums sold in the Top Ten, and all the others sold respectably. With very few exceptions, his songs were dance songs, to be played at parties. He first specialized in the Twist, and later in other dances such as the Limbo Rock.

Dubbed "Chubby Checker" because of a fancied resemblance to Fats Domino, Ernest Evans was one of the many stars created in the orbit around Dick Clark's *American Bandstand*. As Chubby, his first single went nowhere back in June 1960. The very next month, Hank Ballard and the Midnighters, an R&B group, had a minor crossover hit. Its B-side was a catchy song called "The Twist;" within a month, Chubby had a cover of "The Twist" out on his label, Parkway, this time as an A-side. It sold very well, hitting Number 1 for a week in September.

Hank Ballard, perhaps miffed at all this, reissued his original "The Twist" as an A-side three weeks after Chubby released his version. This must be the only case in rock and roll history of an act covering a cover of their own record. At any rate, Ballard's version stalled at Number 28, probably because Chubby Checker didn't just *sing* about the Twist; he appeared on television—frequently—to show teenagers how to do the dance. (Before long, he would appear in several teen movies, performing dance songs of course.)

Chubby kept churning out dance-related singles. "Pony Time" went to Number 1 in the winter of 1961, while "Let's Twist Again" hit the Top Ten that summer. "The Fly," another dance tune, had gone to Number 7 for him in late 1961, when the most peculiar part of Chubby Checker's rock saga was just about to take place.

In November 1961 the second wave of the Twist craze was under way, Chubby's "The Twist" was rereleased by Parkway Records, and the single went to Number 1 a second time. While some records have dropped off the Top 40 and then started selling again after a while, no other song has ever inhabited the top spot on two separate occasions.

Chubby Checker received the very first specifically rock Grammy, the Best Rock and Roll Recording, for "Let's Twist Again." It is readily apparent that Chubby's Grammy was actually a recognition of "The Twist" and its record-breaking performance. "Let's Twist" was a very nice Number 8 back in the summer of 1961, while "The Twist"—having been rereleased in late 1961—had rocketed to the Top Ten, and stayed there for thirteen weeks this time, from December 10, 1961, to March 3, 1962. It was Number 1 for two weeks in January. In other words, it was not really eligible for a 1961 Grammy, but had performed so well in the first weeks of 1962. The 1961 Grammy Award Ceremony was held just over two months after all this, in May 1962; Chubby's triumphant second Number 1 with "The Twist" was the most interesting piece of recent rock and roll news. Unable to give him a crowd-pleasing Grammy for that record, they gave him one for an okay record, with "Twist" in the title.

Immediately following "The Twist" as Number 1 in January 1962 was Joey Dee & the Starliters' "Peppermint Twist," a song from the teen movie *Hey, Let's Twist*. In those weeks there were a total of five Twist records in the Top 40.

Chubby had more Top Ten dance records, including Number 3 "Slow Twistin'" with Dee Dee Sharp and "Limbo Rock" at Number 2. From 1963 on, his singles mostly inhabited the middle of the charts; in late 1964 and 1965, his last two charted singles were bottom feeders at Number 40. The very last was "Let's Do the Freddie," an attempt to cash in on Freddie and the Dreamers' "Do the Freddie," itself only a Number 18 record, and just about the last dance-related hit single by anybody, anywhere, in the classic rock era. (It marked the end of Freddie's career on records, as well as Chubby's.)

Like several of his fellow *American Bandstand* alumni, Chubby helped fuel the growing Oldies movement during the Seventies by performing his old songs again.

Louie, Louie

If you were born after the start of World War II and have wondered what it takes to become President of the United States, perhaps the answer lies in the curious song first recorded in 1956 by its composer Richard Berry. "Louie, Louie," which originally was a mambo and did not become a hit until recorded in a different style by the Kingsmen in 1963, developed into a strange fixture of the classic rock generation. This is particularly true of its chorus which has been sung countless times. (The State of Washington has even adopted "Louie, Louie" as its official rock song.) After Bill Clinton was elected President in 1992, there was a comment that we finally have a President that knows all of the lyrics to "Louie, Louie." From an informal and unscientific poll of people roughly Clinton's age, it seems that few of his contemporaries can actually recite many of the words to the song. Therefore, a possible conclusion is that one thing that separates Clinton from the masses is his mastery of the lyrics of "Louie, Louie."

Most people, however, seem to regard the song's lyrics as unintelligible. (Many people also regard Washington politics as unintelligible. Maybe there is a connection between the two in Clinton's case.) Even the Federal Bureau of Investigation, who examined the words of "Louie, Louie" for alleged obscenities, came to the same confused conclusion as most others. Yet Berry's one notable contribution has been extensively recorded, with some claims to being the most recorded song. In addition, it has been a favorite of fraternities, including the motley bunch in the 1978 film, *Animal House*.

There were other hits in 1963, including: "Blue Velvet," crooned by Bobby Vinton, written in 1951 by Bernie Wayne and Lee Morris; "Dominique," sung by the Singing Nun, written by Soeur Sourire with English lyrics by Noel Regney; "He's So Fine," sung by the Chiffons, written by Ronald Mack; "Fingertips," recorded by Stevie Wonder, created by Henry Cosby and Clarence Paul; "I Will

Follow Him," recorded by Little Peggy March, written by Arthur Altman, Norman Gimbel, Del Roma, and J. W. Stole; "My Boyfriend's Back," sung by the Angels, created by Robert Feldman, Gerald Goldstein, and Richard Gottehrer; "Sukiyaki," originally titled "Ueo Muite Aruku" in Japanese, recorded by Kyu Sakamoto, written by Ed Rohusuke and Hachidai Nakamura; "Puff, the Magic Dragon," sung by Peter, Paul, and Mary, created by Leonard Lipton and Peter Yarrow; "Walk Like a Man," recorded by the Four Seasons, written by Bob Crewe and Bob Gaudio; and the Number 1 in record sales, "Sugar Shack," recorded by Jimmy Gilmer and the Fireballs, written by Keith McCormack and Faye Voss. One wonders how many of these song lyrics Clinton remembers.

Nineteen sixty-three was also the year of a major tragedy, the assassination of John F. Kennedy, the President with whom Bill Clinton has several attributes in common. From what is known of Kennedy, however, knowledge of the lyrics of "Louie, Louie" is probably something not shared by both.

Mr. Bo Jangles

One of the most striking songs of 1968 was Ennio Moricone's composition "The Good, the Bad, and the Ugly." From the famous "spaghetti western" of that name, starring Clint Eastwood, the piece was recorded by Hugo Montenegro.

The "good" seemed to apply to "Mister Bo Jangles" or just "Bo Jangles." His dancing and entertaining ways brought smiles to many faces during 1968 and during the run of the musical *Dancin'*, from which Jerry Jeff Walker's song was taken. (Sammy Davis Jr. made a fine recording.) Another "good" that year was O. C. Smith's recording of "Little Green Apples," which won a Grammy. (Bobby Russell wrote the song.)

The leading candidate for "bad" in 1968 was probably the narrow-minded "Harper Valley P.T.A." Sung by Jeannie C. Riley, Tom T. Hall's composition later spun off into a 1978 movie starring Barbara Eden.

Scanning the rest of the 1968 hits, there doesn't seem to be a viable candidate for "ugly." Among the other songs were: "Love Is Blue," played by Paul Mauriat and written by Bryan Blackburn, Pierre Cour, and Andre Popp; "People Got to Be Free," recorded by the Rascals and written by Edward Brigati and Felix Cavaliere; "Honey," sung by Bobby Goldsboro and written by Bobby Russell; and "I Heard It Through the Grapevine," originally recorded in 1967 by Gladys Knight and the Pips and recorded again in 1968 by Marvin Gaye.

Ah! Now we have at last found the ugly! It was not the two recordings of "Grapevine," nor the song itself, written by Norman Whitfield and Barrett Strong. The ugly applies to the raisins advertised in TV commercials in the 1980s, using "Grapevine" as the theme. California raisins are healthy and delicious, but they would not win a beauty contest.

Mr. Sandman

It may have been just a coincidence that "Mister Sandman" came out in the same year as the early rock classic "Sh-Boom." In any case, the 1954 recording of "Mister Sandman" by the Chordettes was like a softer female response to or echo of "Sh-Boom," sung by the male group, the Crew-Cuts. (Note that both songs had the word "dream" in the lyrics, "Bring me a dream" in "Sandman," and "Life could be a dream" in "Sh-Boom.") A year later, Pat Ballard's "Sandman" composition was itself the recipient of an echo with the appearance of the 1955 Christmas song "Mister Santa," that used the same tune but new words by Ballard. (Incidentally, Ballard is also known as Francis Drake Ballard.)

Ballard did not just write "mister" songs. For example, in the same year that "Sandman" was recorded, his 1928 Ballard ballad "Oh Baby Mine" was popularly revived, not coincidentally riding on the success of "Sandman." However, there were plenty of other "mister" songs during the classic rock era. In 1956 Jerry Bock, Larry Holofcener, and George Weiss collaborated on "Mister Wonderful" or "Mr. Wonderful." DeWayne Blackwell's "Mister Blue" appeared in 1959. In 1960 the novelty "Mr. Custer," by Fred Darian, Al De Lory, and Joseph Van Winkle produced plenty of smiles and sales. "Mr. Lonely" by Gene Allan and Bobby Vinton was successful in 1964. The great Bob Dylan wrote "Mr. Tambourine Man" in 1965. Jerry Jeff Walker's "Mr. Bojangles" was a hit in 1968. Toward the end of the era, Joseph Broussard and Ralph G. Williams wrote the 1971 song, "Mr. Big Stuff."

So anyone living during the classic rock era and who felt like "Mr. Lonely" or "Mr. Blue" or had the luck of "Mr. Custer," could have one's spirits lifted by the music of "Mr. Tambourine Man" and the dancing of "Mr. Bojangles" and end up feeling like "Mr. Wonderful" or "Mr. Big Stuff."

The Purple People Eater

Here's a trivia puzzle to spring on your friends. What do cattle drives and the Minnesota Vikings professional football team have in common? The answer is "purple people eaters." The 1958 novelty "The Purple People Eater" was recorded and written by Sheb Wooley, later to be one of the stars of the 1959 to 1966 television series *Rawhide*, which portrayed the adventures of a group of cowboys on cattle drives. To complete the strange logic of the puzzle, in the years after the song appeared, the defensive line of the Minnesota Vikings was dubbed "the purple people eaters" because of the color of their uniforms and their skill at catching quarterbacks and swallowing them up with a tackle.

The puzzle and even the song may be sneered at by some or even many, but there was nothing to disparage about the song's success. "The Purple People Eater," with its comic story about an odd otherworldly creature, was tied for Number 1 in record sales in 1958. It beat out several well-known and even classic songs that year, including: "Volare," or "Nel Blu Dipinto di Blu," the original Italian words by Domenico Modugno and Francesco Migliacci, the English words by Mitchell Parish, music by Modugno; "Magic Moments," words by Hal David, music by Burt Bacharach; "Tequila" by Chuck Rio; "Summertime, Summertime" by Sherm Feller and Tom Jameson; "Jingle Bell Rock," written in 1957 by Joseph Carleton Beal and James R. Boothe; and "Witch Doctor" and "The Chipmunk Song" by Ross Bagdasarian (also known as David Seville).

In other words "The Purple People Eater" simply gobbled up these other tasty morsels of 1958.

Tutti Frutti

Little Richard (Penniman) was eighteen when he signed with RCA-Victor, but nothing came of his early recordings back in 1951. He spent 1953 through 1955 with the Tempo Toppers, a group so obscure that only Little Richard's involvement makes them noteworthy. At about this time he was signed to Peacock Records, but again to no end. In late 1955 his contract was purchased by Specialty, a small but interesting outfit in southern California. (Both Sonny Bono and Dr. Demento—Barret Hanson—worked for Specialty at various times.) Little Richard had finally found a home.

"Tutti Frutti" was his first release on the new label. It never topped Number 17, but retained that level of popularity long enough to eventually earn a gold record. The song was also popular enough to come to Pat Boone's attention over at Dot Records, the House of Covers. Boone's version went to Number 12. He also covered Little Richard's next single, "Long Tall Sally." The song went to Number 6 for Richard and Number 8 for Pat. Little Richard's B-side charted as well; "Slippin' and Slidin'" reached Number 33 on its own.

"Rip It Up," like "Tutti Frutti," stalled at Number 17 but nonetheless went gold. Its B-side was "Ready Teddy," a song that didn't quite chart but received a fair amount of attention anyway. Bill Haley & the Comets were the ones to cover "Rip It Up"; their version was less interesting and earned a mediocre Number 25. (Covers have also appeared of "Lucille" and "Good Golly Miss Molly," the latter over ten years after Little Richard's original version.)

The thing about Little Richard was his high energy and outrageous behavior. Covers just couldn't compete with the real thing. People knew about this, too, because almost from the start of his stint at Specialty Records, Little Richard appeared on television and in films. In 1956 he was in Alan Freed's *Don't Knock the Rock*, performing his first two hits. Later that year he did three songs in *The Girl Can't Help It*: "She's Got It," "Ready Teddy," and the title tune. In 1957 he once again worked with Alan Freed in *Mister Rock and Roll*, performing "Keep a Knockin'" and "Lucille." These, plus the frenetic "Jenny, Jenny," were his singles for 1957. They earned Number 8, Number 21, and Number 10, respectively.

In late 1957, Little Richard announced his retirement from show business and his intention to become a minister. Specialty released two more already-recorded singles in 1958, "Good Golly Miss Molly" at Number 10 and "Ooh! My Soul" at Number 31, but Little Richard did as he said he would and left the industry.

By 1961, having earned a degree in theology, Richard Penniman was ordained a minister. He returned to performing in 1963, without, however, giving up his religious commitments.

No new songs came from Little Richard after 1958. He has worked a good deal, including filmed performances of oldies concerts in *Let the Good Times Roll* and *The London Rock and Roll Show* (both 1973). Old performance footage was used in *Rock and Roll: The Early Days* (1985). His next film appearance was quite different, as the protagonist's outrageous neighbor in *Down and Out in Beverly Hills* (1986).

In recognition of his pioneering and innovative work, Little Richard was inducted into the Rock and Roll Hall of Fame in the first year of its existence, 1986. Some of his classmates were Elvis Presley, Chuck Berry, Buddy Holly, Fats Domino, and the Everly Brothers, excellent company indeed.

The Twist

It was like a tornado—powerful, wildly revolving in a circular pattern, and short-lived. It was the biggest dance craze of the 1960s, rivaling the popularity of the "Charleston" fad of the 1920s. After Chubby Checker recorded Hank Ballard's very energetic song "The Twist" in 1960, millions of Americans (and others) were gyrating to the new dance's rhythms. (Referring to an earlier song by Ballard, Johnny Otis, and Etta James, even Henry of the 1954 hit "Dance with Me, Henry" or "The Wallflower" probably did "The Twist.")

While many were twisting, others were copying and imitating. Trying to cash in on the fad, several other twist songs appeared between 1960 and 1962. "Twistin' USA" written by Kal Mann followed "The Twist" in 1960. Mann with Dave Appell composed another twist song in 1961, "Let's Twist Again," sung by Checker. In 1962 came three other twist pieces, "Twistin' the Night Away," sung and written by Sam Cooke; "The Peppermint Twist," written by Joey Dee and Henry Glover; and "Twist and Shout," recorded by the Isley Brothers and written by Bert Russell and Philip Medley. Later on, in 1964, the Beatles would also record "Twist and Shout."

Checker, whose real name was Ernest Evans, also recorded songs that had nothing to do with "The Twist." In 1961 he sang "Pony Time," written by Don Covay and John Berry, and in 1962 he was involved in another dance craze by recording "Limbo Rock," written by Jon Sheldon and William E. Strange. It was a good thing Checker was involved with all these active songs. Otherwise, he might have outgrown his nickname "Chubby" and changed it to "Fats." That would have been awkward, though, for another well-known singer named Domino had already taken that name.

Although the twist lasted longer than most dance fads, it eventually faded away and hasn't been danced to any extent since the

1960s. Ironically, the other and lesser dance craze with which Checker was involved, the limbo, has remained popular into the 1990s. There's a simple explanation for this. When you do the twist, you stand in one place and go nowhere. However, when you do the limbo, you keep on going forward.

Wake Up, Little Susie

It is uncertain whether Little Susie woke up in 1957 when the Everly Brothers sang "Wake Up, Little Susie." But many others woke up when they heard the somewhat odd tones of the song. The young Everly Brothers had a unique sound, a smooth, clear, sort of nasal twang. Combine that with the lively, erratic rhythms created by Boudleaux Bryant and Felice Bryant, and you have something not easily overlooked.

The Everlys recorded three other songs by the Bryants, "Bye, Bye Love" (1957), "Problems" (1958), and "Take a Message to Mary" (1959), plus two written by Boudleaux alone, "All I Have to Do Is Dream" (1958) and "Bird Dog" (1958). A number of years later, Boudleaux also wrote "Love Hurts" (1975). The Everly Brothers even wrote some of their own materials. Don Everly wrote "I Kissed You" or "'Til I Kissed You" in 1959, and Don and Phil wrote "Cathy's Clown" in 1960. Of the several top recordings by the Everlys, "Bye, Bye Love," "All I Have to Do Is Dream," and "Wake Up, Little Susie," are perhaps the most memorable.

Speaking of waking, an earlier song with "waking" in the title was "Waking or Sleeping," a 1943 composition by British composer Ivor Novello. Although Novello wrote nothing that is famous in the United States, the award in his name has been given to a number of outstanding songs.

The Everly Brothers, being countrified Americans, had little chance of winning the British-oriented Novello, which began in 1955. But they were fully eligible for the Grammy which began to be awarded in 1958. Not surprisingly, they never won.

Witch Doctor

If you want to really puzzle your friends with a tricky trivia question, try this. What composer of a very famous popular song of the 1950s was also an actor of some consequence, the collaborator on a successful song with a Pulitzer Prize winning author, and an experimenter with audiotapes? The answer is Ross Bagdasarian. When you give your friends the answer, be prepared for puzzled or even hostile looks, for few people are familiar with Bagdasarian's name.

Quite a few people have heard of David Seville, the pseudonym of Bagdasarian. Seville was the creator of "The Chipmunk Song" or "Christmas, Don't Be Late" (1958), which for good or bad has become a holiday standard. It also spawned various TV programs featuring the three cute rodents and David Seville. The audiotape part of the puzzle relates to the speeded-up audiotapes that Bagdasarian used to create the chipmunk sound. The actor part of the puzzle refers to several 1950s movies in which Bagdasarian played secondary but significant roles. The Pulitzer Prize part of the puzzle refers to Bagdasarian's cousin, William Saroyan, a Pulitzer-winning author who in 1950 collaborated with Bagdasarian on the 1951 hit, "Come on-a My House."

Another hit song by Bagdasarian alone was "Witch Doctor" (1958), sung by David Seville. If you're a little confused by actor/singer/composer David Seville/Ross Bagdasarian/the Chipmunks all in one big jumble, don't look for relief in a recording of "Witch Doctor." As the title implies, the song is more than a little weird.

Yakety Yak

Humor has generally been in short supply within the rock and roll world. Not that rock is humorless; most songs simply have nothing to do with levity, one way or the other. The Coasters were a refreshing exception, a group whose songs were often funny but always good rock and roll.

The Coasters (formerly the Ravens, out in Los Angeles) were stablemates of the Drifters at Atlantic, their name chosen to emulate the senior group's. For all that, the Coasters found Top 40 success earlier. Their debut single failed to chart in 1956, but from 1957 to 1959 they couldn't miss on the airwaves with their innovative music. (Most Coasters songs were composed and produced by Jerry Leiber and Mike Stoller, one of the earliest really potent writing teams in rock.)

Their first charted single in 1957 did well on both sides. "Searchin'" went to Number 3, while its flip side "Young Blood" climbed to Number 8. A year later they topped the charts with "Yakety Yak," followed in early 1959 by the Number 2 "Charlie Brown." Nineteen fifty-nine was their best year; after "Charlie Brown" they had a number 9 in "Along Came Jones" and a Number 7 with "Poison Ivy." The latter, unfortunately, was their last hit. Perhaps the public grew tired of humor.

During 1960 and 1961 the Coasters kept releasing records, but the only ones to chart did so quite poorly. A Number 36 and a Number 37 were followed by their final single, "Little Egypt." That record reached Number 23 and stayed on the charts for six weeks, a sad finale for this buoyant, vibrant group.

The Coasters, like so many of the early vocal and instrumental groups, gained a second life due to the oldies craze that started in the Seventies. It can't be all that satisfying for middle-aged men to sing the hits of their youth, but it probably beats working for a living.

SOME OTHER MILESTONES
AND A FEW PEBBLES

Baby, I Need Your Lovin'

Johnny Rivers is known to some rock and roll aficionados as the king of the cover, and not without reason. Over the course of his career, he had several hits (and near misses) with covers of previously recorded songs, as well as with a number of never-before released records.

Johnny Rivers had thirteen charted hits in the period from 1964 to 1967, with roughly equal numbers of original and cover recordings. His covers were of modestly successful songs, all of which had received airplay on Top 40 stations in the preceding several years. For example, Rivers released covers of "Memphis," "Maybellene," and "Mountain of Love" in 1964, each of which was recorded in front of a live audience in Rivers' rollicking, rocking style; none would be a giant hit, but his versions of "Memphis" and "Mountain of Love" have become standards in the rock and roll canon.

Covers are remakes of records by different artists, but in the rock vernacular there is usually more to it than that. Especially in the mid-to-late 1950s, the term "cover" implied a remake (by a white recording artist) of a record originally cut by a black artist, and therefore not played on the many predominantly white-oriented radio stations. The first "Cover King" was Pat Boone, who recorded several songs after Little Richard, The Charms, Ivory Joe Hunter, or Fats Domino had achieved successes with them, primarily on black R&B radio stations.

In the context of the 1950s this was not unusual, because many good records by black artists were essentially unheard by the white record-buying audience. These songs were available to white artists and their producers without any need to be written or even arranged; all that was required was to copy them.

The rock and roll side of the recording industry was desperate for new material in the mid-1950s. There were relatively few Tin Pan Alley-type composers who could deal convincingly with the rock idiom, and the concept of the performer/composer (e.g., Buddy Holly) was not yet firmly established. The motivation was strong to steal material—legally—from innovative black performers and composers.

Unfortunately, copies, like sequels, are rarely as good as originals. The typical cover version of an R&B hit used the original arrangement. The lazy producer and performer tended to take the first version as their benchmark, and copy it as faithfully, within the scope of their abilities, as medieval scribes. As anyone can attest who has heard, for example, both Little Richard's version of "Tutti Frutti" and Pat Boone's, the white cover version often was smoother, had better production values, and was—sadly—very dull by comparison. Only the audience cynically targeted by the record industry, white teenagers who lacked access to the originals, would be likely to find these saccharine cover versions interesting. It is worth noting in this context that the Diamonds, a vocal group strongly associated with covers, had their two big hits with original releases ("Little Darlin'" and "The Stroll," Number 2 and Number 4 in 1957 and 1958), while most of their covers did poorly.

The concept of covering records started before rock and roll, and did not at first have any racial implications. In the heyday of pop music, during the late 1940s and early 1950s, it was not at all uncommon for record producers to rush competing versions of potential big sellers to market.

A hypothetical example: in 1954, Vaughn Monroe records a new song called "To the Ends of the Earth," and releases it on his usual label, RCA-Victor. Producers at Capitol and Columbia are impressed with the song, but less so with Monroe's version of it. They quickly record covers by, respectively, Frank Sinatra and Tony Bennett, using the original arrangement. They have their competing versions in the record stores within a few weeks of the original release; each sells more copies from that point on than Monroe's does. Eddie Fisher, who would have liked to cut the song as well, cannot do so because he is an RCA-Victor artist, and RCA doesn't want his version to compete with Monroe's. The song, all things considered, is a big hit, but no one version of it is a million-seller. (The composer of "To the Ends of the Earth" makes money no matter whose version sells.)

The prerock and roll cover phenomenon was, just like later covers, all about money. However, in the first case the different versions of a given song competed fairly in the record marketplace, while in the early rock and roll era, cover versions had an unfair advantage over the originals. Time has been the judge of all this, and few if any of the various exploitative cover versions are still played by oldies radio stations—or by anybody else.

Johnny Rivers, the 1960s cover king, represented a newer and much healthier version of the cover. By the mid-1960s, rock was completely integrated, and a good tune would receive airplay on radio stations, even if it was in Japanese. (Kyu Sakamoto had a major hit with "Sukiyaki" in 1963, ending up at Number 1 for three weeks.)

Rivers began his recording career with several covers of minor hits. He followed these with a string of original releases, including the very strong "Secret Agent Man" and "Poor Side of Town." Then, in 1967, Rivers once again recycled known songs. These were "Baby, I Need Your Lovin'," previously recorded by the Four Tops, and "The Tracks of My Tears," released in 1965 by the Miracles. "The Tracks of My Tears," reaching only Number 16 on the pop charts, was part of Smokey Robinson and the Miracles' four-year dry spell without a real hit. The Four Tops' version of "Baby, I Need Your Lovin'," released in 1964, was their first pop chart hit, reaching only Number 11.

In each case, Rivers and the legendary Lou Adler, his producer, must have seen the underlying quality of the song, regardless of its comparative failure as a single. Rivers' covers reached Number 6 and Number 2, respectively; to this day they are played more often than the original versions on that ultimate arbiter of rock and roll, the oldies radio stations.

Ballad of a Teenage Queen

Crossover records are those that perform well on two or more of the music charts, pop, country, and soul (the latter has been called R&B and other names over the years). Sometimes a song by an established performer in one of these genres will crossover, as Charlie Pride's country hit "Kiss an Angel Good Morning" did when it also climbed to Number 21 on the pop charts, early in his career. It was his only crossover to pop. Other performers, such as Elvis, would routinely appear on all three charts with their hits.

Not only songs, but sometimes singers as well, cross from one genre to another. Many major country stars attempted to become pop idols when they first started out, perhaps because the money is even better in the pop market. An early example of this was Marty Robbins. His debut pop single in 1956 was a cover of Guy Mitchell's contemporary hit, "Singing the Blues." His next, "A White Sport Coat (And a Pink Carnation)," was cleverly released during the 1957 prom season, and went to Number 2 on the pop charts.

Robbins' singles in 1958 included "Just Married" and "She Was Only Seventeen," both attempts to stay in the teen market. Neither reached the Top Twenty, and soon after Marty Robbins was a country singer who occasionally crossed over with hits such as "El Paso."

Sonny James released "Young Love" in January 1957, and it quickly reached the Number 1 spot. Tab Hunter's cover of "Young Love," released two weeks later, *also* reached Number 1 that winter, something almost unique in rock and roll history. In fact, Hunter's version took over Number 1 from James', holding it for six weeks.

At only one other time in the classic rock and roll era did two versions of the same song both reach Number 1. Amazingly, it was just weeks after "Young Love" was the chart-topper. Andy Williams held Number 1 for three weeks with "Butterfly," and then Charlie Gracie did so for two weeks with his version. Back in 1945, however, Harry James and Bing Crosby did the same thing with competing versions of "It's Been a Long, Long Time." In 1949, Blue Barron and Russ Morgan had successive Number 1s with "Cruising Down the River," while in 1946 the song "To Each His Own" held onto Number 1 for eight weeks in *three* successive versions, by Eddy Howard, Freddy Martin, and the Ink Spots.

Johnny Cash was the next seeming-stalwart of country music to take a shot at pop stardom. "I Walk the Line" in 1956 was really more of a country tune, but "Ballad of a Teenage Queen" in early 1958 was a pop song without doubt or apology. It reached Number 14, encouraging Cash to try again. "Guess Things Happen That Way" went to Number 11, but "The Ways of a Woman in Love" stalled at Number 24, and from that point on Johnny Cash had appeared on the pop charts only as a country crossover, not a rock wannabe. (There is a great photo of Johnny Cash performing "Ballad of a Teenage Queen" on television, wearing a very stylish mohair sportcoat, that The Man in Black would probably like to destroy.)

Also making a pop debut in 1958 was Conway Twitty, whose lovely "It's Only Make Believe" went all the way to Number 1 that fall. Over the next three years he released seven more pop singles, only twice cracking the Top Ten, and then he too successfully sought country stardom.

The last crossover singer to be discussed here is Charlie Rich, an influential songwriter in both genres. In 1960 he released "Lonely Weekends," a Number 22 hit. Nothing more was heard from him on the pop charts until 1965, when his catchy "Mohair Sam" rather surprisingly failed to climb past Number 21. From that time on he had no pop releases until his country-crossover hits of 1973, "Behind Closed Doors" (Number 15) and the Number 1 "The Most Beautiful Girl."

Be-Bop-A-Lula

In 1956 Gene Vincent formed a band and had an influential Top Ten song, and in 1958 he starred in a movie. By 1960 he was utterly washed up, so much so that he left the country. Back in the summer of 1957, rock and roll fans would have predicted a major career for Gene Vincent and His Blue Caps (his four-man backing combo wore blue hats; he didn't).

Vincent Eugene Craddock, a young enlisted man in the Navy, seriously injured his left leg in a motorcycle accident back in 1955. He wore a steel brace the rest of his life, and was invalided out of the Navy. He started calling himself Gene Vincent, formed a band, and played some pretty good rock and roll. (Bear in mind that people playing bebop, country swing, rockabilly, or rhythm and blues in those days were learning to call it "rock and roll;" they got more gigs and sold more records that way. Deejay Alan Freed had only started using the term in March 1952, Bill Haley and the Comets had only become big in July 1955, and Elvis had only been a household name since January 1956, so the listening public wasn't absolutely sure what rock and roll was, yet.)

Vincent signed with Capitol Records, and released "Be-Bop-A-Lula" in June 1956, only about three months after Elvis Presley's first RCA-Victor single came out. "Be-Bop-A-Lula" did pretty well, going to Number 7 nationally. The band was asked to perform the song in the Jayne Mansfield film *The Girl Can't Help It* later that year. Gene Vincent's friend Eddie Cochran had been in the movie as well, performing "Twenty Flight Rock," a song that never made the charts. (Cochran would also appear in the Alan Freed vehicle *Go, Johnny Go!* with Chuck Berry and others. Gene Vincent performed in the 1958 film *Hot Rod Gang*, but not just as a rock and roller. He was also the costar.)

The band had received a lot of positive attention in 1956 and the following year, but they could not find an adequate song to record.

"Lotta Lovin'" went to Number 13 during the summer of 1957, and a few months later "Dance to the Bop" made it to Number 23, but Gene Vincent could not sell any records after that. A promising debut had led to mediocrity in a very short time, a common story in popular music. Gene Vincent was probably the first newly emerged, post-Elvis act to hit the Top Ten and then fail.

Eddie Cochran gave an eerie impersonation of his buddy Gene, just about a year behind him. He had a minor hit in 1957, a successful record the next year ("Summertime Blues," like "Be-Bop-A-Lula," still gets played on the oldies stations), and a couple of poorly-performing singles in the following months. "Somethin' Else," released in September 1959, didn't even chart on the Top 40. Eddie too had just one good song in him, it seems.

In 1960, both men went to live in Great Britain, where rock and roll was opening up and a couple of American ex-stars could still be hot properties. In April of that year, they were in an accident in Cochran's car; Eddie died at the age of twenty-one, and Gene was seriously injured again. Gene Vincent stayed in Britain until 1967.

Vincent died in 1971, at age thirty-six. Popular music treated him shabbily, as did life in general, but his place as a rock and roll pioneer is secure.

Be My Baby

Phil Spector was an important producer and innovator in rock and roll, as well as (briefly) a highly successful performer. His vocal group, the Teddy Bears, had a Number 1 hit in 1958 with "To Know Him, Is to Love Him;" the group toured with the song and appeared on television. Spector left performing and went into production with Atlantic shortly thereafter, while still a teenager. By the age of twenty he had, with Lester Sill, founded Philles Records.

Philles released Top 40 singles by the Crystals, Bob B. Soxx & the Blue Jeans, Darlene Love, the Ronettes, and the Righteous Brothers, nineteen singles in all, over a five-year period. By his twenty-fifth birthday, in December 1965, Spector was essentially washed up in the creative end of the record business. His influence lingered; many famous recording artists (for example, John Lennon) performed pilgrimages to Spector, involving him in the production of their albums. He even briefly presided over production at the Beatles' Apple Corps.

Spector was notorious for knowing exactly what he wanted and pursuing it in a fashion reminiscent of Captain Ahab. His famed "Wall of Sound" (so called by a British music journalist) is a case in point.

Les Paul had, back in the early 1950s, developed the technique of multitracking. With a primitive four-track tape recorder, Paul was able to record dozens of guitar tracks on a given song. What he put on four parallel tracks could then be recorded onto *one* track, and the process continued indefinitely. His overdubbed guitar work, solo or with Mary Ford's vocals, earned Les Paul twenty-eight straight Top 40 hits in the next few years. Subsequent producers learned to construct a song from numerous tracks, possibly recorded by different artists, on different days, in different studios. For example, Brooklyn high school classmates Neil Diamond and Barbra Streisand had a Number 1 hit with their tender 1978 duet

"You Don't Bring Me Flowers." However spontaneous and appropriate the duet sounds, the two were never in the studio at the same time.

Phil Spector, on the other hand, didn't even like stereo, much less multitracking. He was one of the last producers to record hit songs in real time; when one listens to a Spector production such as "Baby I Love You," one can be sure that every note was recorded at the same moment, in a live performance in one specific studio.

The dense Wall of Sound was Spector's answer to multitracking; he created a palpable rhythmic presence through the simultaneous use of multiple drummers, pianists, guitarists, etc. Since even one error by any one performer could ruin a take in Phil Spector's single-track, mono world, one can soon see how expensive the Wall of Sound approach really was, and why other producers learned to love multitracks.

The Wall of Sound was a great phenomenon, though, like nothing else in rock and roll. (Songwriter Andy Kim had his only two hits in the classic rock era with slavish copies of "Baby I Love You" and "Be My Baby," complete with a decent imitation of the Wall of Sound.)

Spector's first production successes were with the Crystals, a girl group he more or less created in 1961. They (and he) had six hits from 1961 to 1963. The Crystals really caught fire after "He's a Rebel," the Number 1 single actually recorded by Darlene Love and the Blossoms, an unknown backing group that was available when Spector had a brief option on the record. (The Blossoms were better than the Crystals, but the Crystals were already an established act.) In 1962, Philles released two singles by the Crystals, and one by another Spector-manufactured group, Bob B. Soxx & the Blue Jeans (really Bobby Sheen, Darlene Love, and one or two other session singers).

In 1963, Spector produced seven hit singles by four acts, Philles' busiest year. The Crystals released three songs that year, including big hits "And Then He Kissed Me" and "Da Doo Ron Ron," their last charted singles. Bob B. Soxx had his second and last outing, and Spector finally got around to letting Darlene Love record a couple of lackluster tunes under her real name. In the fall of 1963,

Phil Spector released the first single by his new girl group, the Ronettes.

Veronica and Estelle Bennett and their cousin Nedra Talley were go-go dancers at the Peppermint Lounge in New York, and may still be seen at that task in the 1961 teen movie *Twist Around the Clock* (a Twist-oriented remake of *Rock Around the Clock*, the very first rock and roll movie). By 1963 they had met Phil Spector, who became enamored of Ronnie Bennett (they later married). He convinced the three to sing for Philles, as the Ronettes.

The debut single by the Ronettes was a surprise hit. "Be My Baby" (cowritten by Spector, like many other Philles releases) went to Number 2 and was a gold record. The Ronettes weren't exactly great, but they were good enough, they could dance better than anybody else in the music scene, and Ronnie's breathless delivery got the attention of teenage boys all over America.

From the moment the Ronettes started making singles, Bob B. Soxx, the Crystals, and Darlene Love never hit the charts again. The Crystals' last four singles had all reached Number 11 or better; it is a shame that, due to Faustian contracts, their recording career ended so abruptly.

In 1964 the Ronettes released four singles. "Baby I Love You" was pretty good, but too much like their first record; it reached only Number 24. By this time Spector had all his eggs in one basket with the Ronettes, and tried again. The next two singles scored Number 39 and Number 34, but their fifth (and last) single, in November 1964, was back up to a somewhat respectable Number 23. "Walking in the Rain" was a very good song, taken strictly on its own merits. Unfortunately, "Be My Baby" had shown the public what the Ronettes could do, and no subsequent single moved into new and different territory.

Exactly a month after the Ronettes' last Top 40 single, Phil Spector issued the first hit record by a different kind of act than he was used to dealing with. The Righteous Brothers were a "blue-eyed soul" duo from California, with a history of mildly successful recordings over the past couple of years, songs one of them had written. Their singles on Moonglow never reached the Top 40, but it was clear that—with proper handling—they could do better. Spector produced four straight hits for them in about a year, the last four Top 40 singles Philles would issue.

Spector didn't have to create the Righteous Brothers, but he slowed down their delivery, brought them great new material (and some classic oldies), and let them sing. His four singles with the duo were among the very best work Spector ever did, and—apart from one post-Spector single—the only good songs the Righteous Brothers ever recorded. "You've Lost That Lovin' Feelin'" and "Just Once in My Life" were exactly what they needed to become stars.

In 1966, after moving to Verve Records, the Righteous Brothers recorded a second tune by the authors of "You've Lost That Lovin' Feelin'," and carefully did everything just the way Spector had. The result was "(You're My) Soul and Inspiration," their best-selling single. The pair's recording career fell apart fairly quickly afterward, however.

Spector had his greatest success with the Righteous Brothers, producing four Top Ten hits in a row, but his career was almost over at that point. The business of pop music diverged too quickly from his vision of it, and there was no longer any common ground. He continued to work at his idea of great rock and roll, producing what some critics consider a magnum opus, Ike and Tina Turner's "River Deep, Mountain High" in 1966, but it failed to attract the attention of disc jockeys around the country.

Working for Apple Records both before and after the Beatles' breakup, Spector provided the hated, string-laden post-production for "The Long and Winding Road" and other songs on the *Let It Be* album. He also produced George Harrison's very successful solo album, the three-LP *All Things Must Pass*. By that time, increasingly bizarre behavior left Spector essentially unemployable.

Phil Spector was inducted into the Rock and Roll Hall of Fame in 1989, at the age of forty-eight. It had been almost twenty years since his last major production.

Because

Sometimes you have to admire a group, even if you don't really care for their act. A case in point, for many oldies fans, might be the Dave Clark Five. In the early days of 1964's British Invasion, and in the months to follow, they were the second most successful British band in America.

The Beatles, of course, caused and defined the Invasion, but many other groups profited by it. Some, such as Freddie and the Dreamers, or Chad and Jeremy, were never really stars in Britain at all. Their fame was almost entirely an artifact of the British Invasion of the American pop charts, television shows, and so on. But just being British by no means guaranteed success; Cilla Black was what you might call a "minor major" act in England, much like Lesley Gore in the United States, but Black could never get her career out of first gear (1964 pun) in America.

The Dave Clark Five was an emerging band in Britain when the Invasion started, and they were well-positioned to exploit the sudden opening of the formerly quite provincial American market. Dave Clark himself was noteworthy for his business acumen, making the most of the group's opportunities. As a band, the Dave Clark Five was also noteworthy in several ways. Like most groups of that day, it had one vocalist rather than three (or three and a half) like the Beatles, but the vocalist wasn't Dave Clark. Clark also wasn't the guitar hero out in front; in addition to being the group's founder, namesake, and business manager, Clark was the drummer. He may have been the only drummer/leader of a successful Sixties rock and roll band.

The Dave Clark Five differed from other contemporary bands in more ways than that. The regulation Beatle-style combo called for rhythm and lead guitars, a bass, and drums. In the mid-Sixties, if a group differed from that pattern it was probably to accomodate a Herman or Freddie (or a Mick) who could sing but not play an instrument adequately. (Some groups included a keyboard player, but from the perspective of the keyboard-mad generation that followed, they were few, and very low-tech.) The Dave Clark Five lineup included bass, lead guitar, and drums, but also a saxophone and electric organ. This was good, because they weren't particularly talented as musicians. It helped that their sound varied from the norm a little.

They also, very clearly, brought a lot of enthusiasm to their work. Dave Clark Five songs are loud, infectious, and rough around the edges. One somehow doesn't imagine that they spent a lot of time in the recording studio, getting the nuances just right on each track.

Their first American hit, "Glad All Over," is representative of the group's work. Released in early March 1964, it went to Number 6 at a time when the Beatles practically owned the Top Five. Just a month later the band had a Number 4 success with "Bits and Pieces;" this presents a good example of how a song's competition, as much as its innate worth, will determine its chart success. "Glad All Over" did not sell as many records as "Bits and Pieces," but according to over thirty years of oldies radio play, it is by far the better song.

In 1964 the Dave Clark Five released seven singles, earning four Top Ten and three more Top Twenty hits. Among these was "Because," the band's only quiet, tasteful ballad; reaching Number 3, it was the band's second-best finish in the American market. The following year they released five singles, including "Over and Over," their only Number 1 hit. By 1966 the music scene was changing rapidly, but the DC5—as they were also called—continued to record songs that might as well have come out in 1964. With three releases, their best performance in 1966 was "Try Too Hard" at Number 12, but they did keep trying.

During 1967, the band's last year on the charts, the Dave Clark Five released only two singles. One was a cover of "You Got What It Takes" (originally a Number 10 hit, back in 1960, and therefore right up the DC5's alley). It went to Number 7, showing that their enthusiasm and determination could still occasionally pay off. Their next single, seventeenth and last in the series, was a cover of the awful, decades-old "You Must Have Been a Beautiful Baby;" it stalled at Number 35, barely on the chart, and the band gave up at last.

The Dave Clark Five showed what a band could do, just on the basis of grit, lacking much talent or even an appreciation for where popular music was headed. Their unwillingness to let anything get in their way is perhaps best exemplified by a song from their movie *Having a Wild Weekend* (a clone of *A Hard Day's Night*). "Catch Us If You Can" has just the defiant tone that a talent-deficient, but highly successful act such as Bill Haley or Sonny and Cher might have appreciated.

Bye Bye Love

Rock and roll is full of brothers, real and otherwise. The Beach Boys, for instance, were comprised of three brothers, their cousin, and a high school friend. Santo and Johnny were the Farina brothers; Bill Medley and Bobby Hatfield were the Righteous Brothers. John and Paul of the Beatles sometimes called themselves the Nurk Twins. However, the first, finest, and most famous brother act in rock and roll was Phil and Don, the Everly Brothers. Debuting in 1957, they had a style almost more Nashville than rock, but popular with both audiences.

Whenever the Beatles were asked who their biggest musical influences were, the same few names were mentioned: Chuck Berry, Buddy Holly, the Everly Brothers, and a few other American innovators. This is not to say that the Beatles sounded like, or wanted to sound like, any of those performers, but perhaps hearing earlier rock and rollers find their own voices freed Lennon and McCartney to do the same. In one respect the Beatles were quite like the Everly Brothers, though; many of the early Beatles hits were characterized by tight vocal harmonies. Some 1960s-era critics found these harmonies impressive and something new for rock—but the Everlys had been doing it for years.

"Bye Bye Love," their first single, reached Number 2 in the summer of 1957. It was a wonderful example of the debut single that sounds like a mature masterwork, but then the Everly Brothers had been raised in a musical household, and played together for many years before they began to make records. Like several of their early singles, "Bye Bye Love" was written by Boudleaux Bryant, a friend of the family. So was "Wake Up, Little Susie," their second record and first Number 1 hit.

Over the next several years the Everlys churned out song after song, producing in total twenty-six hits on twenty singles, with fifteen in the Top Ten, before they retired. Contrary to the standard explanation, however, their career was not stalled—like many careers were—by the British Invasion of 1964. They had two Top Ten hits in early 1962, "Crying in the Rain" and "That's Old-Fashioned," and then did not release another single until the Invasion was largely over, two and a half years later. In retrospect, knowing that the two would later feud for over a decade (preceding their 1983 reunion at the Royal Albert Hall in London), it is easy to suspect that the thirty-month hiatus during 1962 to 1964 was also a feud.

Whatever the cause, when the Everlys tried a comeback in late 1964, it flopped. Their twenty-fifth single, "Gone, Gone, Gone," only reached Number 31. Their next (and last) charted record was "Bowling Green," which was released in mid-1967. It was on the bottom rungs of the Top 40 for two weeks, almost the worst kind of performance a record can give and still chart. This was a far cry from the time when Everly records hit the charts the way tidal waves hit the beach.

For several years the Everly Brothers occupied a well-defined circle of Rock and Roll Hell—too big to forget, but too long ago to matter, able to perform killer oldies but not to sell new records (similar to the career of Del Shannon). By the early 1970s they split up acrimoniously, coming back together finally in 1983, as mentioned above.

Then, in 1986, the Everly Brothers were in the first group of performers inducted into the Rock and Roll Hall of Fame, along with Chuck Berry, Sam Cooke, Buddy Holly, and Elvis Presley. This acknowledgement of their early and lasting importance to rock and roll may have somewhat compensated for a lot of the frustration of the following two decades. When they began to release singles, Don Everly was twenty and Phil only eighteen; when in 1964 it seemed that their careers were over, they were still only twenty-five and twenty-seven, sad ages to already be washed up.

Good Morning, Starshine

In 1969, *Hair* was a musical, a social phenomenon, a seven-week-wonder, and the source of four Top Ten records, each by a very different act. The play was successful—and notorious—on both American coasts, and cagey record producers mined it for the four songs it contained with commercial appeal. (While *Hair* included other worthy songs, they were evidently too tied to the obscure plot, and/or too obviously obscene, to make large amounts of money as Top 40 singles. However, the original cast recording was quite successful as an album, so obscenity and obscurity paid off in the end.)

The book of *Hair* was written by Gerome Ragni and James Rado, who by no coincidence played the two male leads in the New York production. They also wrote all the lyrics, while the music was composed by Galt MacDermott. None of these three men seem to have achieved much of anything before *Hair*, or after their fifteen minutes of fame elapsed; it would in fact be easy to dismiss the play and its brief notoriety as a foolish fad.

However, *Hair* reflects many of the real concerns of its generation, is dramatically interesting, often achieves wit, and is musically stunning to any true rock and roller. It could not have existed even two years earlier, and would not have been of interest a few years later; *Hair* ought to serve as a handy little time capsule for social scientists in generations to come. (We're talking about the stage play here, not the film version.)

Early in 1969, as America got its first taste of Richard Nixon as president, a new group released the first of the *Hair*-derived singles. The Fifth Dimension was an innovative vocal group, featuring three male and two female singers who blended their voices together like a small but powerful choir. Their recording of "Aquarius/Let the Sunshine In" remains one of the greatest vocal treats of popular music, showcasing the music and their individual voices admirably.

As with their earlier hit, "Up-Up and Away," the overall impression is one of pure joy, a rare commodity in 1969. "Aquarius" quickly became Number 1 on the pop charts. For the Fifth Dimension it was an excellent choice, and helped lay a foundation for one of the more successful careers of their musical era.

The next *Hair* piece to be released was "Easy to Be Hard," a sad but beautiful love song. The vocal group Three Dog Night took this song to Number 2, with a subdued arrangement well suited to the tune and to the lyrics. (For the record, while Three Dog Night had a band backing them, only the vocalists—the original Three Tenors— were usually identified by name.) Like the Fifth Dimension, Three Dog Night was in the early stages of its career, and would go on to rock and roll greatness.

A flash in the pan named Oliver was third in line, with "Good Morning, Starshine," a pleasant bit of fluff. It was his first hit record, going to Number 3. Apart from his recording of "Jean," the lovely and sensitive theme from *The Prime of Miss Jean Brodie*, "Good Morning, Starshine" virtually *was* Oliver's career. The lack of follow-up hits for Oliver is perplexing, for his voice, looks, and manner were all pleasant and his first two records very successful.

Finally, the title song of *Hair*, the irreverent and brash credo of penniless hippies, reached Number 4 in a happy version by a well-dressed, freshly scrubbed family group that would later be cloned as television's Partridge Family. The Cowsills were a bunch of youngsters and their mom, who all made some nice recordings and had three hits in their brief career. Theirs was one of the more appealing flashes in the pan in show business history, though their version of the song "Hair" would likely give shudders to fans of the play. Happily for the Cowsills, the vast majority of people who have ever heard "Hair" have heard their version of it. For the Cowsills, unfortunately, it was three hits and you're out; after "Hair" they were heard no more.

The four singles from *Hair* did pretty well for their performers, all placing in the Top Five chart positions. They also did pretty well (indirectly) for the original cast album, the only place versions of all four songs could be found together.

Green Onions

Back in the prerock and roll days of pop music, instrumental hits were not at all uncommon. During the classic rock era, with its idolization of the singer, hit instrumental songs were much less frequent; once in a great while, however, they would still occur.

An instrumental must be more musically interesting than a vocal, to be able to compete effectively with the latter. Put another way, the successful instrumental is typically a song that would have lost some of its impact if a vocal track were added.

Duane Eddy was the first famous instrumental performer of the rock era, debuting in 1958. As almost all subsequent rock and roll instrumentals would do, Eddy's music depended mightily upon a well-played guitar. Some of Elvis Presley's and Ricky Nelson's hit singles included wonderful guitar passages by Scotty Moore or James Burton, but neither man ever stood in the spotlight of fame himself. Duane Eddy was again the first rocker to become famous strictly as a guitarist. (Les Paul, of course, had done so almost a decade earlier as a pop recording artist.)

Eddy's trademark was the "twangy" guitar sound, often achieved in those technologically simpler days by letting his guitar's sound reverberate in huge chambers, such as empty water tanks. (Much later, several New Age performers would rediscover this simple yet effective aural technique.)

His music doesn't vary enough from one track to another for some listeners, so despite Eddy's more than twenty-five charted singles, only three ever hit the Top Ten. In 1958 it was "Rebel-'Rouser," in 1959 "Forty Miles of Bad Road," and in 1960 a movie theme, "Because They're Young." Eddy also recorded other popular themes, such as Henry Mancini's hit theme song for the television show *Peter Gunn*, and "The Ballad of Paladin" (from the top-rated television series *Have Gun, Will Travel*.)

His Top 40 recording career was over after 1963, but Duane Eddy released enough successful singles to ensure that he is indisputably the rock era's Number 1 solo instrumental performer.

Eddy's opposite number, the rock era's leading instrumental group, is the Ventures. This Tacoma-based band is often erroneously described as a surf group. The Ventures had a very distinctive guitar sound, but played a wide variety of songs. (Would anyone call Richard Rodgers' "Slaughter on Tenth Avenue" surf music? It was one of the Ventures' releases.)

The Ventures' first hit was their first recording. They cut "Walk—Don't Run" in 1959; when they were unable to interest record companies in the single, the band formed their own label, Blue Horizon, and released the single themselves. The song quickly became a hit in the Northwest, and Seattle-based Dolton Records snapped them up with a recording contract. (Dolton was also the label of the Northwest's other major act in those days, the Fleetwoods.)

"Walk—Don't Run," finally on a national label, scampered to Number 2 in mid-1960. (It was held down by Elvis Presley's powerful "It's Now or Never," that was Number 1 for five weeks.) The Ventures only visited the Top Ten twice more, with a new version of "Walk—Don't Run" in 1964, and when they were asked to record a theme song for *Hawaii Five-O*. The latter was a Number 4 hit in 1969, and was heard weekly by millions during the highly successful eight-year run of the television series.

While "Hawaii Five-O" was also the Ventures' last Top 40 hit, they were far from dependent on the singles charts. The band had sixteen best-selling albums during the 1960s, and were extremely popular live performers on stage shows. The Ventures probably covered more hits by other groups (as album tracks) than the next three bands put together.

Duane Eddy and the Ventures were the leading instrumental performers of the classic rock and roll era. Hugh Masekela's band was the most exotic, while Mongo Santamaria's was the funkiest. The *best* instrumental band of the era was Booker T. & the MG's. In a sense this is a trick statement, because in many ways they weren't really what one calls a band. Booker T. Jones and Steve Cropper were top session musicians in Memphis, as were the other members of this quartet; Jones and Cropper went on to become highly successful composers and producers as well. "MG's" stands for Memphis Group; one or more of the band members played on literally hundreds of tracks laid down at Stax Records or other Memphis studios (and, later, anywhere in the country).

Booker T. & the MG's as a separate band emerged every so often, when session work was light, or when they wrote something especially good. "Green Onions" was their first release, a Number 3 hit in late 1962. It has remained an oldies favorite, and was prominent in the *American Graffiti* soundtrack. (In 1961, Cropper and the group's bass player had recorded a Number 3 hit, "Last Night," calling themselves the Mar-Keys. In a sense this was the precursor to Booker T. & the MG's, but Booker Jones was a sixteen-year-old high school student at the time, and didn't take part.)

The group only charted seven times during the 1960s, with three Top Ten hits. Even their misses were often gems, though, like "Hip Hug-Her" in 1967. It barely charted, but was and is a great instrumental tune. Movie themes "Hang 'Em High" (their version was not used in the film) and "Time Is Tight" did much better, Number 9 and Number 6, in the following two years. Those would be the last chart appearances for Booker T. & the MG's, but Cropper and Jones are still going strong in the music industry, thirty years later.

He's a Rebel

Sometimes the title of a song or the name of the group that released it aren't the really interesting part, and "He's a Rebel" is a case in point. It's a great rock and roll song. Released by the Crystals in October 1962, on Philles Records, it went to Number 1 nationally. To this day it is a favorite oldie for many people. The Crystals, a girl group produced by Phil Spector (the "Phil" of Philles), had a total of five other releases in their career but never got near Number 1 again, so "He's a Rebel" is obviously the high watermark of their professional lives.

But none of that matters. What's interesting is that the Crystals didn't actually record "He's a Rebel." It is a well-documented fact that, while their group name appears on the label of the 45 rpm single from Philles, the Crystals had nothing to do with the record. In late 1962, Phil Spector obtained a short-term option to record the song, but at a time when his girl group was out of town. He paid Darlene Love and the Blossoms, obscure session singers, to record all the vocal parts of "He's a Rebel" and he released it over the Crystals' name.

It's still a great song, but it may gall the cognoscenti that Darlene Love, singer and actress, is never given credit for her one big hit. Her other releases for Philles, under her own name, were unable to break the Top Twenty, and her career as a singer languished. (And it may have bothered the Crystals that their most famous song, a song that they were expected to sing in concert, was never really recorded by them.)

Apparently it never bothered Phil Spector, however. His attitude seems to have been that, if he so chose, he would record the janitor singing "Hava Nagila" and still release it as though performed by the Crystals. He controlled the label, owned the group names, and selected and arranged the songs recorded by his groups. Sometimes he even wrote them, often with very high-profile writers such as

Barry Mann and Cynthia Weil. It made economic sense to him to release "He's a Rebel" under the name of his already-established girl group, instead of as by someone nobody had ever heard of, the marvelous Darlene Love.

Another interesting thing about the song is its composer. Gene Pitney, a major recording artist in his own right, started out by providing successful (and not-so-successful) songs to a number of established performers. It took Pitney a while to catch on as a recording artist, and so for several years his songs either went to others or went unrecorded. An early example is "Rubber Ball," which Bobby Vee released in 1960, eventually reaching Number 6 with it. The next year Ricky Nelson recorded the popular "Hello, Mary Lou" and saw it go to Number 9.

Pitney himself started releasing singles in early 1961, and had his first real success in mid-1962 with "The Man Who Shot Liberty Valance," a Burt Bacharach and Hal David song inspired by the movie of the same name. It went to Number 4, one of Pitney's better performances on the charts. Most of the songs he recorded were self-composed, however, and he stopped supplying material to other artists as soon as possible after becoming famous.

The Hunter Gets Captured
by the Game

William "Smokey" Robinson was born in 1940; by 1960 he was already an integral part of Berry Gordy's Motown hit factory. As a member of the Miracles, Robinson was a popular and respected figure in American pop music almost from boyhood. His extensive contributions as a writer and producer are somewhat less well known.

The sad truth is that the Miracles, while they put plenty of records in the Top Ten, experienced long dry periods without hits as well. Their first record was produced in 1958, and Smokey Robinson was still with the group fourteen years and twenty-seven charted singles later. He wrote a great deal of material in that time, more than any one vocal group could possibly use. Some of his greatest successes in pop music happened with songs he gave to other Motown groups to record.

The Miracles' first major achievement was the memorable "Shop Around," a Number 2 single released in December 1960, and Robinson's first gold record. After a couple of lesser songs on their next singles, the Miracles scored again with "You've Really Got a Hold on Me," another Top Ten hit. The group recorded material throughout their long career, as did Smokey Robinson as a solo act, on the Tamla label. This was Berry Gordy's very first Motown label; there would be many more as the years passed. The hits kept coming. "Mickey's Monkey," "Ooh Baby Baby," "Going to a Go-Go," "The Tracks of My Tears," "I Second That Emotion," and "The Tears of a Clown" are merely the better-known of their large repertoire. In 1972 Robinson left the Miracles to go solo. They continued as a (somewhat less) successful group, replacing him with another tenor, and making even more records.

Robinson charted with seven singles in the period from 1973 to 1982; it is hard to believe that he could not have bettered that by remaining with the Miracles, but that is spilled milk. Two of his solo singles did quite well, hitting Number 2 and Number 4. He also continued his activities as a composer; writing had always been a major aspect of Smokey Robinson's career.

Mary Wells was an early arrival at Motown, the first successful female vocalist for any of Gordy's labels (she was assigned to Motown). Among her Top 40 appearances were four in the Top Ten. All four were written by Smokey Robinson. In 1962 she recorded "The One Who Really Loves You," "You Beat Me to the Punch," and "Two Lovers." In 1964, Wells had a Number 1 record with Robinson's "My Guy." Each of these songs, while sung in her distinctive manner, is clearly marked by Robinson's musical and verbal styles. The Temptations, a remarkably prolific Motown group, recorded many Smokey Robinson compositions. Their first successful album, released in 1965, was called *The Temptations Sing Smokey.* As the title indicates, it is an entire album of his material. (The Temptations recorded, not on Tamla or Motown, but on the Gordy label.)

An early girl group, the Marvelettes, were Tamla stablemates of the Miracles. They had ten hits between 1961 and 1968. "Please Mister Postman" was a popular Number 1 song, later covered by the Beatles in 1964 (when they ran short of original material). A lesser hit, but still very popular with pop music fans, was "Beech-wood 4-5789," their fourth single. Late in the Marvelettes' career, they recorded two very distinctive Smokey Robinson songs. One was "Don't Mess with Bill," their last Top Ten hit. (The name Bill turns up in a lot of Smokey Robinson songs, but then he's named Bill.) In 1967 the Marvelettes released "The Hunter Gets Captured by the Game," a witty Robinson tune. It went to Number 13, the group's last good recording.

This by no means exhausts the list of hits—and some misses— Smokey Robinson provided to his colleagues in Detroit. His impact on pop music, while impressive simply as a performer, was even greater as a composer and producer. Smokey Robinson was inducted into the Rock and Roll Hall of Fame in 1987.

I Almost Lost My Mind

As mentioned elsewhere in this volume, Pat Boone was once the king of cover versions. His musical director at Dot Records, Billy Vaughn, produced numerous white covers of black R&B hits for Boone, Gale Storm, and other artists. Depending on one's point of view, covers were a crying shame, a service to the white listening public, or maybe just businessmen exploiting an opportunity.

A close examination of Pat Boone's recording career reveals some interesting patterns. When he began releasing singles in 1955, it was with a cover of the Charms' "Two Hearts," released by them just a few weeks earlier. Boone's version went to Number 16 on the pop charts, a decent debut performance; the Charms' version failed to chart as a pop song. His next four releases also involved covers, and were released contemporaneously with the original versions. Fats Domino's "Ain't That a Shame?" went to Number 10, while Pat Boone's release, his second single, went right up to Number 2 as his first big hit. His third single was the Number 7 "At My Front Door," out only two weeks after the El Doradoes' version that stalled at Number 17. It is not established whether white covers always stole some of the thunder from black originals; clearly, however, they sometimes did.

Boone's next single was an original, the Number 4 "I'll Be Home," but the flip side went to a very respectable Number 12 with "Tutti Frutti." This B-side covered the single by Little Richard, one that only reached Number 17. Boone's B-side outsold Richard Penniman's A-side, an uncommon occurrence. Perhaps encouraged by the performance of "Tutti Frutti," Boone covered Little Richard's next song as his fifth release (and fifth cover). "Long Tall Sally" was on the charts for both of them at the same time, peaking at Number 8 for Pat and Number 6 for Richard. Pat Boone's next single was "I Almost Lost My Mind," his first Number 1 song. This may be called a crypto-cover, for the original was released in

1950 by Ivory Joe Hunter, a gold record for the MGM label. After six years the record found an essentially new teen audience, one that probably did not realize the song's history.

By this point, Boone had charted seven hits on five records, and was an established presence on the youth market scene. From that moment on, all of his recordings were of original material, songs that professional tunesmiths were now anxious to put before the popular vocalist.

His next ten singles were Pat Boone's golden age, a two-year string of great recordings and great hits. Three of the songs went to Number 1, including "Love Letters in the Sand" and "April Love," his signature tune. The *worst* performance of a single during this period was the Number 7 "If Dreams Came True."

After that song, during the summer of 1958, something went wrong with Boone's career. He spent three years without a real hit, although he released nine singles during that period. In May 1961, after so much trying, Boone finally hit the gold again with the wonderful "Moody River," his fifth and last Number 1 single. Another year-long slump followed on its heels. In the summer of 1962 Boone charted a Number 2 hit with the novelty song "Speedy Gonzales," his final successful release.

In retrospect, Boone can have had little to complain about. His thirty-eight charted singles included nineteen real hits, with five Number 1 chart-toppers. His success as a personable young singer led to roles in numerous motion pictures, second only to Elvis Presley as a singer-turned-actor. Unlike Elvis, however, Boone was not limited to pop-singer vehicles such as *Clambake* or *Fun in Acapulco*. His career included plenty of lightweight fare, but also major films such as *Journey to the Center of the Earth*.

I Got You, Babe

The latter half of 1965 saw the arrival of a popular culture phenomenon not unlike Beatlemania, albeit on a smaller scale. Suddenly radio stations were saturated with the music of a duo no one had ever heard of, and quickly their pictures began to appear on teen magazine covers and their names became known. They were Sonny and Cher, a.k.a. Salvatore Bono and Cherilyn Sakisian La-Pierre, soon to be among America's top musical celebrities.

Their first single (and their de facto theme song for years afterward) was "I Got You, Babe." The song climbed to the Number 1 spot nationally, which didn't hurt Sonny and Cher's rise to fame. Neither did the outrageous outfits they wore, with high-heeled boots and fur-covered vests, bright colors and long hair. Within a week of the release date for "I Got You, Babe," the first single by Cher as a solo act was issued. A Bob Dylan tune, "All I Really Want to Do" peaked at Number 15, while (contrary to what people might expect) a month later Sonny's single "Laugh at Me" made it to Number 10.

In fact, the period from August to November of 1965 saw the release of seven records: four singles by the duo, one by Sonny, and two by Cher. As their follow-up to "I Got You, Babe," Sonny and Cher released "Baby Don't Go," arguably the best song they ever recorded. It peaked at Number 18, perhaps because there were three singles by Sonny and Cher, jointly or as solo acts, already on the charts, and another released just two weeks later. Not an intrinsically powerful or particularly interesting act, they had oversaturated the airwaves with their work, and record sales on individual singles began to suffer.

In 1966 the duo released fewer singles in twelve months than they had done in five months of 1965. Sonny and Cher's efforts were "What Now, My Love" and "Little Man," reaching Number 14 and Number 21 respectively. As a solo, Cher had the Number 2 "Bang, Bang (My Baby Shot Me Down)" and "Alfie," the theme from the film of the same name. Her version of "Alfie" went only to Number 32, beaten by Dionne Warwick's excellent recording. "The Beat Goes On" was one of their stronger efforts, which rose in 1967 to Number 6, and the Cher single "You Better Sit Down Kids" went to Number 9. That was to be the last Sonny and/or Cher record on the charts for almost four years.

As mentioned in the opening paragraph, the Sonny and Cher phenomenon resembled Beatlemania more than a little. This was not a coincidence, but rather a well-thought-out strategy. Sonny Bono, the little man who many critics would deride as boring and talentless, using Cher's abilities to achieve stardom, had planned their assault on fame like a field marshall. In 1965, the thirty-year-old Bono and his nineteen-year-old wife had both already failed to make it big in the music business. Sonny worked for Specialty Records as a talent scout, producer, songwriter, and song plugger in the late 1950s. His recordings (as "Don Christy") went nowhere, and then Specialty suspended operations. Sonny took on much the same kind of job for Phil Spector at Philles, learning even more about how success is achieved in the music business. There he met and married a California teenager with a strong, but not overly good, voice. Cher's Beatlemania single "Ringo, I Love You" got a little bit of airplay in 1964, but earned her no fame. (It was released as by "Bonnie Jo Mason.") The couple had also struck out as "Caesar and Cleo."

Sonny cagily observed what behavior mattered most in Beatlemania, and recreated this to the best of his considerable ability. He found the two of them a visual image that would attract attention, good songs to record (many of which he wrote), and a wholesome stage presence. He then released so many singles in a short time that anyone even vaguely interested in the rock and roll world soon knew of Sonny and Cher. The idea was his, the songs were often his, and the leadership was his. Cher has gone on to considerable success, but without the recognition she received from being part of Sonny's machine, she would never have become a celebrity.

Sonny and Cher made two very different films in the 1960s. One, *Good Times*, was a typical dumb teen exploitation movie, not unlike the Beatles' *Help!* in spirit—but far less impressive in execution.

Due to unfortunate production delays, *Good Times* was not released until after Sonny and Cher started their career slump, and the film languished, seen by very few. The second film was the moody and semi-artistic *Chastity*, written by Sonny and starring Cher as an aimless drifter. It very definitely was not what their remaining fans expected from the upbeat, feel-good duo.

After almost four years spent out of the public eye, playing humble venues, Sonny and Cher came back to the big time in 1971 with a CBS-network television variety show. It proved popular, allowing both of them to showcase a growing affinity for acting, and served as a springboard for more records. During the three-year run of *The Sonny and Cher Comedy Hour*, the duo had two Top Ten singles, while Cher as a solo had five releases. Three, "Gypsies, Tramps and Thieves," "Half-Breed," and "Dark Lady," went all the way to Number 1, while "The Way of Love" made it to Number 7. This comeback for them jointly and individually was in many ways better than their earlier success.

During the spring of 1974, Cher sought a divorce and the television series was cancelled despite its popularity. Each had a subsequent program. Sonny's was *The Sonny Comedy Revue*, lasting three months on ABC. Cher's new series was titled simply *Cher*. Its debut broadcast on CBS took place on Sonny's fortieth birthday, February 16, 1975, less than two months after his show ended. *Cher* lasted for less than a year, to be replaced by a reunion of the two in *The Sonny and Cher Show*, also on CBS. It lasted for about eighteen months without much of an audience; the put-down humor perfected by Tom and Dick Smothers, and practiced by Sonny and Cher in their first series, just wasn't funny in the context of a painful divorce.

With the end of their show in August 1977, Sonny and Cher finally parted professionally as they had done emotionally three years earlier, each going on to notable success. Cher won an Oscar in 1988, the same year Sonny became the mayor of Palm Springs. In 1996 he was elected to Congress, and was building a reputation as a serious legislator, when, in January 1998, he died in a skiing accident. Subsequently, in the unfortunate way it often happens, he has begun to receive in death a bit of the critical attention and credit that he was denied in life.

I Want to Be Wanted

One of the defining sounds of American pop music from 1960 to 1963 was the high-pitched, chirpy voice of Brenda Lee. She gets very little attention now, but was once a major star, with achievements impressive by anybody's standards. Born Brenda Mae Tarpley in late 1944, the dynamic Brenda Lee was an authentic professional singer before her seventh birthday. When Decca Records signed her up in 1956 she was eleven, and her debut single came out when she was twelve.

After a start like that, it's a shame that Brenda Lee had to wait until she was fifteen to hit the Top 40. "Sweet Nothin's" reached Number 4, something most performers never achieve. Her next single was the warbly "I'm Sorry," that hit Number 1 for three weeks in mid-1960; it was a two-sided Top Ten hit, as "That's All You Gotta Do" reached Number 6 independently.

"I Want to Be Wanted," another Number 1 song that fall, was another two-sided hit. Even Brenda Lee's Christmas single, "Rockin' Around the Christmas Tree," originally released in 1958 without charting, was a pretty decent hit in 1960, reaching Number 14 this time around. In sum, she had six charted hits on four singles, with four of the hits in the Top Ten and two Number 1s, by her sixteenth birthday.

In 1961, Brenda Lee once again had four singles, six hits, four in the Top Ten. She never had another Number 1 after 1960, but that was nothing to cry about. In 1962 she released another four singles, with three in the Top Ten and a double-sided (minor) hit. For the only time since "Rockin' Around the Christmas Tree," a gimmicky seasonal record, Brenda Lee had failed to put an A-side into the Top Ten.

The following year she had a Number 32 miss, a Number 6 hit, a two-sided (Number 24 and Number 25) mediocrity, a Number 17 and a Number 12. Her career was starting to look a lot more average, with ups and downs. Brenda Lee persevered—she was still only a teenager, after all—but her remaining years as a pop singer were increasingly dismal. In 1964 two singles went to Number 25 and Number 17; in the next three years she charted four more times, twice nearly in the Top Ten.

The handwriting was on the wall, and Brenda Lee made a shift in her material and redefined herself as a country singer. (Like the Everly Brothers, she always was a "countrified" performer, so a huge change was not necessary.) Brenda Lee went country and western in 1971, at the age of twenty-six, and was more successful in that arena.

With twenty-three pop singles, she had twenty-nine charted hits, including twelve in the Top Ten and two Number 1 records. Eleven of those twelve big hits dated from before her eighteenth birthday.

It's Over

As a rock and roll composer and performer, Roy Orbison always struggled. From 1960 to 1964, he could put a couple of records in the Top Ten almost every year, but plenty of other recordings that placed lower showed that Orbison lacked a firm bead on the public's tastes. In fact, if his singles missed the Top Ten, they usually charted at Number 25 or worse; if he missed the bullseye he would also miss the barn.

A singer whose incredible range and skill amazed his peers, Orbison had to toil in local bands for years before obtaining a recording contract, and it would not be until his third record company that his career finally took off. The man who was Elvis Presley's favorite singer, whose biggest fans include Bruce Springsteen and Bob Dylan, played in bands in his native western Texas from the age of sixteen on. He attended North Texas University for a while, and signed a recording contract with the Jewel label. He was with Sam Phillips' Sun Records, the company that gave Elvis and Carl Perkins their starts, from 1956 to 1958. Nothing worked for him there, either.

Only after signing with Monument, and writing new material, did Roy Orbison enter the national stage. He had written songs for acts such as the Everly Brothers during his days at the Memphis-based Sun label. He became highly proficient at telling stories in verse, usually very sad stories. Titles such as "Only the Lonely," "Running Scared," "Crying," and "It's Over" convey very accurately the creative terrain that Orbison inhabited. They were good, even great songs, musically and verbally; Orbison's unearthly voice, combined with his fine material, created a unique niche in rock and roll. Bob Dylan has compared Orbison's range and power with those of opera singers, not in jest.

Roy Orbison had nine Top Ten hits in five years, with many less successful singles interspersed among the gold. His biggest singles were "Running Scared" and "Oh, Pretty Woman" (everyone always forgets the "Oh"), both of which were Number 1 hits. The latter was his last big record, in the fall of 1964. Despite the British Invasion, Orbison's 1964 was about like each of the preceding four years. His material from then on just could not click with the public, though he kept trying for several years. His last three charted singles were with MGM records, after his long-term arrangement with Monument came to an end. He had no better luck at MGM, however.

From the mid-1960s forward, Roy Orbison occupied an unenviable spot in the music business, with major talent but lacking an acceptable outlet. Financially secure, he had little joy professionally for almost the whole of his adult life. Then, in 1988, Orbison joined with Dylan, George Harrison, Tom Petty, and Jeff Lynne to form the Traveling Wilburys. This was an idea so absurd as to be instantly addictive. The five men, famous rockers all, adopted false identities as the five sons (by different mothers) of a traveling rogue named Wilbury. They wrote and recorded an album together, with some of the best rock and roll heard in America for decades.

On the strength of this renewed interest in his work, Orbison recorded new songs and even filmed a performance video for MTV. It was in this upbeat, satisfying context that Orbison spent his last days, before dying of a heart attack on December 6, 1988. He was fifty-two. Orbison had seen his career honored again in another way, almost two years earlier, when he was inducted into the Rock and Roll Hall of Fame.

Kicks

Sometimes being too popular with the younger set can be a real disadvantage, contrary to the beliefs of recording moguls. Paul Revere and the Raiders present an excellent example of this phenomenon. Their primary appeal was to a then newly emerged consumer group, the teeny-boppers, and this had a stultifying effect on the Raiders' career.

Paul Revere (his real name) cannot be blamed for giving his group a name that exploited his own; as show business realists must admit, many a good band has failed to make it big, often for the most banal reasons. A catchy, memorable group name is at least a step in the right direction, career-wise. When the Raiders adopted flashy, vaguely Revolutionary War-era uniforms they cemented their attraction for the preteens and young teens, and branded themselves as fatally hokey and square with everybody else.

And this was too bad, because when one gets past all the hype and the surface issues, Paul Revere and his bunch actually were a pretty good band. They tried to make it as recording artists for several years, charting only once on an obscure label (position Number 38 on a 40-place chart). Finally they signed with Columbia, and began to have some success (and wore the dorky costumes). In late 1965 the band reached Number 11 with "Just Like Me," a decent song that suffered from their relative obscurity. Had the Raiders already enjoyed a hit or two, "Just Like Me" would have hit the Top Five. Their next song, "Kicks," did make it higher, to Number 4. It's a good song, one that spoke presciently about the psychological—and other—costs of drug abuse. In 1966 a lot of music professionals and hip rock and rollers scoffed at the song, but it doesn't seem lame or funny now, so many years and lives later.

The Raiders followed "Kicks" with "Hungry" in the summer of 1966. It reached a respectable Number 6; it's not as good a song as

"Kicks," but it profited from the band's growing popularity. Over the next several months the Raiders released four singles, batting about .500. "Good Thing" and "Him or Me—What's It Gonna Be?" placed at Number 4 and Number 5, while the other two reached only Number 20 and Number 22. Given the airplay that an established group will automatically receive, these numbers are evidence of failure.

By this time the band was quite well known, acting as hosts for Dick Clark's newer, hipper daily rock and roll program, *Where the Action Is*. It presented the band members as real people, in a variety of interesting and picturesque California settings, and increased their popularity with the young teen audience.

Something had to give, though—perhaps the amount of time available to write and rehearse material. At any rate, the next several singles bombed. That is not to say they failed utterly; they charted from Number 17 to Number 27, and some bands would kill for those numbers. Paul Revere and the Raiders, however, had put out five strong records in eighteen months, starting in 1965; now they couldn't seem to do anything right.

In 1970 the lead singer of the group, Mark Lindsay, started a solo career. His distinctive voice was so much a part of the Raiders that many people believed that the band had broken up. Instead, they were about to finally triumph. After four years of failure and re-buffs, the group—now officially renamed just "The Raiders," perhaps to distance themselves from their television personae—had their one and only Number 1 hit, "Indian Reservation (The Lament of the Cherokee Reservation Indian)." The song struck a sympathetic chord with an increasingly aware and sensitive audience, and has remained very popular with rock and roll aficionados.

Lindsay as a solo act had scored a Number 10 with "Arizona" in 1970. His second single, "Silver Bird," stalled at Number 25. The Raiders' follow-up to "Indian Reservation," "Birds of a Feather," likewise made it only to number 23, and the group stopped trying. (Not that it broke up; the Raiders have played in oldies venues from time to time since.)

Not every band can have an unbroken string of hits, and claim fans of all ages. The Raiders suffered at times for their popularity with the least-sophisticated segment of the audience, but gamely hung on and ended their recording career on a strong note. Seen from a distant decade, they seem better than the 1960s acknowledged. Their songs were memorable, sometimes meaningful; they were good musicians; they had heart.

Light My Fire

Nineteen sixty-seven was an amazing year musically, perhaps the most important year that rock and roll would ever see. Innovations and influences were springing up all over the place. Many songs now regarded as classics were issued in 1967; some could get little or no airplay at that time. Someone named Jimi Hendrix released a song titled "Purple Haze," but only a few radio stations would play it. The Youngbloods released the beautiful "Get Together," the anthem of a whole segment of the rock and roll world—but it did not chart until rereleased two years later. Songs cannot become hits if radio stations are too conservative or faint-hearted to play them.

The Beatles released their milestone album *Sergeant Pepper's Lonely Hearts Club Band* in June 1967; astoundingly, and unprecedentedly, no single was, then or later, ever released from the album. "Album rock" was catching on as a concept. Jefferson Airplane became world famous (and very, very influential) on the strength of their album *Surrealistic Pillow*. While two singles from that album, "White Rabbit" and "Somebody to Love," made the Top Ten during the summer of 1967, the Summer of Love, most people just bought the album. Other representative records that summer included "Groovin'" by the Rascals, and the much darker piece "For What It's Worth," by Buffalo Springfield.

Many bands and many songs in the watershed year of 1967 had an influence beyond what mere sales figures would suggest. One of the new bands of 1967 was the Doors, a Los Angeles-based group whose influence is still being felt. Jim Morrison named the band for Aldous Huxley's book on experimentation with hallucinogens, *The Doors of Perception*; drug use and altered states were to figure prominently in the Doors' brief but tortured history.

Morrison and the three other Doors played at a variety of Sunset Strip clubs in Los Angeles, perfecting their repertoire and Jim's bizarre, attention-getting stage presence. Their first recording release was "Light My Fire," a seven-plus-minute single that reached Number 1 in the summer of 1967. Morrison was then twenty-three, an anguished rock poet—and, uncommon for a pop cult figure, actually a pretty good baritone. "Light My Fire" had a hypnotic tune, and its lyrics seemed to be about sex without being overt, so it received a lot of airplay during the same weeks that "Purple Haze" fizzled out.

The Doors, like many an act before and since, became famous more for their comportment and costume than for their music; in fact, the next three singles they released after "Light My Fire" only made it to Number 12, Number 25, and Number 39 (deservedly so). Teenagers wanted to read about the Doors more than listen to them, it seemed. (Foolishly, the group had squandered one of their very best songs, "Crystal Ships," as the B-side on their first single, so it got virtually no airplay.)

With "Hello, I Love You" the Doors recaptured the feel of the dangerous, Dionysian edge they had walked on "Light My Fire." Released in July 1968, the song went to Number 1. It was many months after that before the band, troubled by drug abuse and legal problems, could even get together long enough to cut another single. "Touch Me" went to Number 3 in early 1969, the band's third and last real hit.

Two years later, "Love Her Madly" had already fallen off the charts, after a nine-week run and a Number 11 peak position, when Morrison died in his French villa. His record label had the dark "Riders on the Storm" in record stores by July 24, 1971, three weeks to the day after he died. The single went only to Number 14, a poor sendoff to the Vincent van Gogh of rock and roll, but then it's not exactly an easy song to cuddle up to. One could argue with some validity that the best Doors songs never got on the radio. They were album cuts that couldn't find a radio audience, but surely found an audience in millions of teenagers with phonographs. A major song, "The End," finally found *its* audience as part of the *Apocalypse Now* soundtrack in 1976. Millions heard it, most having never dreamed that there were still important Doors tunes they hadn't experienced.

Morrison was the third of the pop stars to die young and unhappy in less than a year. Jimi Hendrix died on September 18, 1970, Janis

Joplin sixteen days later, and Morrison in another nine months, all as a direct result of drug overdoses. Each was twenty-seven years old. Each had already clearly passed his or her creative peak, after a meteoric career. While their deaths, the Great Dionysian Extinction, were sad and unfortunate, the impact to rock and roll was minimal. Their talents went into decline first.

Memories Are Made of This

In another essay, Traveling Man, several actors were discussed who attempted to become teen idols as singers. Few had any luck at this. Only Ricky Nelson could properly claim to have made the transition, but then he was never a major actor. However, there was another (established) actor who made a try at a singing career, and succeeded, enjoying a string of hits that few full-time singers could claim. Even most rock and roll, or television, trivia experts will fail to recall this person, who had two television shows and six Top Ten hits; how soon we forget.

In her day, Gale Storm was a very well-known television star, whose *My Little Margie* and *The Gale Storm Show* had millions of fans. When she turned to pop music in 1955, Storm began with a cover of the current but minor release "I Hear You Knocking;" her version went to Number 2. On her next single, the A-side, "Teen Age Prayer," went to Number 6. The B-side, a cover of Dean Martin's "Memories Are Made of This" (itself released only three weeks earlier), contended with Martin's version and reached Number 5. This single gave a truly remarkable performance. First, it was a double-sided Top Ten hit, something exceedingly few singers have ever experienced. Second, the B-side bested the A-side, also very rare. Third, the B-side did so at a time when another version of the same song was on the charts as a highly successful A-side version by a well-known singer. All told, this is probably a unique achievement in popular music. (Even the A-side, "Teen Age Prayer," was in a real competition, for Storm's version and Gloria Mann's were released on the same day; Mann's peaked at Number 19, her second and final hit.)

Throughout 1956 and early 1957, Gale Storm continued to release covers of current hits—and to do well with them. In a three-way struggle over "Why Do Fools Fall in Love?," Frankie Lymon reached Number 6, Storm Number 9, and the Diamonds Number 12 in the spring of 1956. Cathy Carr, Storm, and the Charms likewise all released copies of "Ivory Tower" in a four-week period, earning Number 2, Number 6, and Number 11 respectively. Storm's final recording is one of the strangest cases of covering ever, ahem, on record. Dot, Storm's (and cover king Pat Boone's) label, itself released two versions of "Dark Moon" in the same week. Gale Storm's single went to Number 4, and the one by Bonnie Guitar went to Number 6; this cannot have hurt Dot, but doubtless each version kept the other from placing higher, hurting the artists.

Gale Storm's career was cut short by more than one factor. Multiple, competing versions of the same song became less popular over time. Storm may have tired of the effort; she was unlikely to ever become a major teen idol, and certainly did not rely on the recording industry for wealth or fame. Finally, as the 1950s wore on, there was less and less interest in the pop vocal styles of even a few years earlier. Singers such as Eddie Fisher, Jaye P. Morgan, Teresa Brewer, or Patti Page, regardless of their popularity in 1954, rarely hit the charts after about 1957. Gale Storm's career was brief, highly successful, and quickly forgotten, which makes her memorable achievements even more poignant for the audio archaeologist.

Monterey

The Monterey Pop Festival, held on a June weekend in 1967, has been the subject of numerous articles, book chapters, a Top 40 song, and even a documentary film. Often hailed as the first rock festival, and as a rehearsal for Woodstock, Monterey was neither of these things. It was instead a memorable musical event that deserves to be better understood.

To begin with, why Monterey and why a "festival?" There were exceptions, from the East Coast and elsewhere, but most of the bands that played at Monterey were California groups, many from San Francisco and most of the rest from Los Angeles. It would have been easy to schedule a multiband concert in either city, but the impact, musically and socially, of a three-day concert in San Francisco or Los Angeles would have been much less than that made by the hipster invasion of a small, beautiful, and well-known coastal California town.

Rolling Stone magazine became famous overnight by chronicling the festival in its first issue, while Eric Burdon and the Animals postponed the end of their shaky career by celebrating "Monterey" in song. Most Americans did not know that the festival was happening until it was over, and most would never view D. A. Pennebaker's pioneer rockumentary, or learn about the Monterey Pop Festival except through media-derived folklore.

The festival was put together by a number of people, ultimately to be dominated by John Phillips of The Mamas and the Papas and powerful record producer Lou Adler. There is no available account of the decision to locate the event in Monterey, but it isn't too hard to figure out the logic. The need was for a place that could (and would) host a large number of bands and thousands of listeners. This place should be between San Francisco and Los Angeles, but preferably close enough to one of them to facilitate air travel.

In June 1967, San Francisco was just entering what came to be called the Summer of Love; its bands were numerous and influential, and Monterey lay only ninety miles to the south, with its own airport and a world-famous, tourist-beloved setting. Perhaps most important, and clearly reflected in the pop event's formal title, the town had already been for years the venue of the world-famous, tourist-beloved Monterey Jazz Festival. The Monterey Pop Festival brought many performers and a large audience to town, and to play in the county fairgrounds, but it wasn't unprecedented. Perhaps of all the towns up and down the California coast, Monterey and its citizens already knew the drill.

The array of musicians at the pop festival was (and remains) impressive. The Mamas and the Papas were of course to perform, as were the Byrds, the Grateful Dead, Jefferson Airplane, the Steve Miller Band, Simon and Garfunkel, Big Brother and the Holding Company (with Janis Joplin), the Association, Otis Redding, Ravi Shankar, the Paul Butterfield Blues Band, and many, many others. The most important acts, in terms of the folklore that has since grown up around Monterey, were Big Brother, Otis Redding, the Who, and the Jimi Hendrix Experience, the latter making its American debut at the festival. (The Doors, then a just-emerging L. A. superband, were invited to Monterey but refused to come. If they had, then all three of the young dying gods of that generation of rock would have performed at the same concert. Hendrix, Joplin, and the Doors' Jim Morrison all died within less than a year of one another, about three years after Monterey. Otis Redding died within six months of the festival, however.)

The performances at Monterey were organized into five long shows, one Friday evening and one each on Saturday and Sunday afternoon and evening. The Sunday afternoon show was entirely given over to Ravi Shankar, the sitar virtuoso and teacher of Beatle George Harrison. (Perhaps for this reason, rumors abounded at Monterey that the Beatles would make an appearance before the festival ended. The Beatles' former publicist was the official public relations person of the festival, possibly the other reason that such rumors "developed" at that time.)

Most attendees did not know even which groups they would be hearing, due in part to poor publicity and in part to the erratic behavior of performers who arrived late, or not at all. The closest thing to an organized show was that on Sunday evening, featuring among many others the Who, Jimi Hendrix, John Phillips' old singing partner Scott McKenzie, and as the last act The Mamas and the Papas. McKenzie performed the Phillips-authored Summer of Love anthem, "San Francisco (Be Sure to Wear Flowers in Your Hair)," his only hit. And there were many, many flowers at Monterey, tucked in long flowing hair or into the bands of funky hats, or painted on faces or other parts of the body.

Several of the San Francisco-based groups that performed at Monterey had played shortly before at a free outdoor concert in Golden Gate Park, called the Human Be-In. By most valid criteria, the Be-In was the first rock concert. It differed from a Monterey or a Woodstock primarily because it lasted only a single day, and took place in a large city, not a rural or small town setting. The media, then as now, loved the concept of a deluge of (potentially dangerous) young people descending upon a helplessly unhip small town; that image is the one that the documentary film and most other accounts of the Monterey Pop Festival still provide. (Note also that the real motorcycle-gang-invades-small-town incident, the one that Marlon Brando's *The Wild One* is loosely based on, happened at nearby Hollister.)

While it is true, as the legend would have it, that large numbers of attendees came down to Monterey from the San Francisco Bay area, many others were from Carmel, Salinas, Santa Cruz, and Monterey itself. Most were not dressed up as hippies, the fairgrounds were not overfilled, the stadium sat less than 10,000 people maximum, and, worst of all for the Monterey-as-early-Woodstock myth, significant numbers of attendees were soldiers on passes from nearby Fort Ord, then one of the Army's largest bases. What could be less hip, after all, than young soldiers in square civilian clothes? And yet they, and local teenagers, were present in great numbers. So were people in their thirties and forties, unhip by definition. The festival was great, provided a lot of good music, and some less good; many people had an entertaining time for very reasonable prices; but it wasn't much like the media then, or elderly rock and rollers' autobiographies now, say it was.

In the mid-1960s one heard a lot about California on the radio. The Rivieras had their only hit in 1964 with "California Sun," and the Beach Boys praised "California Girls" a year later. In early 1966 The Mamas and the Papas had their first hit with "California Dreamin'," but the real gold rush came in 1967. In March of that year Lesley Gore had her eleventh and last hit with "California Nights;" in June, Scott McKenzie released "San Francisco;" and in August the Animals topped them both with the hybrid "San Franciscan Nights," the best song the group ever recorded.

When Eric Burdon and the Animals released "Monterey" on December 30, 1967, they weren't extolling the virtues of a place or its inhabitants, like all their California-music predecessors. They were eulogizing the Pop Festival, already seven months in the past. The song peaked at a respectable Number 15 on the charts, even though it is little more than name-dropping set to music.

Like many of the band's later songs, "Monterey" was written by the entire group. The Animals, who had in fact performed there, apparently saw the Monterey Pop Festival as an epiphany of hipness. The documentary film also was very selective when it showed people who dressed and acted like hippies, while Eric Burdon and his band listed the coolest and most famous performers. To judge from "Monterey," there were only cool bands there.

One would certainly never guess from the mythic film or Top Twenty single that the performers included Lou Rawls, whose cabaret-style act went over very well with the audience; Laura Nyro, the soulful composer of "Eli's Coming" and other songs, making her debut as a professional performer; Johnny Rivers, the L. A.-based rock and roller who also served as a Pop Festival board member, and whose "square" performance brought down the house; the Association, who led off the first show in their suits and ties; or for that matter many performers who were—and remain—obscure.

What one sees and hears about are the Byrds, Janis Joplin, Jefferson Airplane, the Who, Hendrix—especially Jimi Hendrix, who burned his Fender Stratocaster onstage at the culmination of his act. (Well, he couldn't very well have burned it during his *first* song, could he?) This, perhaps the most famous contrived bit of "spontaneity" in the annals of rock and roll, made Hendrix famous overnight for precisely the wrong reasons. And, as Eric Burdon once said about the burning guitar schtick, Jimi had the bottle of lighter fluid in his boot when he went on stage, didn't he?

Like most myths, Monterey was not really much like its press clippings. It was a pretty good concert, though, especially at five bucks per show.

The Name Game

As Juliet said, "a rose by any other name would smell as sweet," but all names emphatically are not created equal. *Romeo and Juliet* are better names for a play title than *Bob and Philomena* would have been, and of course the same name may be more appropriate in one setting than in another. Norma Jean Baker was correct to believe that she had a better chance of becoming a star as Marilyn Monroe; Marilyn Novak became Kim Novak to avoid sounding like Monroe. Julius Marx wasn't funny, but Groucho was.

Show business is literally full of people who changed their names, for one reason or another. Everyone knows that. It is less well known that many musical groups have struggled to find just the right name, or that, on the whole, their efforts have been justified.

Examples are common enough. The Fab Four tried several names, from the Quarrymen to Long John and the Silver Beatles (shades of *Treasure Island*!) to, finally, just the Beatles. The punning nature of their name, and its hidden homage, were and are largely lost on the public. John Lennon was a demon for puns; he and McCartney were great fans of Buddy Holly's group, the Crickets. "Beatles" was an allusion to the Crickets, with the addition of a punning misspelling that incorporated the word "beat," as in beatnik, backbeat, etc. It was a good, short, snappy name, and no doubt added a great deal to the success of the group. Can anyone imagine "Quarrymenmania," or, for that matter, John, Paul, George, and *Richard*? It just wouldn't have been the same—or as good—without an equivalently inventive and oddball name.

Examples are easily found of groups that failed under one name, then succeeded under another. For instance, the Golliwogs couldn't get anywhere, and neither could the Four Lovers. But as Creedence Clearwater Revival and the Four Seasons they each sold millions of records—with the same personnel and much the same kind of music.

Creedence even dropped the last two words of its name, becoming even funkier, while at least the "Four Seasons" was a less geeky name than many that the group had tried before.

Sometimes a group has changed its name after some initial success, such as when the Young Rascals became just the Rascals in 1968. "Groovin'" is by the Young Rascals, while "It's a Beautiful Morning" is by the Rascals, with no intervening changes in personnel, musical style, recording label, etc.

Disc jockeys on oldies shows are sometimes fond of telling stories about how one group "became" another, such as how Joey Dee and the Starliters were transformed over time into the Young Rascals, or how the American Breed became "Rufus featuring Chaka Khan" (that's the actual name). Since in each case it would be hard to find two bands much more dissimilar, these stories are immediately intriguing and interesting. What they aren't, however, is true.

Joey Dee and the Starliters, the house band of New York's Peppermint Lounge, had a Number 1 record with "The Peppermint Twist" during 1961's twist craze. Over the next couple of years they had four more modestly-successful singles, and even a movie. (*Hey, Let's Twist!* was a fairly average rock and roll exploitation film for its day; that is to say, dreadful.) After 1963 the group broke up, when the British Invasion hastened the end of twist and doo-wop groups. In 1967 two members of the band—but not the front man, Joey Dee—formed the Young Rascals with a couple of their friends. The American-Breed-becomes-Rufus story is similar. The same logic would allow one to conclude that Paul McCartney and Wings "really" was the Beatles, because the earlier band had broken up and a couple of years later one of the guys formed a new band with some old pals, see? Musicians tend to want their careers to continue, and they also tend to play with other musicians they already know and admire, so there is no mystery when former members of group A are found playing together in group B. However, A is not equal to B.

Some of the bewildering name changes groups go through are accurate reflections of struggles for fame and control. "Dawn" became "Dawn featuring Tony Orlando," which in turn became "Tony Orlando and Dawn." Probably that's the name they should have had all along, because it is the most memorable of the three.

However, the group charted Number 1 records under all three names, so it cannot be convincingly argued that the earlier name(s) were somehow holding them back.

Many rock and roll performers' personal name changes were probably for the best, professionally. Ernest Evans wouldn't have been as big a hit on *American Bandstand* as Chubby Checker was; Carole King, sad but true, sold more records than little Carol Klein from Brooklyn ever could.

Sometimes a group or solo performer adopts a second stage name, when unsure whether a certain song will be successful. For instance, Walden Robert Cassoto (Bobby Darin) released his highly successful debut single "Splish Splash" in late July 1958. Just six weeks later, he released "Early in the Morning," as by the Rinky Dinks. He needn't have bothered. The single stalled at Number 24, but in truth several later recordings under his real name did no better, and the legitimatizing name of a recent Top Ten charter might have helped the single. So might less competition; Buddy Holly rushed a cover of "Early in the Morning" into the record stores, only to see that version stall at Number 32.

Francis Castellucio (Frankie Valli) and the Four Seasons released their cover of Bob Dylan's "Don't Think Twice" as by The Wonder Who; though it sure sounded like Frankie, it was a very different song than what they usually recorded. Right in the middle of an impressive string of Four Seasons hits, that single went to Number 12—good for an average band but poor by Four Seasons' standards. The Wonder Who were, not too surprisingly, never heard from again.

When the Turtles broke up, Howard Kaylan and Mark Volman found that they did not hold the contractual right to perform under their own names. They called themselves the Phlorescent Leech and Eddie, and then just Phlo and Eddie, before joining Frank Zappa and the Mothers of Invention—heroes of another interesting name saga.

Perhaps the most peculiar name change on record in rock and roll is that by an artist and composer who had two "one-hit-wonders," five years apart, each under a different name. As Johnny Cymbal he reached Number 16 with the amusing "Mr. Bassman" in 1963, while in 1968 he was calling himself by the much hipper name

"Derek" when he recorded "Cinnamon." That song made it to Number 11, not a bad performance.

And by the way, Shirley Ellis, who had a Number 3 hit with "The Name Game" in 1965, was really Shirley Elliston. Changing *her* name didn't help much, as she only had three successful singles in a short career.

Only You

The Platters occupy a very important niche in the history of American popular music, one of the first (and best) black groups with great appeal to the majority white audience. The mid-Fifties were a time of rapidly changing social and cultural mores, for all that commentators from later decades may prattle on about Eisenhower, hula hoops, and the suburbs. Groups such as the Platters integrated radio before the word integration was part of most peoples' vocabularies.

The group formed in 1953 in southern California. It was a vocal quintet, four men and a woman, with tenor Tony Williams singing lead. By 1954 they had obtained a contract with a minor record label, but their first single was unsuccessful. In 1955, after signing with the powerful Mercury label, things were different. The Platters' first single on Mercury was "Only You," a Number 5 hit in the summer of 1955. It is tempting to call "Only You" their signature tune, but in truth the Platters had several strong songs that they are equally well-known for. "Only You" was only their first hit, but it was one of their finest.

In January 1956, the group released another "signature" song, the powerful "The Great Pretender." It was their first Number 1 hit and their first gold record, and is a perfect example of the restrained yet emotional vocal harmonies of the Platters at their best. Nineteen fifty-six also saw "(You've Got) The Magic Touch," a Number 4 single that is only slightly less than their very best work, as well as three two-sided hit singles. Only one of these produced a major hit, the Number 1 "My Prayer." The other five sides rated from Number 11 to Number 39. Perhaps by this time the Platters were getting a little too much exposure.

Their two releases in 1957 were another tepid two-sided hit, their second record to chart Number 11 *and* Number 23, and a second poor showing with a Number 25. Wisely, the Platters did not release any additional singles for almost a year, until the April 1958 hit "Twilight Time." This went to Number 1, and got the Platters another gold record and a return to the spotlight. In November of that year, "Smoke Gets in Your Eyes," yet another golden Number 1, seemed to guarantee that the Platters were back on target. Instead, it was their last major hit.

After two minor releases in 1959, February 1960 saw the debut of their last Top Ten single, a cover of the old chestnut "Harbor Lights," recorded by Bing Crosby (and a bunch of other people) back in 1950. It's a good song; the Platters' version went to Number 8. Encouraged by this last hit, the group moved in exactly the wrong direction. Their next several singles were the hoary oldies "Ebb Tide," "Red Sails in the Sunset," "To Each His Own," "If I Didn't Care," and "I'll Never Smile Again."

These were hits from as long ago as 1940 and as recently as 1959, by Nat "King" Cole, Tommy Dorsey, Connie Francis, the Ink Spots, and others. None made it higher than the mid-chart, and the Platters seemed to have lost their direction. While the group did not officially disband (indeed, there are vocal groups calling themselves the Platters out there somewhere, performing at state fairs, to this day), Tony Williams left after "I'll Never Smile Again," a good choice for a swan song.

That'll Be the Day

Few careers in rock and roll have been as brief, as bright, or as influential as that of Charles Hardin "Buddy" Holly, who died in February 1959 at the age of twenty-two. His life and untimely death spawned a biographical film, *The Buddy Holly Story*, and a worshipful Number 1 record, "American Pie," written and recorded by Don McLean.

As the film shows, Buddy Holly not only made a name for himself as a performer, and as the composer of his own songs, but as a record producer. This was his greatest innovation. A decade after his death it would not be uncommon for talented performer-composers to produce their own records, but in the late 1950s that was still show business heresy. Most, probably the majority of performers, had little or no say in such basic matters as what songs they would record or when and where they would perform on tour. Producers chose songs, musicians, arrangements, and sometimes even which clothes the singer would wear. Buddy Holly, by his intransigence and his success, was a major force in changing all that, even though the old studio production system persists to this day for some unlucky performers.

Where the Hollywood and folkloric versions of the Buddy Holly story have it wrong is in the implicit conclusion that his promising career was nipped in the bud by the crash of a chartered airplane in an Iowa cornfield. When Buddy Holly, Ritchie Valens, and the Big Bopper fell to their deaths in 1959, Holly's recording career was already essentially over, after only eighteen months and seven singles.

The Crickets, Holly's trio from Lubbock, Texas, burst onto the American pop music scene in August 1957 with "That'll Be the Day (That I Die)." The song reached Number 1, and Holly quickly became famous for his idiosyncratic style of singing and his rapid, hyperkinetic guitar playing. Three months later he released "Peggy

Sue" under his own name, reaching Number 3, while the Crickets' "Oh Boy!" barely broke the Top Ten a month later.

Although there would be two more Buddy Holly singles and two from the Crickets in the following nine months, none would even get close to the Top Ten. Only "Maybe Baby," the third Crickets release (and fourth record by Buddy Holly under either name) did better than thirtieth position on the Top 40. The period from Holly's first Top Ten release to his last was just over four months.

This is not the impression one obtains from *The Buddy Holly Story*, or the way most rock and roll fans seem to remember (or learn) it. However, the numbers speak for themselves, and Buddy Holly was pretty much a flash in the pan in the upper reaches of stardom. Certainly length of stardom has never been an accurate indicator of a performer's importance or influence; the Doors, for example, charted with a mere eight singles in a four-year period, of which only three were really successful. And yet there are Doors fan clubs, Doors cover bands, an Oliver Stone movie, and strong continued interest in this strange and marginally productive band.

Among other bands whose influence was disproportionate to their success or duration, both Jefferson Airplane and the Byrds come to mind. The Byrds helped create a new sound, folk-rock, and launched a number of careers. Various incarnations of the group have released many albums, and former Byrds have participated in several subsequent groups (Crosby, Stills and Nash, and the Flying Burrito Brothers, for example). However, the original group released a total of seven singles in slightly less than two years, of which only two songs made it to the Top Ten. By late 1967, the Byrds as a Top 40 group were finished.

Jefferson Airplane (in its various later avatars, Jefferson Starship, or just Starship) actually had more success in the 1980s than in the 1960s; in their first decade, the group had only two singles, "Somebody to Love" and "White Rabbit." Both songs went to the Top Ten in mid-1967. As far as the Top 40 pop charts go, this was indeed a short career.

Buddy Holly and the Crickets bear a curious similarity to the Byrds or to Jefferson Airplane. All three of these groups enjoyed a very fast ride to considerable fame, but also quickly faded away, at least in terms of their presence on the charts and the radio. Each had a powerfully innovative sound, that rapidly caught the attention of the listening public, but each also shortly seemed to approach self-parody. Only performers capable of musical growth and change, such as the Beatles or the Rolling Stones, are likely to maintain true stardom for years or even decades.

Many performers in rock and roll history have attained a certain success based on a novel sound, but quickly faded when later records repeated the sound without the novelty; Del Shannon is a perfect example. Reaching Number 1 with "Runaway," his first release back in 1961, he only achieved the Top Ten twice more in his four-year, eight-single career. Shannon's highly distinctive vocal sound, that he seemingly could not alter, grew stale rather rapidly.

Buddy Holly was, to some extent, the victim of similar pressures. Unless he was about to metamorphose into something quite different, his musical career predeceased him. We of course shall never know where life would have led Holly, but nothing suggests that he was capable of the kind of evolutionary changes that a Paul McCartney, Brian Wilson, or Stevie Wonder could take for granted.

These Boots Are Made for Walkin'

Nancy Sinatra, first child of the megastar Frank Sinatra, definitely used her parental connections to ease her way into show business. She made her professional debut with her father (and Elvis Presley) on television in 1959, and was able to land roles in a variety of teen exploitation movies in the years to come. (*Get Yourself a College Girl* was one of her films.)

In the mid-1960s Nancy met Lee Hazlewood, a composer-arranger-producer-singer who had produced records for Duane Eddy, among others. He wrote a brash woman's anthem for her, "These Boots Are Made for Walkin'," with a countrified air that appealed to country and pop listeners both. It soared to Number 1, not at all hurt by her familial connections. (Another connection, less obvious, lay in her choice of record label. Her father had founded Reprise several years earlier, although he no longer owned it outright.)

Two months after "Boots," she released a somewhat similar song, "How Does That Grab You, Darlin'?" The newness of her style and voice was already gone, so the single climbed to a respectable Number 7, but not to Number 1. Nancy's next single barely charted at all.

This called for a new strategy. Hazlewood brought forth "Sugar Town," a dreamy, happy ballad that showed Nancy at her best; it reached back up to Number 5. Three months later, she released the amusing "Somethin' Stupid," a romantic duet with her dad. This song was Nancy's second and final Number 1 record. "Love Eyes" (released a scant two weeks after the duet) was propelled to Number 15 by the success of "Somethin' Stupid," but is a very forgettable tune.

In the summer of 1967 began the third and final phase of Nancy Sinatra's brief career. Producer Hazlewood became her new, countrified singing partner. "Jackson" was a durable hit for the two, more memorable than its Number 14 peak position would suggest.

Another solo number by Nancy, "Lightning's Girl," stalled at Number 24. Her last two charted singles, in late 1967 and early 1968, were once again with Hazlewood. "Lady Bird" (the nickname of the current First Lady) went to Number 20, while her swan song "Some Velvet Morning" climbed no higher than Number 26, a sad fate for what is really a very pretty little song.

In fact, Nancy, soloing or in duets with Lee Hazlewood, released a few more singles. Some, like "Summer Wine," were as good as many successful Top 40 records. The public had grown tired of her sound, evidently.

What may have been her very best work passed unnoticed in the summer of 1967. Her soulful rendition of the theme from *You Only Live Twice* was perhaps the only thing right about that James Bond epic. As a Reprise single, however, it spent the whole summer on the *Billboard* Hot 100 charts, never quite surfacing on the Top 40. It is too bad the song never got the recognition it deserved, thus ending Nancy Sinatra's career on a high note.

Tom Dooley

Several of these essays have emphasized that rock and roll is only one of many traditions and genres in American popular music. At the time when rock emerged, it had to contend with the mambo craze (followed by the cha-cha-cha craze). If it had not been for the dominant presence of Elvis Presley, the outcome back in the 1950s might have been very different.

Another growing genre was folk music. More accurately put, it was the re-creation of the American and English folk traditions, mostly by people who consciously learned these traditions as adults. "Folk music" properly should refer to traditions that individuals learned as children in their home cultures. The folk music of the American record industry was what a later, more aware generation would call the coopting (or worse) of other peoples' traditions.

Folk or folklike music was used as a means of publicizing social protest by politically motivated singer-songwriters, going back many decades. Joe Hill is an early example of the folk artist as political commentator. Folk first became successful pop music at the hands of the Weavers, Pete Seeger, and three other politically and musically sophisticated troubadors.

The Weavers had eight hit records from 1950 to 1952, including a Number 1 B-side with Leadbelly's old "Goodnight, Irene" in the summer of 1950, and a Number 2 "On Top of Old Smoky" the following year. Their last hit was "Wimoweh" in 1952; nine years later, it resurfaced as the Tokens' big hit "The Lion Sleeps Tonight." Both versions derive from an obscure South African folk song. The Weavers' leftist political stance made too much trouble for them in the early 1950s, and their career as recording artists came to an abrupt end.

A few other folk (or folklike) performers were in the public eye in those days. Burl Ives released singles and albums from the late 1940s on, to no very great success. Folkies maintained a larger presence in coffeehouses and college auditoriums than on radio or television.

Things began to change in the late 1950s. Interest in folk music and sales of acoustic guitars both grew, feeding upon each other. A handful of folksongs made it to the Top 40 or even the Top Ten, such as Jimmie Rodgers' Number 1 "Honeycomb" and Number 3 "Kisses Sweeter Than Wine" in 1957. The Folk Craze, a major occurrence in American pop music, was about to begin.

Another important precursor of the Folk Craze was, oddly enough, Harry Belafonte. The New York City-born professional actor made a major career for himself by recording authentic (and also sometimes very synthetic) Calypso and other Caribbean folk song styles. In 1956 and 1957, Belafonte released several singles and five top-selling albums.

The first and most popular of the folk groups in the Folk Craze was the Kingston Trio. They got together in San Francisco during 1957, and released the first of many best-selling records the following year. "Tom Dooley" was a Number 1 record, the first folk song to top the pop charts since "Goodnight, Irene" over eight years before. The Kingston Trio's subsequent singles were less successful; where they triumphed was in album sales.

Their debut album, *The Kingston Trio*, was a top seller in 1958, but later albums—when the group had achieved greater fame— were even better. *Here We Go Again, The Kingston Trio at Large, Sold Out,* and *String Along* (all released during 1959 to 1960) were among the best-selling albums of the twentieth century. (No other folk group came close to the Trio in popularity.) Their thirteen other albums released by 1965 all sold well, too.

It was clear to everyone in the music business that folk music would sell; scouts for major record labels searched for new groups, and had little trouble uncovering them. Capitol had the Kingston Trio. Columbia signed the Brothers Four, Bob Dylan, and the New Christy Minstrels. RCA got the Limeliters, Vanguard landed Joan Baez, Judy Collins went to Elektra, and Warners ended up with Peter, Paul, and Mary. (These are only some of the more famous performers.)

Even Allan Sherman's folk and other parodies (on Warners) were best sellers from 1962 on. At about the same time, on the Mercury label, the Smothers Brothers began to sell records of their subtler, wittier folk parodies, many of them written by Tom Smothers' college roommate, the multi-talented Mason Williams.

Some of the new folk acts sold a lot of singles as well as albums. The Brothers Four (a quartet of frat boys from the University of Washington) had a Number 2 hit with "Greenfields" in 1960; the New Christy Minstrels hit the Top Twenty with "Green, Green," while Peter, Paul, and Mary had numerous folklike hits. In 1962 "Lemon Tree" barely charted, but "If I Had a Hammer," "Puff the Magic Dragon," "Blowin' in the Wind" and others did much better. (When PP&M recorded actual folksongs, such as "Stewball" or "Go Tell It on the Mountain," these did poorly. It was sophisticated songs in the folk manner that really seemed to be popular.)

Some famous performers began their careers in these folk groups. When lead singer Chad Mitchell left the Chad Mitchell Trio, he was replaced by John Denver. Jim McGuinn, later to form the Byrds, played with the trio as well. Kenny Rogers and Barry McGuire were New Christy Minstrels; famed singer Glenn Yarbrough started out as a Limeliter. Founding member Dave Guard left the Kingston Trio, to be replaced by John Stewart, a successful singer and songwriter for decades to follow. Scott McKenzie and his friend John Phillips of The Mamas and the Papas both started out as two of the Journeymen, a lesser folk group. Erik Darling of the Rooftop Singers had been a Weaver, and before that a Tarrier; another Tarrier was Alan Arkin.

The Folk Craze ran its course by the mid-1960s, having brought folk and rock together through the Byrds and Bob Dylan. In a way, folk-rock was an unfortunate merging; it didn't have a lasting effect on rock, but killed off pure old folk for a generation of performers.

Traveling Man

Attempts to turn fame into fortune are at least as common in show business as in real life. Singers try to become actors, though Elvis, Sinatra, and Cher are among the very few to achieve real success in film. Actors try to become singers—and here the ratio of successes to failures is higher, because if enough people buy your records, you are by definition a successful singer. Many actors with average or better voices (and way above average looks) have sought to shore up their vulnerable starhood with Top 40 appearances. (The money is nice, too.) Quite a few have made it, at least for a while.

Of all those who tried, only one actor ever became a major singing success story, perhaps because he was never more than a "minor" actor. Ricky Nelson was born into a show business family, his father a bandleader, his mother the band's vocalist; Ozzie and Harriet became radio personalities and then television stars, and their young sons Dave and Ricky did too. Ricky parlayed exposure on television into major stardom as a rock and roller.

Ricky Nelson's greatest successes were "Poor Little Fool" in 1958 and "Traveling Man" in 1961; the latter was a two-sided hit, with the Number 9 "Hello Mary Lou" as its flip side.

In an on-again, off-again career he managed a very impressive thirty-five hit records, including eighteen in the Top Twenty and two at Number 1. His hits were mostly during the late 1950s, but he charted as late as 1970, and again in 1972 (the wonderful "Garden Party"). Of all the television personalities who cracked the Top 40, Rick Nelson was probably the only one who would have succeeded without a leg up from Hollywood, although it is fair to say that he would not have become quite so famous strictly on his own merits.

Among Hollywood's other, less-gifted aspirants to musical greatness, many achieved one or two decent hits, only to see their momentum stall. In 1957, Tab Hunter scored a Number 1 with the credible "Young Love," but his subsequent records failed to enter the Top Ten, and by 1959 he was finished. Shortly after Hunter's big hit, another young Hollywood actor gave rock and roll a chance. Sal Mineo released "Start Movin' (In My Direction)"— surely one of the least attractive song titles of the decade—in May 1957, reaching Number 9. His inevitable follow-up single, "Lasting Love," failed to make the Top Twenty. At about the same time, Tony Perkins released a single or two, and made Mineo look good by comparison.

In 1959 and the following year, two singles on the Warner label would seem to virtually incarnate the hoped-for actor-to-singer process, although neither one succeeded at the transformation. Edward (also known as Edd) Byrnes was a minor star but a major pop cult phenomenon on the Warner Brothers' television program *77 Sunset Strip*. (Byrnes played "Kookie," the hipster parking attendant; for those who do not know the show, perhaps it will suffice to say that Henry Winkler's "Fonz" is a toned-down version of Kookie.) Byrnes and Warners' starlet Connie Stevens cut a record titled "Kookie, Kookie (Lend Me Your Comb)" that reached Number 4. Stevens, who played a minor character in Robert Conrad's *Hawaiian Eye*, also released "Sixteen Reasons" by herself in 1960; it peaked at Number 3. Neither she nor Byrnes ever followed up on their (compared to the rest of these people) major success on vinyl, although each continued in acting.

Annette Funicello, of Mouseketeer (and later, *Beach Party* film) fame, had five hits in 1959-1960. Only her first, "Tall Paul," cracked the Top Ten. Annette's fellow Disneyite Hayley Mills had a Number 8 hit with "Let's Get Together," a song from her 1961 film *The Parent Trap*, but "Johnny Jingo" the next year peaked at Number 21, and her singing career too was called off for lack of popular interest.

The year 1962 saw a veritable plague of television actors shooting for musical stardom, none very successfully. It began with Shelley Fabares of *The Donna Reed Show*, whose "Johnny Angel" was released on March 17, eventually becoming Number 1 in the land. (Her next record, "Johnny Loves Me," stalled at Number 21, and that was the end of *her* singing career.) On the same record label, owned (like their television show) by Columbia Studios, her

Donna Reed sibling Paul Peterson released his first single only two weeks after "Johnny Angel." The two actors had records on the Top 40 charts at the same time; Peterson's was "She Can't Find Her Keys," which peaked at Number 19. (Its flip side was a duet between Peterson and Fabares, "Highly Unlikely.") In December 1962 Peterson ran against form and achieved a Number 6 with his second single, "My Dad" (Carl Betz?). Subsequent efforts returned to the familiar Hollywood exploitation pattern and failed to chart.

George Maharis also released a single in 1962, "Teach Me Tonight." The handsome star of *Route 66* only reached Number 25 in his one tour of the Top 40. (Even Nelson Riddle's instrumental version of the *Route 66* theme did about that well, three months later.) The other two actor-singers who made their debuts in that year managed to perform a little better. Johnny Crawford, who played the son of *The Rifleman* on television, made the Top Ten with "Cindy's Birthday," and then Numbers 14, 12, and 29 over the next half-year or so, before calling it quits.

Heart-throb Richard Chamberlain earned a Number 10 with the theme from his own program, *Dr. Kildare*, but his next two singles were less successful. In a move that has since been emulated by Shaun Cassidy, Cheryl Ladd, and many other struggling artists, Chamberlain covered old hits rather than find and cut new songs. Apparently at least some producers believe that listeners are predisposed to enjoy old favorites sung by new celebrities. It almost never succeeds, and reeks of greed. Richard Chamberlain's covers of "Love Me Tender" and "All I Have to Do is Dream" did alright, at Number 21 and Number 14 respectively, but not well enough to propel his singing career forward.

After 1963, there was a pause in the attempts of actors to become singers, perhaps because the multiple efforts of the preceding years were so generally abysmal. Then in 1965 Patty Duke, star of her own television program, issued two singles. "Don't Just Stand There" reached Number 8, while its successor "Say Something Funny" neared the Top Twenty; after that Duke, too, retired from the fray. (She, like many of the actors under discussion here, would also occasionally sing on television.)

What all of the would-be singers discussed here have in common is that, with the exception of Rick Nelson, none were successful in launching any kind of lasting career. For some, their already-established celebrity was enough to generate interest in their first couple of singles, but the quality of those records was never good enough to make listeners want more. Each was a musical flash in the pan, and for good reason.

Turn Me Loose!

Since at least as far back as the 1930s, there has been a well-established role in American popular music for the good-looking young crooner whose audience is disproportionately female. Bing Crosby was the premiere crooner of the 1930s, Frank Sinatra of the 1940s, and Eddie Fisher of the early 1950s. When pop was overwhelmed by rock and roll, Elvis Presley became the chief crooner, by then known more accurately as a "teen idol," for the rest of the decade. However, Pat Boone, who was always more of a pop singer than a rock and roller, kept the crooner tradition alive.

It is by no means coincidental that all five of the aforementioned men were quite handsome. Of course, all were fine, even great, singers as well. As record producers in the later 1950s sought to adapt to the new, bewildering genre that was rock, more than one developed the idea that it might be possible to foist handsome young men of dubious talent off on the public, and to do so very profitably.

This reprehensible idea was made easier to put into practice by the growing tendency for live television performances to be "lip-synched;" singers moved their lips in time with their records, but did not actually sing. This permitted a producer to make records with poor-quality singers, who only had to get each note right once. The late 1950s/early 1960s were also, and for the same reason, the era of the echo chamber and other techniques for covering up a weak voice.

The key element in the manufacture of a teen idol—some of whom, it must be said, were great singers, such as Dion—was and is proper presentation. Many of the idols of the late 1950s came from Philadelphia, the home city of Dick Clark and his extremely influential television program *American Bandstand*. A good-looking young man could go on the show and obtain access to the vast horde of American teenagers, by effortlessly lip-synching a song that he had laboriously strained to sing correctly for the single. (Naturally, no one "performing" on the program or in the studio audience ever mentioned that the singing was faked, even though it was immediately obvious to everyone who watched the program.)

An interesting commentary on this whole process is that, by and large, the recruitment and presentation to the public of untalented teen idol wannabes . . . didn't work. The buying public generally has more sense than the music industry would like to believe. Manufactured teen idols might become moderately famous, but they rarely grow rich.

Some examples will illustrate this point. Among the young men who were propelled toward stardom in the late 1950s was Tommy Sands. Recording for Capitol in 1957 and 1958, he had three charted releases and one hit, the unsubtly titled Number 2 "Teen-Age Crush." Other releases charted at Number 16 and Number 24, or failed to chart at all. Producers can control film and television appearances, if not the public's buying habits, so Sands starred in a small number of films, such as *Babes in Toyland*, but his closest brush with stardom probably was his five-year marriage to Nancy Sinatra.

Frankie Avalon (Francis Avallone) was a Philadelphia boy who became famous on an "amateur hour" television program, and began recording (with an anglicized name) at the age of seventeen. Avalon released eleven singles for Chancellor over a four-year period, 1958 to 1962. The first six singles produced eight hits in 1958 and 1959, some quite successful. His fourth release, "Venus," went to Number 1, as did his seventh, "Why?"

Avalon's last four singles languished in the Sargasso Sea of forgotten songs, the Bottom 20 of the Top 40, and his recording career ended quickly. A pretty face and pleasing personality do not compel the purchase of records, a primarily aural medium, for very long. Even fans eventually require some show of talent. Avalon, sadly, is a mediocre singer. He did better as an actor in a string of youth-oriented films, and rode that wave for several years.

Bobby Rydell (Robert Ridarelli) was Avalon's friend and bandmate (both played in Rocco and the Saints, a Philadelphia dance band, while in high school; Frankie trumpeted while Bobby drummed). He signed with Cameo and released sixteen singles, including six hits, between

1959 and 1963. Two were double-sided hits, a sure indicator of popularity. The high points of Rydell's career were "Wild One," a Number 2 single in early 1960, a Number 4 cover of "Volare" that summer, and his last charted single, the Number 4 "Forget Him" in December 1963. Rydell was a businesslike artist who kept churning out singles despite rebuffs, and it is satisfactory that he was able to finish strong with what was only his fifth Top Ten record.

Bobby Vee (Robert Velline) and his band, the Shadows, briefly filled in for Buddy Holly on tour after the fatal plane crash in 1959. On the strength of that, Vee was able to sign with Liberty Records in 1960, and produced singles for them over the next eight years. He was only sixteen when his debut single, "Devil or Angel," went to Number 6. He is better known for "Rubber Ball," a Number 6 written for him by Gene Pitney, the Number 1 "Take Good Care of My Baby," the Number 2 "Run to Him," and Number 3 "The Night Has a Thousand Eyes."

Vee comes closer than most teen idols to being an actual singing star, like Dion or Paul Anka. However, the "manufactured teen idol" stigmata are clearly present; over half of his records were unsuccessful, but relentlessly pushed through television appearances and the like.

Bobby Vinton (Stanley Robert Vinton) recorded for Epic from 1962 until 1975; he released twenty-five charted singles between 1962 and 1969. About one third were decent hits. Vinton led off with a Number 1, "Roses Are Red," but the next five singles in a row were poor. Only after a full year of waiting did he score again. "Blue on Blue" reached Number 3 and "Blue Velvet" Number 1 in the summer of 1963, his Golden Age. In December he went to Number 1 again with "There! I've Said It Again," a good example of how a song's competition, as much as its innate worth, can determine success. "Blue on Blue" is a much better song, but could not make it to Number 1 with the competition it faced at that earlier time.

In late 1964, Vinton scored another Number 1 with "Mr. Lonely," followed by two years and six unsuccessful singles. He had a couple of minor hits in the late 1960s, before remaking himself as "the Polish Prince" (that would have a completely different meaning now) in the 1970s. There are several quite good Vinton songs, and like Bobby Vee, he really could sing, but way too much of the material he recorded was just plain bad.

This leads to the last teen idol under discussion here, in some ways the ultimate of the species. When Frankie Avalon's brief career was about over, the head of the Chancellor label went looking for a successor, one might say the "hair apparent." He found an even younger, even prettier boy with a mediocre voice but a great name. Fabian (Forte) was only fifteen in 1959 when he began his rise to quasi-stardom, and only sixteen when his singing career was over.

In thirteen months Fabian (the first rock and roll performer known by one name through media manipulation, not popularity) released seven singles. The first, the optimistically titled "I'm a Man," peaked at a very low Number 31, but "Turn Me Loose," his signature song, made it to Number 9. "Tiger" next went to Number 3, his highwater mark.

Fabian's fifth single again hit Number 9, the theme from the Stuart Whitman film *Hound Dog Man* (about dogs, not Elvis). Fabian began to find his real strength by costarring in the movies; his good looks and general amiability translated into several film roles for him. He acted in *North to Alaska*, *Five Weeks in a Balloon*, and numerous other popular movies.

His other singles pottered along at Number 29, Number 31, and finally only two weeks at Number 39. Everybody called it quits at that point, and he went on to a mildly successful film career and touring on an oldies program with his old Philadelphia friends Frankie Avalon, Chubby Checker, and Bobby Rydell. Of all these would-be teen idols he was the least skilled and least successful, but somehow also the least pretentious and annoying.

Under the Boardwalk

The Drifters were a fairly popular group during the early 1960s, and could always be counted on for good harmony. Theirs is a strange and, for the most part, unknown saga, unique in the annals of rock and roll. The group has been made up of different singers at different times, because their manager copyrighted and owned the group name. When a Drifter made the boss angry, he could be summarily fired and some unknown new singer hired, on five minutes' notice. At least some of the Drifters were on salary, earning no royalties however well their records might sell.

The Drifters varied from four to five men. At various times the lead singer was Clyde McPhatter, Ben E. King, Johnny Moore, David Baughan, Bobby Hendricks, Rudy Lewis, or some other guy the manager liked. The group was formed in 1953, and from 1954 to 1959 they released at least eight singles that failed to chart on the Top 40; some were successful on the R&B charts. The Ertegun brothers of Atlantic Records had faith in the Drifters and stayed with them throughout the life of the group.

The original Drifters featured Clyde McPhatter, who left the group for a reasonably successful solo career in 1954. That year they released their first single, "Such a Night," and their first R&B hit, "Honey Love." The latter became a gold record, but was largely unknown to the Top 40 audience. In 1958 Treadwell fired the entire group, including Johnny Moore, and hired the Five Crowns to be the next batch of "Drifters."

At last in 1959 the new crew broke through into success. "There Goes My Baby" went all the way to Number 2, in the first chart appearance for anybody calling himself a Drifter. (The success was the former Five Crowns'—but they weren't famous under that name, and didn't own their current one. The music business can be Faustian at times.) A quick follow-up single, "Dance with Me," did fairly well, reaching Number 15 and selling a lot of records.

Their next release is a paradox. Not overly popular at the time, "This Magic Moment" reached no higher than Number 16, but has proven over the four succeeding decades to be one of the greatest vocal hits of the period. It is a Ben E. King masterpiece, presaging the work he would later do as a solo performer.

The group's biggest release would follow. The Number 1, gold record "Save the Last Dance for Me" became the Drifters' signature song. However, almost every time they struck gold, their manager and producers rushed out one or two inferior follow-ups; they did so after "Last Dance," as usual. The public is rarely fooled, and the lesser songs receive notably lesser sales. The two singles that followed the hit this time earned Number 17 and Number 32, a new low for the group since they first hit the Top 40. It would be two years and four more singles before they had another hit.

At about the same time, in 1960, Ben E. King left the Drifters. Within a year he would release the major hits "Spanish Harlem" and "Stand by Me" (the latter is his most famous song). For the next three years, newcomer Rudy Lewis was the lead Drifter.

When the Drifters finally had another hit, it was a great one. "Up on the Roof" brought them out of their slump with a Number 5 gold record, and a perennial oldie to boot. For once, the next single was a good one as well, the popular "On Broadway." (A young Phil Spector can be heard playing the excellent guitar solo on this Number 9 hit.) *Then* the curse of the Drifters took effect; the following single, "I'll Take You Home," was eminently forgettable.

In 1964 Rudy Lewis died, and the manager brought back one of the mid-1950s Drifters, Johnny Moore, who sang lead on their last three charted singles. During the summer of 1964 the group had its final big hit, "Under the Boardwalk." A conscious effort to evoke the mood and magic of "Up on the Roof," it is that very rare thing, a sequel better than the original. It marginally outperformed the earlier record, too, coming in at a pleasing Number 4. *Its* sequel, a boardwalk-evoking "I've Got Sand in My Shoes," reached a disappointing (but fair) Number 33.

Finally, in December 1964 the Drifters released what turned out to be their final Top 40 hit. It wasn't bad at all. "Saturday Night at the Movies" was a lighthearted romp, more of a Coasters than a Drifters song, but it finished out their recording career with a respectable Number 18. Since then, various combinations of Drifters have sung their songs, in oldies venues all over the country (and in Europe), under the watchful eyes of their manager and his heirs. This ungainly and unpleasant arrangement may not have resulted in a particularly admirable distribution of wealth, but it did produce a half dozen world-class songs we wouldn't have heard otherwise.

The Wanderer

Dion Di Mucci was one of the teen idols who emerged after the rise of Elvis in 1956 and the rise of Ricky Nelson in 1957. Unlike most of his idol colleagues, Dion had talent for the long haul, not just a brief synthetic stardom.

Born in 1939, Dion was only seventeen when he formed his first group, Dion & the Timberlanes. A year later it was a different backing trio, the Belmonts. They signed with the Laurie label, and Dion & the Belmonts had their first Top 40 hit while Dion was still only eighteen. The single reached Number 22, a reasonable achievement for a debut.

The next couple of records went to Number 19 and Number 40, but then, in the spring of 1959, they struck gold at last with "A Teenager in Love." The song went to Number 5, and their next release hit Number 3. Dion, in addition to a very good voice, had a real talent for infusing his vocals with emotion. When he sang a passage such as "Why must I be . . . a teenager in love?" he sounded sincerely unhappy and perplexed.

The group's sixth and seventh charted singles were very unwise covers of familiar songs. Dion & the Belmonts did well by "When You Wish Upon a Star" and "In the Still of the Night," but both singles charted briefly and badly.

When Dion recorded next, it was as a solo act. Apparently, it was the right move—the Belmonts as a trio had a couple of minor hits and then faded away, while Dion went on to have ten big hits, seven of them in a row immediately after going solo in late 1960.

His first single after leaving the Belmonts behind was "Lonely Teenager," a Number 12 hit. Dion was writing or cowriting most of his own material, and sometimes many months went by without a single. Almost a year passed between "Lonely Teenager" and the next hit, "Runaround Sue," but it was worth the wait. The new record went to Number 1, Dion's only chart-topper, and made believers out of those fans who'd missed the Belmonts.

The following single just missed Number 1. "The Wanderer" was very popular, but competed—during the Twist craze—with Chubby Checker's "The Twist," Joey Dee's "Peppermint Twist," and Gene Chandler's moronic (but fun) "Duke of Earl." Bad timing for Dion. He owed something to the Twist, though, for Dion performed in two Twist movies in 1961, *Teenage Millionaire* and *Twist Around the Clock*.

Over the next couple of years, several strong singles by Dion came out. "Lovers Who Wander," "Ruby Baby," "Donna the Prima Donna," and three other Top Ten hits bracketed three lesser tunes. After late 1963, when he was twenty-four, Dion had no further pop hits for a five-year period. Then, in a changed style, he released the powerful "Abraham, Martin, and John." This song so summed up the feelings of people stunned by their losses that, for many, it is somehow the only Dion song.

Dion has become a committed Christian and, apart from an occasional nostalgia tour reunion with the Belmonts, he has performed only religious music for many years.

You Don't Own Me

Back in 1963 master producer Quincy Jones discovered seventeen-year-old Lesley Gore, already a professional singer but not yet signed to a recording contract. Jones quickly rectified that lack, and her most famous release, "It's My Party," just as quickly went to Number 1 on the Mercury label. It's a sad song; her second single was the happier sequel, "Judy's Turn to Cry," a Number 5.

It seemed that Lesley Gore had struck gold with her songs about uneasy relationships, so her third release went back to this familiar territory. "She's a Fool" is another romantic triangle, with poor Lesley the unhappy one. It earned her another Number 5, her third major success in three tries.

Next came "You Don't Own Me," her most interesting song. In an era of "I Will Follow Him," "(I Want to Be) Bobby's Girl," "Johnny Angel" and the like, "You Don't Own Me" was a slap in the face. This time, Lesley is directly addressing her boyfriend, and negotiating their relationship in terms that sound dangerously close to equality.

The public loved it, and the record spent three weeks as Number 2. ("I Want to Hold Your Hand" was firmly entrenched as Number 1 at that time, so in a sense one could claim that Lesley Gore's Number 1 was among the first casualties of the British Invasion.) On this song more than any other, her ability to project a quietly determined and strong persona was evident, without ever getting in the way of the material.

Her fifth single, "That's the Way Boys Are," reached only Number 12. It was time to bring something new to the equation, but her label gave Lesley Gore only warmed-over repeats of what she had already done. "I Don't Want to Be a Loser" was the next single, and spent only one week on the chart at Number 37. Songs can't do a whole lot worse than that and leave a record of their existence.

Her career had just gone through one of the most precipitous dives in rock and roll history, but it was slightly ameliorated by her seventh single, a year and a half after she started recording. "Maybe I Know" was a great song, with all the old fire. A few months earlier it would have reached the Top Five; coming after the inert "Loser," it stalled at Number 14, and was off the charts after six weeks. Her next single was poor, while the ninth, a tie-in to her movie role in *Ski Party* (a Beach Party movie in the mountains) did much better. "Sunshine, Lollipops, and Rainbows" went to Number 13.

Following one more minor effort, Lesley's eleventh and final charted single was the very nice "California Nights." It peaked at Number 16, a position that once would have been laughable for a Lesley Gore release. By 1967 she hadn't hit the Top Ten in over three years, so Number 16 wasn't such a bad finale.

Lesley appeared in another teen flick, *Girls on the Beach,* and as an assistant villainess on an episode of *Batman* on television. When Lesley stopped recording in 1967 she was just twenty-three. The times and tastes had passed her by, to some extent, but better material might have prolonged what—briefly—had looked to be a truly great career.

You've Lost That Lovin' Feelin'

The Righteous Brothers were one of a number of rock and roll acts that called themselves brothers, but weren't. It made for a memorable group name, though, and one of the earliest and best acts in rock and roll *was* made up of real brothers—the Everlys—so maybe later brother wannabes were trying to evoke the quality (and success) of Phil and Don.

Bill Medley and Bobby Hatfield linked up as the Righteous Brothers in 1962, and began releasing singles the next year. It wasn't until they came to the attention, and under the influence, of Phil Spector in late 1964 that anything started really happening in their career, however. Spector signed them to his Philles label, handpicked and produced their songs, and suddenly the Righteous Brothers were a major force in rock and roll. Their first Philles release was "You've Lost That Lovin' Feelin'," a long, romantic ballad that spotlighted the duo's ability to turn on what came to be known as "blue-eyed soul."

The disc jockeys of that day were often unwilling to play songs longer than three minutes, so Phil Spector labeled the single as three minutes and five seconds. It was in fact closer to four minutes, but by the time its real length was known, "You've Lost That Lovin' Feelin'" was on its way to Number 1 on the Top 40. The song was a collaboration between Spector and the writing partnership of Cynthia Weil and Barry Mann.

Another famous partnership would provide the Brothers with their next single, "Just Once in My Life," a fairly obvious attempt to duplicate the magic of their first hit. It was written by Carole King, Gerry Goffin, and—once again—Phil Spector. (One is free to speculate just how much, or how little, Spector may have brought to some of these collaborations; Mann and Weil, or Goffin and King, didn't seem to need anyone else's help on other Top Ten songs.) A decent record, "Just Once in My Life" peaked at only Number 9;

perhaps it would have done better a few months later, but Spector rushed it to the record stores on the heels of their first hit, and it lacked originality and impact.

Phil Spector was known for his innovative "Wall of Sound," a production technique that utilized multiple drummers and other instrumentalists to create stunning backgrounds for many of the groups whose records he produced. However, Spector knew when *not* to use the Wall, too; his Righteous Brothers sessions are much more traditional than most Spector productions, letting nothing obscure the vocal fireworks.

For their third and fourth Philles singles the Righteous Brothers recorded "Unchained Melody" and "Ebb Tide," both established oldies that were well-chosen to match the Brothers' voices and style. The two singles made it to Number 4 and Number 5, respectively, very good performances for cover versions.

At this point, after a year of fame, the duo badly needed something new to prevent their career from stalling and their public persona from being typecast. What they got was something old and something new. Cynthia Weil and Barry Mann wrote "(You're My) Soul and Inspiration," a lovely song that held the Number 1 spot for three weeks in early 1966, the Righteous Brothers' most successful record, and definitely one of their best. However, it was uncannily like their first two singles, and really did nothing to propel their careers forward. The Righteous Brothers had been frequent performers on both *Shindig* on ABC and its rival *Hullabaloo* on NBC throughout 1965; overexposure on television, especially for a group with only one sound, was a mistake as well.

Medley and Hatfield had already severed their relationship with the Svengali-like Phil Spector; "Soul and Inspiration" was their first single for the Verve label, but it was also their last good record. No longer under Spector's wing, they wrote their own songs, and Medley produced the singles. These efforts simply did not measure up, and so the duo had no charted singles from late 1966 until the unspeakable "Rock and Roll Heaven" in 1974.

It must not be assumed that the Righteous Brothers would somehow have remained at the top, had they stayed with Phil Spector. Spector was the quintessential early 1960s producer, but by 1966 the early 1960s were over and he had lost his grasp of the evolving rock and roll genre. The Righteous Brothers basically had one way of singing, one sound, and couldn't move past that point. It was a good sound, occasionally a beautiful one, but that isn't good enough to permit a prolonged stay at the top. In rock and roll, groups that can't change are rapidly relegated to oldies status.

THE BEST AND THE WORST
OF CLASSIC ROCK

The Best Classic Rock Song

Over the years, there has been much debate as to the best or ultimate song of the classic rock period, excluding "Rock Around the Clock," the early mini-masterpiece that gave the era its jump start. The senior author prefers the upbeat "Good Vibrations," the highly creative and innovative 1966 composition by Brian Wilson and Mike Love of the Beach Boys. Not only is it a clearly superior song, its message and tone were very compatible with the cultural characteristics of the turbulent yet "laid back" 1960s. "Good Vibrations" appealed both to people in the mainstream and people in the counterculture, although some people may not regard the composition as a true rock song.

This appeal to diverse sectors of American culture also applies to, in the senior author's opinion, another leading candidate for best classic rock song. The other piece is the mystical and marvelous 1968 phenomenon "Aquarius." Written for the hit musical *Hair* by lyricists Gerome Ragni and James Rado and composer Galt Mac-Dermot, "Aquarius" is definitely at home with the 1960s counterculture yet it falls so well on the ears of mainstream listeners. "Aquarius" is a brilliant and delightful piece with durability, and is a splendid candidate for best classic rock composition.

The Worst Famous Classic Rock Song

There is no shortage of candidates for the worst highly successful or famous song of the classic rock period. The senior author, never hesitant to avoid controversy, feels that several of the early songs of the Rolling Stones could fit this dubious honor, but possibly the leader of a very large pack might be the Beatles' "All You Need is Love," a 1967 hit written by John Lennon and Paul McCartney. Not only is it a weak and insipid song artistically, it is also a very pretentious song, with four very wealthy white young men arrogantly suggesting to the world, including the poor and downtrodden, that all you need is love to solve the globe's many social and economic problems. It was post-Maharishi psychobabble.

If the reader is of the opinion that the celebrated Beatles could do nothing wrong, another possible candidate, in the opinion of the senior author, is Gerry Goffin and Barry Mann's 1961 "Who Put the Bomp?" Although there have been a number of very good nonsense songs over the years, and "Who Put the Bomp?" is lively and in a perverse way interesting, one gets the impression that the "bomp" is the sound of lyrics hitting the bottom of the artistic barrel. Perhaps one thing that helps make "Bomp" look so bad is its contrast to the fine ballad "Will You Love Me Tomorrow?," written in the very same year by Goffin and Carole King.

CLASSIC ROCK MEETS DISCO,
AND BOTH DISAPPEAR

Disco Duck

In style, disco was a sort of cross between the swing music of the 1930s and 1940s and rock music of the 1950s, 1960s, and early 1970s. Appealing to an older audience than the teenagers who were the primary support for rock, and also appealing to those who felt alienated from the white male dominated field of classic rock, disco was more sexually explicit than its musical predecessors. Most of all it centered on dancing, dancing, and dancing.

First appearing in 1974, disco was the big rage until around 1979 when it began to be absorbed by the relentless tide of change in popular music. Discotheques had been around for years, but with the disco fad many more discotheques were opened to large and enthusiastic mobs of patrons. If someone went into the discotheque business early, there was considerable money to be made. However, those who developed discotheques toward the end of the 1970s often saw their money go down the drain when disco fairly rapidly sank into oblivion.

During the brief reign of disco, the supporters of rock and roll were often hostile to the campy dance alternative to rock. On the television comedy series *WKRP in Cincinnati*, the character Johnny Fever, a disc jockey, was always disparaging disco. In addition, a real disc jockey, Steve Dahl of Chicago, burned hundreds of disco records before a 1979 crowd attending a major league baseball game.

Even the song that perhaps was the most representative composition of the disco years, Rick Dees' 1976 curiosity "Disco Duck," indirectly or inadvertently went along with the antidisco sentiment. Whenever a rock aficionado heard the music of the despised rival, the response would be "Disco—Duck!"

Stayin' Alive

One of the main characteristics of the disco fad of the mid-to-late-1970s was the general absence of good and enduring songs. Perhaps the major exceptions to this overall lack of notable music came in the 1977 movie, *Saturday Night Fever.* John Travolta, the male star of the disco film, rocketed to stardom because of his role, and the Australian singing group, the Bee Gees, also zoomed to the top of the pop music world because of the songs that they sang for the film.

Brothers Barry, Robin, and Maurice Gibb (they got their name from the initials of their leader Barry), wrote and recorded several good pieces for *Saturday Night Fever.* The fine love ballad "How Deep Is Your Love?," which won a Novello Award, was possibly the best, but "Night Fever," "More Than a Woman," and "Stayin' Alive" were also well received. With these and other hits, such as "Grease" (1978), sung by the three Gibbs and written by Barry, "Thicker Than Water" or "Love Is Thicker Than Water" (1977), sung by another brother Andy Gibb and written by Barry and Andy, "I Just Want to Be Your Everything" (1977), sung by Andy and written by Barry, and "Shadow Dancing" (1978), sung by Andy and written by all four Gibbs, the Bee Gees were one of the top groups of the late 1970s and early 1980s.

Of all their songs, "Stayin' Alive" is probably the most important. Not only was it Number 1 in record sales in 1977 and one of the leading symbols of disco, it was one of the most ironic of the songs of the late 1970s. Because classic rock came to an end around the mid-1970s, the disco craze, which vigorously danced in at about the same time, has been blamed for the demise of classic rock and roll. This is partly true, but other types of music, reggae and the varieties of hard rock, which began to make inroads by the early 1970s, were also involved in the passing into history of the generation of classic rock. Songs such as "Stayin' Alive" helped make classic rock a thing of the past, but couldn't manage to keep disco alive for very long. Disco and classic rock violently clashed in the mid-1970s, and neither was alive by the beginning of the 1980s.

Title Index

Subject Index

Order Your Own Copy of
This Important Book for Your Personal Library!

THE CLASSIC ROCK AND ROLL READER
Rock Music from Its Beginnings to the Mid-1970s

_____ in hardbound at $49.95 (ISBN: 0-7890-0151-9)

_____ in softbound at $19.95 (ISBN: 0-7890-0738-X)

COST OF BOOKS _____	☐ **BILL ME LATER:** ($5 service charge will be added) (Bill-me option is good on US/Canada/Mexico orders only; not good to jobbers, wholesalers, or subscription agencies.)
OUTSIDE USA/CANADA/ MEXICO: ADD 20% _____	
POSTAGE & HANDLING _____ (US: $3.00 for first book & $1.25 for each additional book) Outside US: $4.75 for first book & $1.75 for each additional book)	☐ Check here if billing address is different from shipping address and attach purchase order and billing address information. Signature _____
SUBTOTAL _____	☐ **PAYMENT ENCLOSED: $** _____
IN CANADA: ADD 7% GST _____	☐ **PLEASE CHARGE TO MY CREDIT CARD.**
STATE TAX _____ (NY, OH & MN residents, please add appropriate local sales tax)	☐ Visa ☐ MasterCard ☐ AmEx ☐ Discover ☐ Diner's Club
	Account # _____
FINAL TOTAL _____ (If paying in Canadian funds, convert using the current exchange rate. UNESCO coupons welcome.)	Exp. Date _____ Signature _____

Prices in US dollars and subject to change without notice.

NAME _____

INSTITUTION _____

ADDRESS _____

CITY _____

STATE/ZIP _____

COUNTRY _____ COUNTY (NY residents only) _____

TEL _____ FAX _____

E-MAIL_____
May we use your e-mail address for confirmations and other types of information? ☐ Yes   ☐ No

Order From Your Local Bookstore or Directly From
The Haworth Press, Inc.
10 Alice Street, Binghamton, New York 13904-1580 • USA
TELEPHONE: 1-800-HAWORTH (1-800-429-6784) / Outside US/Canada: (607) 722-5857
FAX: 1-800-895-0582 / Outside US/Canada: (607) 772-6362
E-mail: getinfo@haworthpressinc.com
PLEASE PHOTOCOPY THIS FORM FOR YOUR PERSONAL USE.